Sacred Fire

Sacred Fire

THE QBR 100
ESSENTIAL BLACK BOOKS

MAX RODRIGUEZ, Founder, *QBR: The Black Review*
ANGELI R. RASBURY
CAROL TAYLOR

Foreword by CHARLES JOHNSON

John Wiley & Sons, Inc.
New York • Chichester • Weinheim • Brisbane • Singapore • Toronto

Copyright © 1999 by Max Rodriguez and Angeli R. Rasbury. All rights reserved.
Published by John Wiley & Sons, Inc.
Published simultaneously in Canada

The authors gratefully acknowledge permission to reprint excerpted material (page 169) from *Blacks,* a collection of poetry by Gwendolyn Brooks. Copyright © 1981 by Gwendolyn Brooks.

Excerpt (page 177) from *for colored girls who have considered suicide/when the rainbow is enuf* by Ntozake Shange. Copyright © 1975, 1976, 1977 by Ntozake Shange. Reprinted with the permission of Simon & Schuster.

This publication is designed to provide accurate and authoritative information in regard to the subject matter covered. It is sold with the understanding that the publisher is not engaged in rendering professional services. If professional advice or other expert assistance is required, the services of a competent professional person should be sought.

Library of Congress Cataloging-in-Publication Data:

Sacred fire : the QBR 100 essential black books / [compiled and edited by] Max Rodriguez, Angeli R. Rasbury, Carol Taylor; foreword by Charles Johnson.
    p. cm.
   Includes bibliographical references (p.) and index.
   ISBN 0-471-24376-0 (cloth)
   1. Afro-Americans—Books and reading. I. Rodriguez, Max.
II. Rasbury, Angeli R. III. Taylor, Carol.
Z1361.N39S22 1999
[E185]
016.973'0496073—dc21   98-35060

Printed in the United States of America

10 9 8 7 6 5 4 3 2 1

To my father, who kept his eyes on the prize;
my mother, who introduced me to Bach, Billie, and Bustelo;
and my brother, who found his own way.

—Max Rodriguez

For my nieces and nephews, who already show
a love for black books.

—Didi

O Black and Unknown Bards of long ago,
How came your lips to touch the sacred fire?

—James Weldon Johnson
"O Black and Unknown Bards"

Contents

Origins, Ancestors, and Memory

Community and Identity

Politics, Nationalism, and Revolution

Soul and Spirit

Sisters' Stories

Brothers' Lives

Acknowledgments

The editors would like to thank the following for their generous assistance in the compilation of our list of 100 great books: Malaika Adero, Molefi Kete Asante, William M. Banks, Amiri Baraka, Betty Winston Bayé, Herb Boyd, Ed and Miriam Carter, James Fugate, Archie Givens, Suheir Hammad, Charles Johnson, Rosalind Oliphant Jones, Jacqueline C. Jones, Ph.D., Andre Kelton, Paul E. Logan, Zakiyya McCloud, Sonia Sanchez, Anne Allen Shockley, the staff of Afrikan World Books, the staff of Brother's Books, the staff of Nkiru Books, the staff of Sisterspace and Books. We would also like to thank the many supporters of QBR who recommended books, including Reinaldo Cummings, Jr., Dorothea Moore, Loretta J. Hargrove, Sandra D. Cahse, Rita Woods, and Margarita Smith-Phillips.

Max Rodriguez would like to honor those who have come before us, whose struggle has garnered for us life and the begrudging respect of survival. He offers love and gratitude to his wife, Melba, without whom QBR could not have been sustained. He offers gratitude to Jeri Love-Graves and Patrick Lee, the original QBR team; to every QBR contributor and writer; to supporters and volunteers who, through QBR, have expressed their love of books and black people—what a combination; to QBR editors Tonya Bolden, Susan McHenry, and Leslie Lockhart; to the writers and recorders of revolution and accommodation: Haki Madhubuti, Sonia Sanchez, Paul Coates, Glenn Thompson, Kassahun Checole; to the QBR advisory board, who gave me hell *and* tremendous support; to Chris Jackson, my editor at Wiley, an astounding individual as deep in his knowledge of African American literature as patience. He drove me firmly but gently, and always with good direction. Finally (and first), I offer a deep and reverent gratitude to the All for being allowed. Thank you.

Angeli R. Rasbury would also like to thank Shanida Smith, Monique Fleming Berg, and her family for being so patient with her and supportive.

Foreword
by Charles Johnson

As we approach a new century, it is difficult to resist the temptation of composing briefs for the best artistic products—novels, poetry, plays, and motion pictures—of the last hundred years, though clearly such selection by its very nature must be provisional and woefully incomplete. Often they become lightning rods for controversy, because at century's end we are still immersed in what many call the Culture Wars. Consider the literary world's flap over the haphazardly selected "100 Best English-Language Novels" compiled by the editorial board of the Modern Library, a canon that included only three black books (*Native Son, Invisible Man,* and *Go Tell It on the Mountain*), all of them unquestionably superior and seminal works of art, but written exclusively by males and published before 1955 or, put another way, prior to the civil rights and Black Power movements. It was a statement saying, in effect, that the last half-century of black literary production is unworthy of notice, or that the jury is still out on the enduring value of these texts. Fortunately, this Waspish catalogue soon lost all credibility and was judged capricious once the bungling selection process was revealed (one editorial board member confessed to recommending books he had not read), just as a giggle factor now clings to the "100 Top American Films" announced by the American Film Institute. That much-publicized list included not a single motion picture written, directed, or produced by persons of color. (What? No Charles Burnett? No Oscar Micheaux?)

Thus, Max Rodriguez, publisher of QBR and author of the book in your hands, is dead-on right when he says in his introduction that black Americans still live "within a society that has institutionalized its efforts to relegate blackness to the bottom rung." This book you hold, this "view of the African American literary mind, circa 1999," is a necessary antidote to the nervous tokenism of the Modern Library list, to the aesthetic apartheid practiced by the American Film Institute, and to this culture's intractable resistance to recognizing the contributions of the African Diaspora. But readers *will* ask, and so must I, the inevitable question: Is QBR's inventory of literary excellence complete, coherent, and consistent?

If I were to sift through black writing in *one* genre only (novels, say), looking for literary gold, my criterion would be identical to and not differ one iota from that of Albert Murray, who wisely informed us in *The Blue Devils of Nada* that fine art is distinguished by its "range, precision, profundity, and the idiomatic subtlety of the rendition." With Murray as my guide, I would hunt for books that exhibited and promoted in their readers a refinement of language, perception, and reflection. The majority of authors cited here do just that; they are watershed thinkers like the polyhistor W. E. B. Du Bois, magisterial storytellers like Ralph Ellison, and writers whose works—from slave narratives to contemporary cultural critiques—have proven to be essential for a firm grasp of both black and American history.

Yet, no list of 100 will please everyone, and some readers will kvetch about the omissions, fine writers, and first-rate, elegant minds who somehow fell through the cracks: groundbreaking science fiction writer Samuel Delany; Pulitzer Prize–winning Poet Laureate Rita Dove; Clarence Major, our magister ludi of literary experimentation; essayist Gerald Early, a craftsman who writes with clarity and astonishing precision; the late Leon Forrest; MacArthur poet Jay Wright; the ubiquitous black intellectuals—the prolific Thomas Sowell from the right and Henry Louis Gates from the left.

I could go on, of course. Whenever we choose to tally books for a new "canon" of black writing, there will be objections, counter-lists, and fungible choices. More important, though, the very enterprise of making a checklist compels us all, as readers, to question the presuppositions and values we bring to literary judgments. It forces us, if nothing else, to define our own aesthetic position. Is a work "essential" because it was a bestseller? (In that case Stephen King and Irving Wallace are essential.) Because it is "political"—i.e., one that jibes with our own political views? Or won a prestigious award? Or do we gravitate toward certain authors because they are celebrities and appear charming, witty, and well dressed under the klieg lights on *The Oprah Winfrey Show*? Needless to say, none of this has much of anything to do with literary and intellectual achievement, though it does reveal the merely commercial or marketing aspects of contemporary publishing, where too often books are just commodities to be sold—as we sell burritos and toilet paper—and authors are not bellwethers for the life of the mind, but salespersons primarily concerned with profits and the bottom line.

So yes, every list raises interesting questions. Yet what was said in defense of the Modern Library canon—that it briefly galvanized street sales and got more people reading its number one choice, James Joyce's *Ulysses*—can be said as well for the QBR inventory. If it encourages black people to read, it also serves the goal of achieving black *freedom*. No, I do not mean this merely in a "political" way (though surely reading these texts serves this end), but rather in the deepest philosophical sense. Look around you. What do you see? We are enveloped, I daresay, by what Saul Bellow in his essay "Culture Now" called "an amusement society, like decadent Rome." Many Americans watch eight hours of television daily—ready-made images they *passively* receive, even as they consume the endless, often vulgar products of a Hollywood that targets adolescents as its primary audience. In the midst of formulaic entertainment, in a popular culture where "dumbing down" is the rule, *reading* becomes the most radical of all enterprises.

Open any novel. What is there? Black marks—signs—on white paper. First they are silent. They are lifeless, lacking signification until the consciousness of the reader imbues them with meaning, allowing a fictitious character like Bigger Thomas, say, to emerge hugely from the monotonous rows of ebony type. Once this magical act takes place in the mind of the reader, an entire fictional world appears, redivivus, in his consciousness: "a vivid and continuous dream," as novelist John Gardner once called it, one that so ensorcells us that we forget the room we're sitting in or fail to hear the telephone ring. Put simply, the world experienced within any book is *transcendent*. It exists for consciousness alone (Bigger exists *only* as a mental construct, like a mathematical entity). But, as Jean-Paul Sartre describes so well in his classic work, *What Is Literature?*, the rare experience found in books is the "conjoint effort of author and reader." It is dialectical. While the writer composes his "world" in words, his (or her) work requires an attentive reader who will "put himself from the very beginning and almost without a guide at the height of this silence" of signs. Reading, Sartre tells us, is *directed creation*. A contract of sorts. "To write is to make an appeal to the reader that he lead into objective existence the revelation which I have undertaken by means of language." Do you get it? I hope so. For each book *requires* that a reader exercise his orbific freedom for the "world" and theater of meaning embodied on its pages to *be*. As readers, we invest the cold signs on the pages of *Native Son* with our *own* emotions, *our* understanding of poverty, oppression, and fear; then, in what is almost an act of thaumaturgy, the powerful figures and tropes Wright has created reward us richly by returning our subjective feelings to us transformed, refined, and alchemized by language into a new vision with the capacity to change our lives forever.

This magic rests in your hands, as readers. It is a power to co-create and travel through numerous imaginative and intellectual realms that you can invoke at any time, anywhere. If film is a communal experience, as so many have claimed, then reading is the triumph of individual consciousness and man's freedom. And, despite the issues raised by any list of "essential" books, QBR's evolving canon is a splendid way to begin flexing the muscles of our minds and honoring black literary artists by allowing their too often marginalized contributions to find a place to permanently live within us.

Seattle, Washington
1998

Introduction

QBR: The Black Book Review was established five years ago to provide a forum for the critical review and celebration of books that captured our voices, our stories, and our lives. We've taken it as our responsibility and mission to praise and admonish our writers, as needed, and to expose their work to our readers in an unprecedented way.

This book is an outgrowth of that mission. While we have traditionally exposed our readers to the work of our best contemporary writers, for the purposes of this book, it was our intent to gather a consensus on the literature that has most impacted us as a community across the years. Not just the latest flowering of critically and commercially successful literature (although it's good that we continue to develop as a market), but the classics: the works that represent the record of our collective experience. We wanted to find out how important the written history of our experience is to us today. So we asked.

Our request was very simple and straightforward: Name ten books by authors from the African Diaspora that have had the greatest impact on you. We asked everyone. (I know, I know, but we *almost* asked you.) We asked scholars and historians (they read, too); bookstore owners and book buyers; members of reading clubs and attendees at QBR's literary series. (I even asked my sister.) We drew from this survey a range of books that identified the issues and philosophies that we, as a people, felt were most critical, and that were written by the artists who most eloquently and powerfully presented these issues to the world.

This book, however, is not a statistical journal. What you will find are the results presented in a most informative and, yes, opinionated manner. The editors of QBR gathered the numerous responses, selected the titles most often cited, and supplemented them with our own recommendations. We then categorized those books into sections we believe speak directly to the heart of our matters: Origins, Ancestors, and Memory; Community and Identity; Politics, Nationalism, and Revolution; Soul and Spirit; Sisters' Stories; Brothers' Lives. Our final step was to offer brief commentary on each book, summarizing its plot or thesis, talking about what makes it special, and placing it, whenever possible, within the context of its time.

I have often spoken about the way interest in our books has historically waxed and waned. It would be easy to say that every thirty years since the mid-1800s, the beginning of Reconstruction, there has been a spike of interest in the literary affairs of the "Negro." Following the international interest in Frederick Douglass's freedom cry, the writing of Booker T. Washington held sway; Charles Chestnutt and Paul Laurence Dunbar were the anointed of the 1900s; Alain Locke ushered in Harlem's New Negro Movement in the late 1920s and early 1930s; Amiri Baraka, Haki Madhubuti, and Sonia Sanchez *slapped!* us to consciousness as the Black Arts Movement spread Stokely's fire in the 1960s; Sheharazod Ali's *The Black Man's Guide to Understanding the Black Woman* was the flint, and Terry McMillan's *Disappearing Acts* was the fire of the 1990s commercial renaissance.

In fact, every resurgent period of interest in African American literature corresponds to intense social changes. The Civil War marked the voluntary conscription and arming of a previously enslaved population; the mass migration of a disenfranchised public followed. The development of an urbane African American cultural aesthetic was followed by a call to black power. Today's literature reflects the economic and social progress wrought from Malcolm, Martin, urban unrest, open-door policies, and affirmative action. Accommodation and demand, protest and personal introspection mark this current period of African American literature.

Still, what we hoped to identify within this book were not only the books that serve as the literary landmarks of our social movements but also those critical and illuminating works that, due to the social stillness of the moment, fell quietly from the shelves yet survived by dint of word of mouth alone. We also wanted to add representative books from our brothers and sisters in Africa and the Caribbean, whose experiences have so closely paralleled the experiences of African Americans.

We anticipate that arguments will be made around the inclusion or exclusion of one book or another within this list of the essential one hundred. This, too, is part of our process. For certainly, when one discusses essential African American books, one can easily surpass one hundred.

Still, I would be remiss in not recommending Toni Cade Bambara's *Gorilla, My Love,* Wole Soyinka's *Ake,* Gayle Jones's *Corregidora,* and Paul Beatty's *White Boy Shuffle* or Sapphire's *Push,* both stylistic breakthrough novels of the '90s. These, too, should be enjoyed.

A number of noteworthy books that direct readers through African American literary history can be found in bookstores and libraries. The most recent of those, the *Norton Anthology of African American Literature,* joins the *Oxford Companion to African American Literature* and Howard University Press's *The New Cavalcade: African American Writing from 1760 to the Present, Vols. I* and *II,* as excellent primers to our world in literature. Those anthologies, along with this book, support a strong argument for the recognition of an African American literary canon, a functional canon that serves as a respite—a community safehouse—to which to turn when the going gets rough. Yes, the books in our canon must work as literature, but they must also reach the heart. And they must speak to communal truths.

The *Webster's Seventh New Collegiate Dictionary* definition of canon as "a criterion or standard of judgment" begs the question, Whose standards? What cultural criteria are to be met in order to gain inclusion within the list of books deemed "authoritative"? This will continue as a hotly debated issue, given the continuing shift in the American population, the "browning" of the American classroom, and the increasing number of culturally diverse voices being brought to print. Perhaps it is time to develop a more functional, world literary canon—a more inclusive and accepted body of work that serves cultures individually and nurtures a sense of community globally.

African American literature is the story of the African in the new Americas. It is a history of a people in transition and inner turmoil as we seek, still, to find a place within a society that has institutionalized its efforts to relegate blackness to its bottom rung. Ours, then, is an autobiography of protest and struggle for recognition, of achievement and survival.

Our earliest achievements in public letters and writings, protestations to enslavement, were autobiographical: the slave narrative. Even then, and beyond the telling of their plight, the writing was an attempt at proving an intellectual and moral capability and, by extension, the humanity of the enslaved African. Even the reality of post-Reconstruction and the advent of a covert American apartheid could not dim our urge to freedom.

And so with emancipation, we packed our belongings, knowing that if only the opportunity existed, we would show we were possessed of the will to thrive. To St. Louis, Chicago, New York, and all points north, east, and west, we migrated in search of better lives as free women and men, free to grow as a community, free as individuals to contribute to the ideal that was America.

It is from this community history that QBR selects the one hundred most representative books within the African experience in the Americas—books that are significant in that they represent visions and aspirations, or a turning in thought, attitude, or perspective within our evolution as citizens in the New World.

And because they mark the passage of our time on this earth, because they contain our parents' wisdom and ours, because they validate our sense of *I am,* and because they leave an indelible record of our contribution to the cultures of the world, we deem them essential both to us and to those who follow. We encourage you to create your own personal list of books so that you may pass our selections, along with yours, on to your friends and loved ones. Our compilation of the books with the greatest impact on us will be a project that lasts into the new millennium; we will continue to record these works on our web site (www.QBR.com). We would be honored to post your favorites. E-mail us or reach us by post.

May you read and prosper. We continue . . .

—Max Rodriguez

Origins, Ancestors, and Memory

Commentary

by Charles Brooks

The late John Henrik Clarke, in his essay "Why Africana History," stated: "History, I have often said, is a clock that people use to tell their political time of day. It is also a compass that people use to find themselves on the map of human geography. History tells a people where they have been and what they have been. It also tells a people where they are and what they are. Most importantly, history tells a people where they still must go and what they still must be." Dr. Clarke powerfully underlined the importance of grasping and understanding African and African American history because of its connection to the collective fate of a people. Simply put, "If you don't know your past, you don't know your future."

Writers from throughout the African Diaspora have created—and not without struggle—an impressive body of work documenting their origins as a people and reclaiming their right to remember the past. This has been one of the central functions of African American literature. Why has this task been so important? Because our history has often been erased, misrepresented, and used as a tool against us, when in fact it should be the most powerful tool of our empowerment. The truths of our history have been twisted and threatened with extinction—a situation that should be as lamentable to other peoples of the world as it is to people of African descent. Why? Because the real story of our origins, our ancestors, and our quest to remember is a compelling and, ultimately, deeply inspiring story—a gift bequeathed by our finest writers to us and to the world.

This section, "Origins, Ancestors, and Memory," profiles and excerpts nineteen works, spanning two hundred years. These works speak volumes about who we were and who we are, and they provide a vision for what we have yet to achieve. They also provide an opportunity to share the hopes and dreams, pains and sorrows of our ancestors. The section begins by profiling two vital slave narratives, the first literary device used by African Americans to tell their story: *The Interesting Narrative of the Life of Olaudah Equiano* by Olaudah Equiano, and the redoubtable *Narrative of the Life and Times of Frederick Douglass* by Frederick Douglass. It also includes two of the earliest works of fiction created by African Americans, *Clotel* by William Wells Brown and *Our Nig* by Harriet E. Wilson. These early literary efforts were created as a response against the oppressive social institution of slavery. These books do more than retell the familiar story of slavery—they tell it from the perspective of the men and women who lived through it, who felt the pain of bondage and abuse, and who, instead of crumbling, took pen and paper in hand to speak out and make sure the horrible truth would not be ignored or forgotten.

Also profiled are works of history that chronicle the experiences of Africans from the earliest civilizations of antiquity to the contemporary era. Works such as John Hope Franklin's *From Slavery to Freedom,* Lerone Bennett's *Before the Mayflower,* and Ivan Van Sertima's controversial *They Came Before Columbus,* pioneering works of history that describe the varied experiences of people of African descent—not just the story of recent oppressions. Other works in this section speak to the need of black people interpreting the African and the African Diaspora historical experience for themselves. Included in this category is the seminal classic *Stolen Legacy* by George James.

Finally, the section includes works from contemporary writers of fiction who have taken on the work of remembering and rehumanizing our ancestors by reimagining their lives and struggles through highly imaginative storytelling techniques. Toni Morrison's heartbreaking *Beloved,* David Bradley's *The Chaneysville*

Incident, and Octavia Butler's startling *Kindred* are three splendid examples of this act of creative remembrance at work.

This collection of books articulates the commitment that people of African descent have made to document their historical experience in their own words. These books are tools we can all use to advance our understanding of humanity. Enjoy!

Charles Brooks is a freelance journalist and writer. He contributes to the New York Amsterdam News, The Source, The Black World Today, *and the* Black Collegian.

The Interesting Narrative of the Life of Olaudah Equiano, or Gustavus Vassa, the African, Written by Himself (1789)

Olaudah Equiano

Memoir

Published in England in 1789 and in the United States in 1791, *The Interesting Narrative of the Life of Olaudah Equiano* was the first slave narrative to be written without the aid of a ghostwriter or an editor. The clear, intelligent, and ardent voice of Equiano was among the first African voices to tell the story of the journey from Africa to America; his autobiography is considered the father of the slave narrative, the first literary form that black folks used to have their say.

Unlike most other slave narratives, Equiano begins his story in Africa—the idyllic land of his youth. He offers a detailed account of African cultural life and society prior to the European encroachment. Africa was a land "rich and fruitful" whose inhabitants were simple, noble, and in love with life: "We are almost a nation of dancers, musicians, and poets." His rose-tinged memories of a bright and humane existence in Africa are followed by descriptions of the agonies brought on by encounters with brutish and fearsome Europeans: war, the atrocity of the Middle Passage, and enslavement. By juxtaposing the peaceful, humane, and progressive land of his birth with the crude, animal-like behavior of the Europeans, Equiano flipped the script on the usual expectations of his primarily white audience, who typically assumed *they* were the civilized ones. As his story continued, Equiano stressed the importance of hard work (he purchased his own freedom with money he earned) and the crucial role of Christian faith in his life.

This first manifestation of the African American genius for autobiography—a genius that would later give us the lives of Frederick Douglass, Malcolm X, Maya Angelou, and countless others in their own words—gave eloquent voice to the experience of the voiceless millions who made the journey from Africa to America. And like the memorable books produced by Frederick, Malcolm, and Maya, Equiano's book is both a fascinating tale and a story with a mission: to describe and protest the enslaved condition of his people. Pre-dating Frederick Douglass's *Narrative of the Life of Frederick Douglass, an American Slave* by some fifty years, Olaudah Equiano's *Life* did for abolitionists in Great Britain what Douglass's *Narrative* did for the movement in the United States: It exposed the horrors of slavery while simultaneously holding the mirror of blame to the European, and it lent a human face to enslaved Africans, around which a slave reform movement could develop. As much a surprise to the world as it was "interesting," its passion and quality of prose made it the most influential literary work by an African American in the eighteenth century.

The Narrative of the Life and Times of Frederick Douglass: An American Slave, Written by Himself (1845)

Frederick Douglass
Memoir

When it was first published, many critics doubted that *The Narrative of the Life and Times of Frederick Douglass* had even been written by Frederick Douglass. As odd as it may seem now, that criticism was not completely unfounded: In the mid-nineteenth century, the antislavery movement produced hundreds of slave narratives, many of them ghostwritten by white abolitionists and tailored to create sympathy for their movement. But this book, by this remarkable man, was different. The tag line at the end of the book's subtitle—*Written by Himself*—was vitally important. Although clearly written with the abolitionist cause in mind, this book is not merely a political tract. True, its dispassionate prose brought to light the "injustice, exposure to outrage, and savage barbarity" of slavery as Douglass observed and experienced it. But it also brought to life an uncommon man and the particular concerns seared into him during his experience of bondage. Douglass recounts that during slavery, he and his people were denied life's fundamentals: faith, family, education, the capacity for bold action, a sense of community, and personal identity. Douglass saw reclamation of these things as the key to his and his people's survival, redemption, and salvation.

The autobiography opens with a description of the aspects of his own life that Douglass was never allowed to know: the identity of his father, the warmth and care of his mother (who was a stranger to him), and even the fact of his own date of birth. As a child, he suffered from and observed savage beatings firsthand, including the fierce beating of his Aunt Hester at the hands of their master, Captain Aaron Anthony. As he grew older, Douglass liberated himself in stages: mentally, spiritually, and, eventually, physically. His mental freedom began when he was taught to read and write and realized the power of literacy; his spiritual freedom came when he discovered the grace of Christianity and the will to resist his beatings; his physical freedom arrived when he finally escaped to the North.

After escaping, Douglass was committed to telling the world about the condition of the brothers and sisters he left behind. Aside from telling Douglass's personal story, his autobiography takes us to the fields and the cabins and the lives of many slaves to reveal the real human cost of slavery. Douglass focused on the dehumanizing aspects of slavery: not just the beatings, but the parting of children from their mothers, the denial of education, and the sexual abuses of slave masters. He ends the book with this statement: "Sincerely and earnestly hoping that his little book may do something toward throwing light on the American slave system, and hastening the glad day of deliverance to the millions of my brethren in bonds—faithfully relying upon the power of truth, love, and justice, for success in my humble efforts—and solemnly pledgeing myself anew to the sacred cause, I subscribe myself, Frederick Douglass."

The book was an incredible success: It sold over thirty thousand copies and was an international bestseller. It was the first, and most successful, of three autobiographies that Douglass was to write. The other two, *My Bondage and My Freedom* (1855) and *The Life and Times of Frederick Douglass,* update the story of his life and revise some of the facts of his earlier autobiography.

Clotel: or, The President's Daughter, A Narrative of Slave Life in the United States (1853)

William Wells Brown
Novel

After his 1834 escape from slavery, William Wells Brown became a noted activist, orator, journalist, and memoirist in the cause of abolition. When he published *Clotel; or, The President's Daughter* nineteen years after his escape, he also became the first African American novelist. *Clotel* was a complicated mix of literary genres—part melodrama, part escape narrative, part love story—but it is not surprising that the first African American novel was first and foremost a novel of political protest, a genre that would be well-tread by Brown's literary progeny.

Clotel was also the first abolitionist novel produced by a black man who had himself escaped bondage, so Brown's exhaustive chronicling of the shameful behavior of white Americans in the face of slavery is written with knowing detail and passion. Brown named names and pulled no punches, denouncing the hypocrisy of religion and democracy, clergymen and politicians. He also explored troubling themes that have recurred throughout African American literary history: color envy among African Americans, the exploitation of black women, the struggles of nurturing a black family under oppressive conditions, and the maddening chasm between the ideals of American democracy and freedom and the reality of black life in America.

The novel tells several stories (in fact, it opens with Brown's own story of escape) but primarily follows the life of Clotel, the enslaved daughter of Thomas Jefferson and his mulatto housemaid, Currer. The novel opens with Clotel, her mother, and her sister Althesa being sold on the auction block to different masters. Clotel is sold to Horatio Green and becomes his concubine. She develops a genuine emotional attachment to Green and has his child, Mary. When Green marries, his new wife forces him to sell Clotel while retaining Mary. The novel then follows Clotel's exciting escape from her new master, from Mississippi to Louisville, Cincinnati, Richmond, and, finally, Washington, D.C., where the novel's final drama unfolds in the shadow of the nation's Capitol.

The assertion that Jefferson had children with his enslaved mistresses was so controversial that the complete, unexpurgated version of the book was not published in the United States until 1969. Wells released the book in several editions and under different titles during his lifetime, and although it never did achieve the success of other antislavery novels published in the period, notably *Uncle Tom's Cabin,* it has endured as one of the first powerful fictional salvos in the ongoing battle for justice and equality in this Land of the Free.

Even with her short hair, Clotel was handsome. Her life had been a secluded one, and though now nearly thirty years of age, she was still beautiful. At her short hair, the other servants laughed, "Miss Clo needn't strut round so big, she got short nappy har well as I," said Nell. . . . "She thinks she white, when she come here wid that long har of hers," replied Mill. . . . The fairness of Clotel's complexion was regarded with envy as well by the other servants as by the mistress herself. This is one of the hard features of slavery.

—from *Clotel*

Our Nig, or, Sketches from the Life of a Free Black, in a Two-Story White House, North (1859)

Harriet E. Wilson
Novel

I t is the relatively obscure writer Harriet E. Wilson who has earned the title of Mother of Black Women's Fiction. *Our Nig,* the first novel by an African American woman, transports the reader of the African experience in America to the North— the Promised Land—*freedom.* The time: circa 1859; the place: Boston, or its environs. Through Alfrado, the novel's female protagonist, Wilson adds to the American literary palette the first of many black heroines who evince moral rectitude and strength of character. But Alfrado's life was no crystal stair. As Wilson describes it, the "freedom" afforded blacks in the North was a chimera; the "shadows of slavery"—racist abuse, servitude, limited opportunity—fell hard on New England's black citizens and particularly hard on black women.

After the death of her father, a black man, Frado is abandoned by her white mother and her mother's new black lover. Frado becomes a servant for a white family, the Bellmonts. While Mr. Bellmont and his sons are kind-hearted men, Frado is chronically mistreated and tormented by Mrs. Bellmont, a diabolic woman intent on destroying Frado's spirit through scoldings and physical violence. Frado withstands the worst of Mrs. Bellmont and eventually rebels, refusing to be beaten, much to the shock of her mistress. She leaves the Bellmont household and eventually marries Samuel, a con man who claims to be a former slave and makes his living as an abolitionist orator. When Frado becomes pregnant, Samuel takes off, leaving her alone and in desperate poverty.

"Yes, *yes!* " she repeated sarcastically, "you know these niggers are just like black snakes; you *can't* kill them. If she wasn't tough she would have been killed long ago. There was never one of my girls could do half the work."

"Did they ever try?" interposed her husband. "I think she can do more than all of them together."

"What a man!" said she, peevishly. "But I want to know what is going to be done with her about getting pious?"

"Let her do just as she has a mind to. If it comforts her, let her enjoy the privilege of being good. I see no objection."

"I should think *you* were crazy, sure. Don't you know that every night she will want to go toting off to meeting? and Sundays, too? and you know we have a great deal of company Sundays, and she can't be spared."

"I thought you Christians held to going to church," remarked Mr. B.

"Yes, but who ever thought of having a nigger go, except to drive others there? Why, according to you and James, we should very soon have her in the parlor, as smart as our own girls. It's of no use talking to you or James. If you should go on as you would like, it would not be six months before she would be leaving me; and that won't do. Just think how much profit she was to us last summer. We had no work hired out; she did the work of two girls—"

"And got the whippings for two with it!" remarked Mr. Bellmont.

"I'll beat the money out of her, if I can't get her worth any other way," retorted Mrs. B. sharply.

—from *Our Nig*

It is at this point that Frado decides to write the story of her life. The novel ends on a poignant note, with Frado hopeful that sales of the book will allow her to care for her financial needs.

While it was a sentimental novel, *Our Nig* told a tough story in realistic and often strikingly beautiful language, without the melodrama or happy endings of contemporary novels and autobiographical narratives. In certain facets, Frado is a remarkably modern character: she was a working-class and ultimately independent woman who found spiritual strength in resistance. The clarity and realism with which Wilson rendered Frado may come from the fact that, in all likelihood, Frado's story was literally the story of Wilson's life. Wilson herself suffered for years as a servant to a difficult employer and was abandoned in pregnancy by a good-for-nothing con man and had to turn to writing to support herself. As noted by the editors of *The Norton Anthology of African American Literature*: "Thus African American women's fiction originated in necessity, if not virtual desperation, but took form and meaning in Wilson's eloquent testimony."

Up from Slavery (1901)

Booker T. Washington
Memoir

The history of the African in America has often been personalized or embodied within one individual, one spokesperson who represented the sentiments of the moment. In the South of the 1890s, Booker T. Washington stood as the often controversial personification of the aspirations of the black masses. The Civil War had ended, casting an uneducated black mass adrift or, equally tenuous, creating a class of sharecroppers still dependent on the whims of their former owners. Black Reconstruction, for all its outward trimming, had failed to deliver its promised economic and political empowerment. While an embittered and despairing black population sought solace and redemption, a white citizenry systematically institutionalized racism.

From this Armageddon rose this Moses, Booker Taliaferro Washington, who was born in 1856 in Virginia, of a slave mother and a white father he never knew. But he gave no indication in his autobiography of the pain this almost certainly caused him: "I do not even know his name. I have heard reports to the effect that he was a white man who lived on one of the nearby plantations. But I do not find especial fault with him. He was simply another unfortunate victim of the institution which the nation unhappily had engrafted upon it at that time." After Emancipation, Washington began to dream of getting an education and resolved to go to the Hampton Normal Agricultural Institute in Virginia. When he arrived, he was allowed to work as the school's janitor in return for his board and part of his tuition. After graduating from Hampton, Washington was selected to head a new school for blacks at Tuskegee, Alabama, where he taught the virtues of "patience, thrift, good manners and high morals" as the keys to empowerment.

An unabashed self-promoter (Tuskegee was dependent upon the largesse of its white benefactors) and advocate of accommodation, Washington's "pick yourself up by your bootstraps" and "be patient and prove yourself first" philosophy was simultaneously acclaimed by the masses, who prescribed to self-reliance, and condemned by the black intelligentsia, who demanded a greater and immediate inclusion in the social, political, and economic fabric of this emerging nation. Washington's philosophy struck a chord that played like a symphony within the racial politics of the times. It gave a glimmer of hope to the black masses; it created for whites a much-needed locus for their veneer of social concern—funds flooded into Tuskegee Institute; and finally, the initiatives of the black intelligentsia, led by W. E. B. Du Bois, were, for the moment, neutralized.

Washington "believed that the story of his life was a typical American success story," and he redefined "success" to make it so: "I have learned that success is to be measured not so much by the position that one has reached in his life as by the obstacles which he has overcome while trying to succeed." His powerfully simple philosophy that self-help is the key to overcoming obstacles of racism and poverty has resonated among African Americans of all political stripes, from Marcus Garvey to Louis Farrakhan.

Ignorant and inexperienced, it is not strange that in the first years of our new life (after slavery) we began at the top instead of at the bottom; that a seat in Congress or the state legislature was more sought than real estate or industrial skill; . . . No race can prosper till it learns that there is as much dignity in tilling a field as in writing a poem. It is at the bottom of life we must begin, and not at the top.

—from *Up from Slavery*

Black Reconstruction in America: An Essay toward a History of the Part Which Black Folk Played in the Attempt to Reconstruct Democracy in America, 1860–1880 (1935)

W. E. B. Du Bois
History

In *Black Reconstruction in America,* Du Bois applies his keen eye to the question of America's post–Civil War Reconstruction, and why it failed. Emancipation for African Americans did not bring on a glorious new beginning for them. Besides not getting their promised forty acres and a mule, the former slaves were denied the vote, denied equal educational opportunities, and cheated out of their livelihood by the sharecropping system. Reconstruction, a never-to-be-repeated opportunity to genuinely change the nature of race relations in the South, only delayed the reestablishment of white dominance over the lives of black southerners.

The brilliantly written and exhaustively researched *Black Reconstruction in America* was completed in 1935 while black southerners still lived under the stifling reign of Jim Crow. Du Bois considered this work to be his magnum opus. In addition to cataloging the reversals of the post-Reconstruction South, Du Bois presented Reconstruction as a lost opportunity for all Americans. He describes the Civil War, the emancipation of slaves, and Reconstruction as being part of a dramatic revolutionary movement that created, for an all-too-brief historical moment, true democracy in America. And he portrays African Americans as bold actors in that drama, rather than as just passively manipulated pawns in the power games of northern and southern whites. But in the end, he insisted that equal rights for blacks were still missing from American society. Du Bois used strong language and commonsense reasoning to make the case that even under the best circumstances, it would take black people time to shake off the effects of slavery, but in a still-hostile South and without the protection of the American government, it was insanity to expect blacks to make quick advancements.

In *Black Reconstruction*, Du Bois points to the failures of Reconstruction to adequately reconstruct American society so that its black citizens could move forward fully enfranchised and with equal rights under the law. *Black Reconstruction* gives a penetrating analysis of how Reconstruction fell short of creating true democracy for all Americans and instead began a new process of discrimination and disenfranchisement for free black citizens. The effects of America's failure to live up to its promises and ideals are still being felt by its people—both black and white.

The unending tragedy of Reconstruction is the utter inability of the American mind to grasp its real significance, its national and world-wide implications. . . . We apparently expected that this social upheaval was going to be accomplished with peace, honesty and efficiency, and that the planters were going to quietly surrender the right to live on the labor of black folk, after two hundred and fifty years of habitual exploitation. And it seems to America a proof of inherent race inferiority that four million slaves did not completely emancipate themselves in eighty years, in the midst of nine million bitter enemies, and indifferent public opinion of the whole nation. If the Reconstruction of the Southern states, from slavery to free labor, and from aristocracy to industrial democracy, had been conceived as a major national program of America, whose accomplishment at any price was well worth the effort, we should be living today in a different world.

—from *Black Reconstruction*

From Slavery to Freedom: A History of African Americans (1947)

John Hope Franklin
History

W riting in the *New Republic* about the scholarly contribution of historian John Hope Franklin, the late Roy Wilkins noted, "John Hope Franklin is an uncommon historian who has consistently corrected, in clear, vigorous language, the misreading of this country's rich heritage." Similarly complimentary is the more recent assessment by historian Nell Irvin Painter, who praised Franklin for his "great intellectual integrity" and open identification of himself "as a black person concerned with black people." The combination of rigorous, authoritative scholarship and unabashed affection that Franklin brought to his subject—his people—remains the standard by which subsequent histories have been judged.

From Slavery to Freedom, originally published in 1947, was in its seventh edition in 1999. It is usually referred to as the authoritative history of African Americans. Beginning with the pre-Diasporic African states and institutions, the narrative follows the African "forced migration" to the Caribbean, the early American colonies, and Latin America. The major focus of the text is, of course, on the United States. Recent editions have brought the African American experience through to the Black Revolution of the 60s and 70s and expanded the coverage of African states and contemporary issues. Its in-depth discussion of slavery remains one of the most authoritative accounts of the "peculiar institution."

Franklin once said, "It was necessary, as a black historian, to have a personal agenda." At the same time, his history has remained redoubtable over the years, in part owing to his politically objective point of view. From its first edition through its current incarnation, the book never adhered to the fashionable ideology of the day, whether Marxism or Afrocentrism, but let the history speak for itself. In fact, historian Earle Thorpe has noted that at its initial publication in 1947, there were mixed reactions to the work from the black intellectual community. He concedes, however, that despite the conventionality of its content and interpretation, "the objectivity of the author, his temperateness in tone, thorough grasp of his materials, and scholarly presentation make the work a significant contribution." Not a radical history, but thorough, durable, and essential.

Stolen Legacy (1954)

George G. M. James
Nonfiction

*S*tolen Legacy stands among the first scholarly works that have attempted to recover the "lost" history of early African civilization. George G. M. James was a professor of Latin, Greek, and mathematics. It was his interest in the roots of Greek philosophy and the seemingly "immaculate conception of Western civilization" that brought him to ask such questions as Who were the Greek scholars? Who were their teachers? How did what they learned fit into the contemporary Greek worldview? And, when James considered the fates of the greatest of them—Anaxagoras was imprisoned and exiled, Socrates executed, Plato sold into slavery, and Aristotle exiled—he wondered why they were considered to be undesirable citizens in their own land.

Could it be that Greek philosophers were so mistreated because they imported a foreign and therefore subversive worldview? For example, Pythagoras, the "father of geometry" and the first Greek philosopher, was purported to have traveled to Egypt. He settled in Italy and practiced a simple, communal life, the goal of which was to live in harmony with the divine. To that end, he prescribed a regimen of purification that included dietary restrictions and periods of silence and contemplation. He taught the kinship of all life and the immortality and transmigration of the soul.

Stolen Legacy argues that Greek philosophers were not the originators of Greek philosophy, but that they derived it from Egyptian priests. James posits that Greece during this period of "enlightenment" was, in fact, constantly engaged in war and internal conflict, creating an environment not conducive to the evolution of philosophy. He bluntly states that Greek philosophy was the offspring of the Egyptian Mystery System and that the Egyptians educated the Greeks.

Upon its publication in 1954, *Stolen Legacy* was not well received; however, it has remained in print to this day as a controversial chronicle of the possible African origins of classical civilization. Even if you don't agree with all of James's conclusions, the questions he asks and the theories he asserts are fascinating to anyone interested in studying classical civilizations from an African-centered perspective.

Before the Mayflower (1966, latest rev. ed., 1988)

Lerone Bennett Jr.

History

*B*efore the Mayflower grew out of a series of articles Bennett published in *Ebony* magazine in 1962, regarding "the trials and triumphs of a group of Americans whose roots in the American soil are deeper than the roots of the Puritans who arrived on the celebrated *Mayflower* a year after a 'Dutch man of war' deposited twenty Negroes at Jamestown." Bennett's history is infused with a desire to set the record straight about black contributions to the Americas and about the powerful Africans of antiquity. While not a fresh history, it provides a solid synthesis of current historical research and a lively writing style that makes it accessible and engaging reading.

After discussing the contributions of Africans to the ancient world, *Before the Mayflower* tells the history of "the other Americans," how they came to America, and what happened to them when they got here. The book is comprehensive and detailed, providing little-known and often overlooked facts about the lives of black folks through slavery, Reconstruction, America's wars, the Great Depression, and the civil rights movement. The book includes a useful time line and some fascinating archival images.

Bennett, who attended Morehouse College, was a reporter in Mississippi before becoming the first senior editor of *Ebony*. He has published several books on the black experience, as well as a biography of Martin Luther King Jr. Bennett hoped to astonish the reader with "the richness of the Negro's heritage," to illustrate that their story is "relevant to the struggle of all men." With *Before the Mayflower,* he succeeded brilliantly.

Civilization started in the great valleys of Africa and Asia. Blacks, or people who would be considered blacks today, were among the first people to use tools, paint pictures, plant seeds and worship gods. In the beginning, black people marched in the front ranks of the emerging human procession. They founded empires and states. They made some of the critical discoveries and contributions that led to the modern world.

—from *Before the Mayflower*

Two Thousand Seasons (1976)

Ayi Kwei Armah
Novel

"That we the black people are one people we know. Destroyers will travel long distances in their minds and out to deny you this truth. We do not argue with them, the fools. Let them presume to instruct us about ourselves. That too is in their nature. That too is in the flow of their two thousand seasons against us." With this searing indictment, Ayi Kwei Armah tells us of the way of our ancestors, and of our prophesied two-thousand-year walk in the valley of the destroyers.

How often have we looked for some direction, some inkling of information regarding our ways advent to the Great Intrusion, that period prior to our open-armed welcome of the Muslim hoard? How often have we sought some glimmer, some fraction of insight into ancient societal Africa and the communal spirit, our birthright, which guides us silently through resistance and survival?

Entwining fable and fact, Armah delivers both a saddening and a scathing account of our fall from grace. He tells, also, of the way that we left behind: "Our way is reciprocity. The way is wholeness. Our way knows no oppression. The way destroys oppression. Our way is hospitable to our guests. The way repels destroyers. Our way produces before it consumes. The way produces far more than it consumes. Our way creates. The way destroys only destruction."

Armah spares no one in his indictment. In our treason, black people too are guilty. If there is only one book within this collection that one must read, this is it.

They Came Before Columbus (1976)

Ivan Van Sertima
History

According to standard history, the first African Americans emerged from the holds of slave ships, shackled, confused, and already defeated by their European masters. *They Came Before Columbus* is a compelling, detailed, and exhaustively researched documentation of the presence and legacy of black Africans in America before Columbus. Van Sertima, an anthropological historian from Rutgers University who is also a gifted writer, painstakingly sifts the documentation of centuries of research into a cohesive narrative that aims to prove that Africans predated Columbus in America and that their contributions as artisans, agricultural scientists, and linguists are still seen in present-day America.

Van Sertima's controversial claims stem from historical, navigational, archeological, linguistic, oral, and botanical evidence of a pre-Columbian African presence in the Americas. Van Sertima cites Indian words and religious and cultural practices apparently derived from the Mandingos and other African nations. Records indicate that Indians spoke of trading with Africans. Oral histories from West African griots talk of expeditions across the Atlantic. American nicotine and cocaine have been found in the bodies of entombed Egyptians. And there were even confirmed sightings by European explorers, including Vasco Nuñez de Balboa, who allegedly stumbled across African prisoners of war in an Indian camp, and the Spanish priest Fray Gregorio García, who wrote, "Here we found slaves of the lord—Negroes—who were the first our people saw in the Indies."

Van Sertima's work has come under fire from numerous critics. But each reader can draw his or her own conclusions based on the provocative and truly fascinating evidence presented here. A work of great importance and popularity, *They Came Before Columbus* argues that it was Africans who crossed the Atlantic first and that those ingenious first "African Americans" left behind tantalizing clues of their presence.

The Mande people of West Africa created a center of plant domestication around the headwaters of the river Niger circa 4500 B.C. Black Africans contributed the bottle gourd, the watermelon, the tamarind fruit and cultivated cotton to Egypt. . . . Black gods and gods with Negro features have been found among the American Indians. It is hard for many to imagine the Negro-African figure being venerated as a god. He has always been represented as the lowliest of the low, at least since the era of conquest and slavery. His humiliation as a world figure begins, in fact, with the coming of Columbus. The Negro-African as a backward, slow and uninventive being is still with us . . . the memory of his cultural and technological achievements before the day of his humiliation seem to have been erased from the consciousness of history.

—from *They Came Before Columbus*

Roots: The Saga of an American Family
(1976)

Alex Haley
Novel

Roots is the fictionalized account of Alex Haley's family history and an epic narrative of the African American experience. For many African Americans, the novel and the history-making television miniseries it begot were pivotal in their understanding and appreciation of their origins. The story traces Haley's family history from the imagined birth of his ancestor Kunta Kinte in an African village in 1750 to the death, seven generations later, of his father in Arkansas. Based on fifteen years of research by Haley, the novel is a combination of fact and fiction—it is often referred to as faction—that puts a human face on the suffering of black people through the ordeal of the Middle Passage, slavery, and Jim Crow. Its combination of compelling, affectionate storytelling and informative history has had a revolutionary effect on the way Americans—black and white—think about the history of a people.

The story, like that of Olaudah Equiano, begins in an idyllic African world destroyed by Europeans. Haley's description of Kinte's journey to America in the hold of a slave ship is harrowing and indelibly memorable. Kinte is enslaved in America but is still proud, refusing to forsake his African name or heritage. He passes on stories of Africa to his daughter, Kizzy, who bears a child, Chicken George. George is a successful cockfighter whose father is also his master—a common situation in the time of slavery but one that is treated with unusual sensitivity here. George passes the stories of his grandfather on to his children, including Tom, who marries a part-Indian woman named Irene. Tom and Irene have eight children, one of whom is Haley's grandmother.

She passes the family stories to her daughter, who passes them on to Haley. Haley, in turn, tells the story, from Kunta Kinte to Chicken George, to his own grandmother, to his children.

Haley has been accused of plagiarism and his book has been criticized for historical inaccuracies, but the novel holds up as a powerful representation of the full African American saga. Haley tells the story of his family—and, by extension, the story of all black people whose family histories are lost in the mists of time—with an immense amount of respect and tenderness. Amidst the undeniable misery of slavery and Jim Crow, he always reveals the outstanding characteristics that sustained his family—spirited resistance, cunning survival instincts, and a will to remember and pass on. James Baldwin captured the book's appeal when he wrote, "Alex Haley's taking us back through time to the village of his ancestors is an act of faith and courage, but this book is also an act of love, and it is this which makes it haunting."

Sally Hemings (1979)

Barbara Chase-Riboud
Novel

Almost twenty years ago, Barbara Chase-Riboud made literary history when she published *Sally Hemings*. The novel spent six weeks on the *New York Times* best-seller list, sold 1.6 million copies worldwide, and breathed life into an historical enigma.

Sally Hemings details one of the greatest and most controversial stories in America: the tempestuous love affair between Thomas Jefferson, third president of the United States, and his quadroon slave, the extravagantly beautiful Sally Hemings. Epic in proportion yet rendered in exquisite detail by a writer with the eye of a historian and the heart of a storyteller, Barbara Chase-Riboud illustrates the story of Sally Hemings—Thomas Jefferson's half-stepsister, mistress, the mother of his children, and the slave he would never set free.

Sally had lived happily at Monticello, the Jefferson plantation in Virginia, for many years. It was when she was sent to join the Jeffersons in Paris, when she was fourteen and Thomas forty-four, that he fell hopelessly in love with her. "The return to Virginia and to slavery had been a shock to me. In Paris, we had both forgotten what it meant to be white or black, master or slave."

By chronicling the tempestuous lives of two families, one black and one white yet both inextricably linked, *Sally Hemings* shows irrefutably one of the prime peculiarities of the peculiar institution: that love and bondage often went hand in hand.

She had never contemplated freedom. Freedom, to Sally Hemings, was a vague, glimmering place no one ever returned from to prove it really existed.

—from *Sally Hemings*

The Chaneysville Incident (1981)

David Bradley
Novel

David Bradley's second book, *The Chaneysville Incident*, took ten years to complete. A deeply moving work set in the mountains of Pennsylvania, it received the PEN/Faulkner Award as the best novel of 1981. John Washington, the novel's hero, is a history professor and scholar, a man with an impressive mastery of his academic world, a proud rebuke to stereotypes of black intellectual inferiority. But he is utterly detached from his heritage; he is a historian of other people's history who wants to believe that his identity as a black man goes no further than the color of his skin. John is nevertheless driven by circumstances and his own demons to go back home, to the mountains of Pennsylvania, and back in time, to the lives of his ancestors, to uncover the truth about his father and his father's father and, ultimately, about himself.

The novel opens with Washington, the consummate professional whose demons are well contained deep within his subconscious, having reached a critical point in his life. His girlfriend, Judith, demands a greater emotional commitment, which he finds he is unable to give. When he is summoned back to the town of his birth by an urgent message advising him of the imminent death of Old Jack, the only one of the three men who reared him still living, he begins an introspective journey that challenges his willingness and ability to expiate his demons. With the help of the dying Jack, he enters a personal history he had staunchly avoided because of an emotionally inaccessible father and the contempt that he holds for his mother. Washington uncovers the mystery of his father's suicide; learns the heroic truth of how his great-grandfather, an ex-slave, was killed when caught helping twelve runaways; discovers that his contempt for his mother is misplaced; and creates within himself a place of compassion where commitment to Judith can grow.

The heroes of *The Chaneysville Incident*—John Washington; his father, Moses; and his grandfather, Brobdingnag C. K.—stand apart as strong, contemplative, intellectual men. Each, in his own way, uses tools of logic and creativity to invent ways of understanding and surviving in an illogical, hostile world. But they are also men who draw their strength from and give their lives for family, community, and heritage. As John grows up, his disconnection from family, community, and heritage lead him to an unbalanced life—strong intellect, malnourished spirit—and a tormented psyche. In beautiful and precise prose, Bradley tells the story of how that balance between intellect and spirit was regained, and how an intelligent reclamation of one's heritage can be a source of strength and peace.

Beloved (1987)

Toni Morrison
Novel

When Toni Morrison was an editor at Random House, she edited *The Black Book*, an anthology/scrapbook of African American history. While working on the book, she ran across a newspaper article about a woman named Margaret Garner, a runaway slave who killed her children, slitting the throat of one and bashing in the skull of the other, to prevent them from being recaptured by the slave hunters hot on their trail. This upside-down story of motherly love expressed through child murder haunted Morrison for many years and finally manifest itself in fictional form in her Pulitzer Prize–winning fifth novel, *Beloved*. A poetic chronicle of slavery and its aftermath, it describes how that inhuman ordeal forced cruel choices and emotional pain on its victims and gave them memories that would possess them long after they were released from their physical bondage. Morrison uses the story to address a key question for black people then and now: How can we let go of the pain of the past and redeem the sacrifices made in the struggle for freedom?

The novel's main character, Sethe, escapes from a plantation where she was viciously abused and perversely cherished by her master for her "skills" as a childbearer. When the slave hunters come looking for her, she kills her infant child to prevent her from becoming a slave. After slavery, Sethe finds work and devotes herself to her surviving daughter, Denver, but is haunted by memories of cruel life on the plantation she escaped and by the vindictive spirit of her murdered infant, Beloved. Paul D., an almost supernaturally charming former slave from the same plantation as Sethe, arrives and temporarily banishes the ghost of the infant Beloved. But Beloved returns in an older and more dan-

Not even trying, [Paul D.] had become the kind of man who could walk into a house and make the women cry. Because with him, in his presence, they could. There was something blessed in his manner. Women saw him and wanted to weep—to tell him that their chest hurt and their knees did too. Strong women and wise saw him and told him things they only told each other: that way past the Change of Life, desire in them had suddenly become enormous, greedy, more savage than when they were fifteen, and that it embarrassed them and made them sad; that secretly they longed to die—to be quit of it—that sleep was more precious to them than any waking day. Young girls sidled up to him to confess or describe how well-dressed the visitations were that had followed them straight from their dreams. Therefore, although he did not understand why this was so, he was not surprised when Denver dripped tears into the stovefire. Nor, fifteen minutes later, after telling him about her stolen milk, her mother wept as well. Behind her, bending down, his body an arc of kindness, he held her breasts in the palms of his hands.

—from *Beloved*

gerous form and sets out to destroy Sethe's household by seducing Paul D., driving Denver away from her mother, and feeding on Sethe's body and spirit.

Beloved is both beautiful and elusive: beautiful for its powerful and captivating language, and elusive not just because of its reliance on visions of haints and apparitions, but in its narrative interweaving of the past and present, the physical and the spiritual. For all of its supernatural elements, however, *Beloved* is most notable as a powerful tribute to the real-life struggles of a generation of black men and women to reconcile the horrors of the past and move on. The spirit of Beloved and the recurring memories of the tribulations Sethe endured on the plantations she lived on and escaped from were both testaments to the tangibly powerful hold that slavery had on her. In the end, she is able to recover her life only by finding within herself and her community the spiritual tools strong enough to exorcise her of this haunting. In this, Sethe's struggle is the struggle of all African Americans: the struggle to redeem ourselves, our families, and our communities from the wreckage of the past even as we honor the sacrifices made for survival.

Kindred (1988)

Octavia Butler
Novel

Using the techniques of science fiction, Octavia Butler in *Kindred* tangles in a startlingly unique and imaginative way with some of the most fundamental questions about slavery: How does one become mentally enslaved? What is the nature of the slave-master relationship? What is the relevance of slavery to modern-day descendants of slaves?

Dana Franklin, a black woman writer, is celebrating her twenty-sixth birthday in 1976 when she is snatched from her Southern California home and transported to the bank of a river in the antebellum South where she saves the life of a young white child who appears to be drowning. When the child's parents arrive, they begin to beat Dana; when the child's father attempts to shoot her, she is transported back to the twentieth century. The child is Rufus Weylin, whom Dana later discovers is to be the father of one of her ancestors, a child born of Weylin's rape of Alice Greenwood, one of his slaves. Thus, the preservation of his life is critical to Dana's survival. She is transported to the nineteenth century whenever his life is in danger, and she returns to the twentieth century whenever *her* life is in danger.

She begins to develop an attachment to Rufus; in every life-saving encounter with him, she attempts to teach him not to fall into the racism endemic in his family and southern society. In essence, she tries to save both his body and his soul. But her trips back in time are too infrequent to have any lasting effect on Weylin, who buys into the racist and sexist system that surrounds him. Dana takes an interest in the Weylin slaves, particularly Alice, and uses her literacy and knowledge of modern medical skills to help them. But in order to guarantee her own existence in the future, she also must encourage Alice to have sex with Rufus. Eventually, Dana too is made a slave and forced into an intimate understanding of the horrors of slavery and her own limitations.

The tension of the oddly symbiotic relationship between Dana and Weylin makes this book a riveting read. By transporting a modern-day African American woman into slavery, Butler vividly brings to life the hardships endured by the slaves. Dana frequently compares her strength and survival skills to those of the enslaved women and finds herself wanting. In the end, Dana finds the strength to break free of her physical slavery and the hold that the past has on her, while ensuring her own survival in the present, but she can never again forget the struggles of her exploited ancestors.

Spirits of the Passage: The Transatlantic Slave Trade in the Seventeenth Century
(1997)

Madeline Burnside and Rosemarie Robotham
Nonfiction

How can one sunken vessel represent three hundred years of history? Black scuba diver Mel Fisher's discovery of the *Henrietta Marie*, a slave ship that foundered off the coast of Florida in 1700, served as the inspiration for the writing of *Spirits of the Passage*. This sunken merchant slaver, with its many accoutrements of "the trade" still intact, became the earliest "living" monument to the greatest of all human crimes—the ownership and enslavement of humans for profit.

A beautifully illustrated book, *Spirits of the Passage* relates the history of the transatlantic slave trade through passages of narrative and attractive, informative photographs and drawings. It begins with an overview of the world circa 1400 that quickly dispels the myth of the Portuguese as the originators of the African slave trade. That ignoble honor belongs to the Moors of North Africa, a Berber people who in the mid-fifteenth century were Europe's main procurer of all races of slaves—black and eastern European alike.

Spirits of the Passage describes the antecedents to the transatlantic slave trade: the hegemonist philosophies of the Portuguese, the Spanish, the Dutch, and the English governments; the social and economic hardships of life in London that led to the English settlement of the New World; and the constant internecine warfare among African tribes, which made prisoners abundant, expendable, and available to meet the exploding demand for exported human labor. Tribal warfare, along with the avarice of some African elders, became the wedge used by Europeans to feed their expansionist greed.

The book then presents a description of the infamous Middle Passage, a harrowing history of survival, murder, acceptance, mutiny, and suicide. The book concludes with the arrival in the New World, and the rest, as they say, is (our) history. *Spirits of the Passage* is a deeply informative and engrossing book.

Community
and Identity

Commentary

by Robert Fleming

Community and *identity* are two of the most important criteria used to evaluate the humanity, potential, and spiritual worth of a people. Despite the political, economic, and social oppression that has plagued us since our forced introduction to these shores, our troubled march toward full equality in the face of overwhelming odds has been nurtured by our faith in our worth as individuals and our connection to each other. When protesters during the bloody southern civil rights campaigns of the mid-sixties carried signs reading I AM A MAN, every black person in America knew exactly what was being said. At that moment, we snatched back the power to define ourselves.

It was our sense of community, our blood-tie forged by ancestral love and mutual history, that provided us with the backbone to withstand our often brutal lives with an eye on the promised land of tomorrow. Our sense of a collective identity prevented us from completely falling victim to the powerful negative stereotypes and myths manufactured by the pro-slavery establishment. Our entrenched self-knowledge prevented us from buckling under the flood of pseudoscientific theories concocted to reduce our status to that of a childlike, primitive beast of burden. We never really believed we were niggers.

We knew it would not be easy to reverse bigoted views that many whites embraced and traced back to the Good Book and the tale of the Children of Ham. If you were not entirely human, how could you love your woman or children? How could you maintain a family? How could you appreciate the lush harmonies of music or admire the breathtaking beauty of a flower in full bloom? Or create anything of lasting wonder from your limited powers of reason and imagination?

49

We never really bought their Darwinian theories about us. If we had, we would no longer exist. We knew the truth. We knew how it felt to face indignity and injustice on a daily basis, we knew how it felt to be wounded on a spirit level, we knew what it meant to be an outsider. Yet we found ways to sustain ourselves. The mission of African American writers under these maddening circumstances has often been to use words as weapons in the war for self-definition, the war waged for the demise of Topsy, Sambo, and Uncle Tom. Writers included in this section of *Sacred Fire* fully understood this and structured their contributions to stress a deep commitment to truth and emotional honesty about our lives in a manner not commonly found in books written about us by whites.

The writers, in their dual roles of observer and interpreter, knew exactly what Claude McKay meant when he said "No white man could have written my books." Imagine Andrew Hacker or Studs Terkel, both considered astute chroniclers of our American experience, capturing the essence of black urban existence as sociologist St. Clair Drake did so aptly in his landmark study, *Black Metropolis: A Study of Negro Life in a Northern City*. Imagine any white writer assembling such a marvelous array of our finest Harlem Renaissance voices with the skill that editor Alain Locke achieved in his 1925 collection, *The New Negro*. Imagine Anne Tyler or Jane Smiley creating the complex relationship between Milkman Dead and his love-crazy cousin Hagar found in Toni Morrison's masterpiece *Song of Solomon*. Or Cheever or Updike conjuring up so realistically the struggle of Franchot to use the "square life" to escape the steely clutches of the ghetto in Richard Wright's riveting *Black Boy*.

Maybe Frantz Fanon, the sage observer from Martinique, explained it best in these few lines from his groundbreaking collection of essays *Black Skin, White Masks: The Experiences of a Black Man in a White World*: "I am black: I am the incarnation of a complete fusion with the world, an intuitive understanding of the earth, an abandonment of my ego in the heart of the cosmos, and no white man, no matter how intelligent he may be, can ever understand Louis Armstrong and the music of the Congo."

What Fanon is saying: Accept no substitutes. We can speak for ourselves. The real sound of Soul. The real style of Negritude. We know when it is real, no matter what the form, what the genre. If we browse the works of leading white science fiction writers such as Ray Bradbury, Philip K. Dick, or Ursula LeGuin, nothing there can compete with the blend of wise social commentary and poetic magic found in Octavia Butler's road novel *Kindred*. When Ralph Ellison takes us inside the helter-skelter consciousness of his narrator in his award-winning 1952 novel, *Invisible Man,* during his visit with Jim Trueblood, the black sharecropper, we see the question of identity and old racial myths handled with a sensibility foreign to the European aesthetic.

Just how much does identity matter? If there is any doubt as to whether McKay's statement rings true, a glimpse at this passage detailing the cry of the black soul from James Baldwin's highly accomplished first novel, *Go Tell It on the Mountain*, published in 1953, should set the record straight: ". . . And now in his moaning, and so far from any help, he heard it in himself—it rose from his bleeding, his cracked-open heart. It was a sound of rage and weeping which filled the grave, rage and weeping from time set free, but bound now in eternity; rage that had no language, weeping with no voice . . ." This is a cry that almost every black person afflicted with prolonged exposure to a hostile white world can understand.

In the years after slavery, Jim Crow and legalized segregation served as constant reminders to the descendants of the transplanted African of the bitter reality of color prejudice. Even today, after the changes brought on by the civil rights movement, the world can still be an unfriendly place, and in the minds of many, *a nigger is still a nigger,* regardless of achievement or status.

Some writers included here—such as Paul Robeson, Carter G. Woodson, John Edgar Wideman, Paul Laurence Dunbar, and Margaret Walker—exhibit no fear of not belonging, cherishing the role of the outsider without any sense of hesitation or ambivalence. The words *submission* or *inferiority* are nowhere to be found in their lexicon. They're not concerned with acceptance, total assimilation, or being on one's best behavior. Even in writings concerning the black immigrant experience like that in Edwidge Danticat's stirring short-story collection, *Krik? Krak!,* there exists a savvy knowing about the role of the outsider in an America of contradictions, an America of skin color privilege and status quo.

What is celebrated in the words and images of the writers in this section of *Sacred Fire* is individual freedom and the collective power of the alienated, the disinherited, the marginal. These writers wrote to survive, to avoid total assimilation and annihilation, to maintain a power of choice in their daily lives not guaranteed by the ballot box. Style and soul, along with smarts, were essential weaponry in these outsiders' arsenal. These elements of our identity and community were the unique things that set us apart aesthetically from all others, isolated us artistically from Western tradition, separated us spiritually from the American experience.

Yet we always knew who we were, and we spoke up when it was time for us to tell them who we were. Without this wisdom, without this knowledge gained from the many obstacles overcome, we would be a people devoid of strength, a people to be pitied. These writers on the front lines knew that and produced enduring works with this axiom in mind, ever trumpeting the triumphs of the past, ever respectful of the steep losses along the way, ever vigilant of the dangers ahead. This section of *Sacred Fire* is an affirmation of their intellectual brilliance, moral courage, and spiritual power.

Prize-winning journalist Robert Fleming is the author of The Wisdom of the Elders.

Lyrics of Lowly Life (1896)

Paul Laurence Dunbar
Poetry

It is both poignant and ironic that *Lyrics of Lowly Life,* Paul Laurence Dunbar's third volume of poems and the one to gain him a national reputation, should also contain the two poems that would most clearly represent him and reflect the artistic conflict that would torment him throughout his life.

In "We Wear the Mask," the poet speaks of the need to present a false face to the world while suffering inner torment:

> We wear the mask that grins and lies
> It hides our cheeks and shades our eyes,—
> This debt we pay to human guile;
> With torn and bleeding hearts we smile,
> And mouth with myriad subtleties.

And then from "When Malindy Sings":

> G'way and quit that noise, Miss Lucy—
> Put that music book away;
> What's de use to keep on tryn'?
> Ef you practice t'will you'r gray,
> You can't sta't no notes a-flying
> Lak de ones dat rants and rings
> From the kitchen to the big house
> When Malindy sings.

The conflict that tormented Dunbar, one that remained unresolved throughout his short life (he died at age thirty-three), involved his reputation as a poet: While he longed to be taken seriously and to be acknowledged for his poems in standard English, the racial proscription of the country would allow him place only for his mastery of "Negro dialect." A good deal of nineteenth-century white America's love of his dialect poetry was based on his benign images of laughing "darkies" and "coons" eatin' and fishin' and dancin' on the plantation.

But in his standard poems, Dunbar showed a more philosophic bent, musing in the Romantic tradition about the natural world and life itself. And while his dialect poems seem to indicate a counterrevolutionary Tom, his standard poems reveal a man with an evolved racial consciousness that, on rare occasions, borders on militance. Poems such as "We Wear the Mask" and "Frederick Douglass" remain sublime testimonies to the difficulties of black life in America. Fortunately, in the century since Dunbar's death, his reputation has come to rightly rest with these and others of his challenging and lyrical standard English poems.

The Conjure Woman (1899)

Charles W. Chestnutt
Novel

C harles W. Chestnutt was the most widely read and influential African American fiction writer of his time and the first ever brought to press by a major publishing house. *The Conjure Woman* introduced the verbal and philosophical richness of African American folk culture to a white readership largely ignorant of true southern black life. Even today, this collection is thought to be among the best representations of life on a southern plantation to be found in American literature.

The Conjure Woman is a collection of "conjuring tales" written in rich dialect. Each of the stories masterfully portrays both the inhumanity of plantation life and the cunning wisdom used by many to survive post–Civil War neoslavery. The stories are more accurate than those written by contemporary writers like Joel Chandler Harris, whose Uncle Remus stories fondly portray life on the plantation. Chestnutt's stories more often reflect the true conditions of plantation life, if in slightly muted tones: forced separation of loved ones, the greed of the slave masters, and the ready violence to be found on the plantations.

Chestnutt's later—and more straightforward—explorations into biracialism, miscegenation, and racisim (*The House Behind the Cedars, The Marrow of Tradition,* and *The Colonel's Dream*) met with so tepid a commercial response that Chestnutt decided to return to his private legal practice in order to support his family. But *The Conjure Woman* has ensured his reputation as a groundbreaking writer of fiction that truthfully tells the stories of slave life.

The Souls of Black Folk (1903)

W. E. B. Du Bois
Nonfiction

"**H**erein lie buried many things, which if read with patience may show the strange meaning of being black here in the dawning of the Twentieth Century."

Born in Massachusetts in 1868, William Edward Burghardt Du Bois was the foremost black intellectual of his time—and mind you, his time stretched all the way from Reconstruction to the civil rights movement of the 1960s. A man of staggering intellect and drive, he was the first black to hold a doctorate from Harvard University. Du Bois wrote three historical works, two novels, two autobiographies, and sixteen pioneering books on sociology, history, politics, and race relations. He was a founder of the NAACP, pioneering Pan-Africanist, spirited advocate for world peace, and tireless fighter for civil rights during the darkest days of Jim Crow.

Du Bois was also a prophet: At the turn of the century, he wrote in the "forethought" of this seminal collection of essays that "the problem of the Twentieth Century is the problem of the color line." That statement has resonated throughout this turbulent century and remains just as fresh today as in 1903. *The Souls of Black Folk,* a collection of fourteen powerfully written essays that are by turn testimony and autobiography, stands as a monumental achievement and quite possibly his most influential work. The book is both a vivid portrait of the conditions facing freshly emancipated black folk at the turn of the century and a still-relevant discussion of the dilemma of race in the United States. It was here that Du Bois introduced his influential concept of "double-consciousness": the struggle of black people trying to define themselves as both black and American.

What makes these unflinching, luminous, and troublesome essays so powerful is that each builds upon the other to try to answer questions about race that have perplexed, enraged, and divided America for over a century. Written in part to counter Booker T. Washington's prevailing strategy of accommodation, *The Souls of Black Folk* created a fresh way of looking at and protesting the multifaceted oppression of black people.

Your country? How came it yours? Before the Pilgrims landed we were here. Here we have brought our three gifts and mingled them with yours: a gift of story and song . . . the gift of sweat and brawn to beat back the wilderness, conquer the soil, and lay the foundations of this vast economic empire two hundred years earlier than your weak hands could have done it; the third, a gift of the Spirit. . . . Are not these gifts worth the giving? Is not this work and striving? Would America have been America without her Negro people?

—from *The Souls of Black Folk*

Cane (1923)

Jean Toomer
Novel

*C*ane is Jean Toomer's acclaimed exploration of the American racial temperament of the 1920s. Using his own life as a model, Toomer explores the issues of race and identity that simmer just below the fragile American social veneer. Organized in three sections, these stories and vignettes are also interspersed with poetry. Toomer's brilliant interweaving of black folk culture within themes of miscegenation, black sexuality, and racial identity and conflict turned this novel into a literary high point.

Toomer's book represented and served to introduce the now self-aware and emergent "new" Negro. In fact, the author himself was embraced by the white literary avant-garde as a modernist of the first order. While initially a commercial failure, *Cane* is now considered a twentieth-century masterpiece.

Men had always wanted her, this Karintha, even as a child, Karintha carrying beauty, perfect as the dusk when the sun goes down. Old men rode her hobby-horse upon their knees. Young men danced with her at frolics when they should have been dancing with their grown-up girls. God grant us youth, secretly prayed the old men. The young men counted the time to pass before she would be old enough to mate with them. This interest of the male, who wishes to ripen a growing thing too soon, could mean no good to her.

> . . . Her skin is like dusk,
> O can't you see it,
> Her skin is like dusk,
> When the sun goes down.

—from *Cane*

The New Negro (1925)

Alain Locke
Anthology

Alain Locke is the acknowledged Father of the Harlem Renaissance. A highly educated man and the first African American to be awarded a Rhodes scholarship, Locke served as the bridge between a burgeoning literary expression centered in Harlem, New York, and the mainstream literary world. He brought the star writers of the renaissance, including Countee Cullen, Langston Hughes, and Claude McKay, broad literary attention and patrons—wealthy supporters who provided financial support for struggling writers and artists. In this landmark anthology, Locke set forth the defining characteristics of the new Negro who was emerging in America's northern cities: literary, artistic, cosmopolitan, and urbane.

Published in 1925, *The New Negro* is an anthology of poems, stories, and essays edited by Locke that includes such luminaries as W. E. B. Du Bois, James Weldon Johnson, Angelina Grimké, Hughes, Cullen, and McKay. It became a "Who's Who" of the Harlem Renaissance and its defining text. Like the renaissance itself, *The New Negro* was a symbol of the literary fruit of the great migration of blacks from the rural South to the urban North. Locke was sure that Harlem was fast becoming a new mecca of black artistry and one of the world's cultural capitals, an assertion that was not hard to argue on the basis of the outstanding work represented in this volume.

The best of the work created during the renaissance—the criticism of Du Bois, the poetry of Johnson and Hughes, the fiction of McKay—has endured. And the Harlem of the 1920s and 1930s remains one of the iconic places in African American history: full of jazz, creativity, and beautiful black people on the move. But what became of the new Negro, that artful and cosmopolitan urbanite? There were lofty expectations, to be sure, but in retrospect and beyond the stardust, the Harlem Renaissance presented to the new Negro a hard lesson: the real work of the culture lay in assuring its permanence, not just basking in the flow of transient praise and voguishness. The artists of the renaissance were heavily dependent on the patronage of their fellow New Yorkers downtown, and Harlem's renaissance died out with onset of the Great Depression, when the patronage stopped flowing in even as Harlem's most enduring artists continued to produce important work. Nevertheless, the spirit of the so-called new Negro, the spirit of vital black urban creativity embodied in the works found in this collection, lives on.

In Harlem, Negro life is seizing upon its first chances for group expression and self-determination. It is—or promises at least to be—a race capital. That is why our comparison is taken with those nascent centers of folk-expression and self-determination which are playing a creative part in the world today. Without pretense to their political significance, Harlem has the same role to play for the New Negro as Dublin has had for the New Ireland or Prague for the New Czechoslovakia.

—from *The New Negro*

The Blacker the Berry (1929)

Wallace Thurman
Novel

Wallace Thurman's brilliantly sly novel *The Blacker the Berry* is about skin color, blackness, and the color bias of "golden browns," "mulattos," "high yallers," and "nearly whites" against the "dark browns," "blue-blacks," and "Hottentots."

This is the tragic tale of Emma Lou Brown, a very dark sister whose indigo complexion gives her endless grief and humiliation at the hands of her lighter-complected family. Emma Lou's relatives "couldn't stomach" black people. After years of being the darkest spot of color in her near-white black family, Emma escapes to Harlem, hoping to fit in or at least to disappear. "More acutely than ever before Emma Lou began to feel that her luscious black complexion was somewhat of a liability, and that her marked color variation from the other people in her environment was a curse. Not that she minded being black, being a Negro necessitated having a colored skin, but she did mind being too black. . . . Why had her mother married a black man? Surely there had been some eligible brown-skin men around."

The Blacker the Berry is clever, beautifully written, sharp, and searing. Emma is every black woman who has ever been told to wear a hat for fear of getting any darker, who has cursed her African features, or who has been told to choose a lighter mate to lighten her offspring. Every line, word, and phrase in Thurman's bitter masterpiece is pure truth; therein lies its power.

The Mis-education of the Negro
(1933, latest rev. ed., 1969)

Carter G. Woodson
History

C arter G. Woodson has been called the Father of Modern
Black History. He was a central, commanding figure in
the study, writing, and teaching of African American history and
the first historian to successfully use sound scholarship to refute
the prevailing myths and racist views about black Americans and
their history. Among his contributions to American life is Black
History Month (originally dubbed Negro History Week), which
Woodson established to promote the study of African American
history.

Woodson's 205-page monograph, *The Mis-education of the
Negro,* reflects his profound concern for setting the record
straight. His thesis, as outlined in his Preface, could well apply
today: "The so-called modern education, with all its defects,
however, does others so much more good than it does the
Negro, because it has been worked out in conformity to the
needs of those who have enslaved and oppressed weaker people."
He was concerned with the way African American identity had
been warped by racist approaches to history and education; he
foresaw the ways that such a warped history would be internal-
ized by black students who would never know of the achievements of their forebears, only of their humiliations and
sufferings.

In the book's eighteen chapters, Woodson presents a systematic critique of the education system and offers a plan for change
that would create a system that informs black students about
their own history and addresses their unique challenges. The

current proliferation of African American studies programs, Afro-centric schools, and multicultural curricula all bear Woodson's stamp. Still, *Mis-education* remains a biting indictment of a public school system whose promise of education of the masses has still been left sadly unfulfilled.

The Ways of White Folks (1934)

Langston Hughes
Short Stories

I f you are not yet familiar with Langston Hughes, then his collection *The Ways of White Folks* (named in homage to Du Bois's classic *The Souls of Black Folk*) is the perfect introduction to his mordant wit and unerring eye for detail and his sly and direct prose.

These stories move from poignant to funny, to seething with rage, often within a paragraph. And life, as it is painted here, is bleak and unchanging until death. Hughes's characters inhabit a world where people are mean because they can be, and where hard work is all that is guaranteed; these were the harsh realities for blacks in America in the twenties and thirties. If, as Du Bois contended in his book, "the problem of the twentieth century is the problem of the color line," this collection allows Hughes to illustrate that point time and again. He demonstrates to white readers what he and his black readers knew: "White folks is white folks, South or North, North or South." This is the concept he used to structure his seemingly mundane yet tragic tales.

"Cora Unashamed" reveals how lifelong servitude can render the servant almost invisible, even to herself. In "Passing," a mixed-race black passes for white, forever denying his race and family: "I felt like a dog, passing you downtown last night and not speaking to you. You were great, though, didn't give a sign that you even knew me, let alone that I was your son."

From North to South, light to dark, prosperous to dirt poor, all the stories are bound together and made powerful by the fact that they were all regular occurrences at that time in the United

States. Within his simple stories, Hughes offered a barbed and trenchant analysis of white behavior and black behavior. Like his poems, the cruel accuracy of *The Ways of White Folks* is a reminder to Americans of some hard truths about the ridiculous and tragic ways skin color warps our lives.

Black Boy (1945)

Richard Wright
Memoir

[Wright] came like a sledgehammer, like a giant out of the
mountain with a sledgehammer, writing with a sledgehammer . . .

—John Henrik Clarke

*B*lack Boy is Richard Wright's unforgettable story of growing
up in the Jim Crow South. Published in 1945, it is often
considered a fictionalized autobiography or an autobiographical
novel because of Wright's use of fiction techniques (and possibly
fictional events) to tell his story. Nevertheless, the book is a lyrical and skillfully wrought description of Wright's hungry youth in
rural Mississippi and Memphis, told from the perspective of the
adult Wright, who was still trying to come to grips with the cruel
deprivations and humiliations of his childhood.

Life in the pre–civil rights South was intensely alienating for
young Richard. At every turn, his desire to communicate was
stunted, whether by family members who insisted he "hush!" or
by teachers who harassed and mocked him. He was surrounded
by people he considered contemptibly ignorant, people who willingly allowed their lives to be restricted by tradition and authority
no matter how illegitimate or self-destructive. Whether they were
racist whites or passive, uncompassionate blacks, his fellow southerners viewed Richard's independence and intelligence with suspicion and scorned and humiliated him for his family's poverty.
He lashed out by hitting the streets: He was already drinking by
the time he turned six, and he fought constantly. He finally found
his outlet in writing; by the end of the book, he decided that
there was nothing he could ever do to improve his life in the
South and committed to moving to Chicago to pursue his art.

When first published, *Black Boy* was considered by many to be an angry attack on the racist South because of Wright's hard-hitting portrayal of the racism he faced, not to mention his already-acquired reputation as a "protest writer." But the book's value goes deeper than that: Wright bears witness to the American struggle for the right of self-definition. His own quest to escape the suffocating world of his childhood and find a place where he could freely exercise his individuality, creativity, and integrity was ultimately successful. But *Black Boy* also offers insight into an entire culture of people, both black and white, who had unthinkingly accepted a narrowly prescribed course of life. As Wright put it, "[though] they lived in America where in theory there existed equality of opportunity, they knew unerringly what to aspire to and what not to aspire to." Despite Wright's stifling environment, his story is inspirational for its portrait of how a black boy shucked off the limited expectations of those around him and dared to aspire.

From Richard Wright's Black Boy
to Kendrick Lamar's Black
Boy Fly

Black Metropolis: A Study of Negro Life in a Northern City (1945)

St. Clair Drake and Horace Cayton
Nonfiction

The cry "Up North!" and the city of Chicago became synonymous as America's second city absorbed the masses during the great black migration of 1910 to 1940. This great migration was a watershed event in American history, transforming the lives of millions of black people and the cities to which they flocked. It had the obvious outcome of turning a primarily southern, rural people into one identified, for better or worse, with the inner cities of the American North and West.

Originally published in 1945, the award-winning, two-volume *Black Metropolis* is the work of two eminent social scientists, anthropologist St. Clair Drake and sociologist Horace Cayton, trying to describe what this massive movement of people had wrought. It takes as its subject for study one of the largest black communities in the world, at the time, Chicago's inner city, nicknamed Bronzeville. Richard Wright wrote the preface to the 1945 edition. In it he said:

> Chicago is the city from which the most incisive and radical Negro thought has come; there is an open and raw beauty about that city that seems to either kill or endow one with the spirit of life. I felt those extremes of possibility, death and hope, while I lived half hungry and afraid in a city to which I had fled . . . it was not until I stumbled upon science that I discovered some of the meaning of the environment that battered and taunted me. . . . *Black Metropolis,* Drake's and Cayton's scien-

tific statement about the urban Negro, pictures the environment out of which the Bigger Thomases of our nation come.

This study is critical in locating the site and tracing the circumstances under which southern dreams of freedom and prosperity up North were dashed. It is critical to understanding the modern history of the disenfranchisement of the African American.

Invisible Man (1952)

Ralph Ellison
Novel

*I*nvisible Man—incredibly, Ralph Ellison's first and only novel—is one of the lasting masterpieces of American literature. It chronicles the existential journey of an unnamed black man attempting to discover his identity and role in a hostile and confusing world that refuses to acknowledge his existence.

Within the story of the protagonist's quest for definition, Ellison offers a vivid and unforgiving examination of the shortcomings of the self-serving black bourgeoisie, clumsy white philanthropists, dehumanizing American industry, and unrealistic revolutionary movements. The narrator jointly tells his own, personal coming-of-age story—one that takes him from the deep South to the streets of Harlem, from workaday jobs to revolution, from a black college to (literally) a hole in the ground—and the symbolic story of the unfinished coming of age of his race in America. Ellison skillfully manages to tell both stories without ever reducing his narrator to a flat symbol of everyblackman, allowing the story to work successfully on both levels.

The novel also benefits from Ellison's rich narrative style, which drew from a heady mix of influences. He incorporated the jazzy rhythms and vivid imagery of black American speech, music, and folklore in his tale, while also showing the influence of white writers such as Melville, Twain, and Dostoyevsky.

Invisible Man is an essential book, whether read as an intriguing coming-of-age story, an incisive portrait of an individual's quest for identity, or a powerful indictment of the absurdity of racism that remains fresh and relevant today. Ellison's stylish prose speaks to the individual and collective need to acquire self-knowledge, self-definition, self-illumination—to become visible to ourselves.

I am not a spook like those who haunted Edgar Allan Poe; nor am I one of your Hollywood-movie ectoplasms. I am a man of substance, of flesh and bone, fiber and liquids—and I might even be said to possess a mind. I am invisible, understand, simply because people refuse to see me. Like the bodiless heads you see sometimes in circus sideshows, it is as though I have been surrounded by mirrors of hard, distorted glass. When they approach me they see only my surroundings, themselves, or figments of their imagination—indeed, everything and anything except me.

—from the Prologue to *Invisible Man*

Go Tell It on the Mountain (1953)

James Baldwin
Novel

*G*o *Tell It on the Mountain* is considered to be James Baldwin's greatest novel. Like much of Baldwin's writing, it draws heavily on his own intense childhood experiences with religious doubt, racism, sexual ambivalence, and a complex relationship with a difficult father. The entire book takes place on the fourteenth birthday of John Grimes, the son of a fire-and-brimstone revivalist preacher, who finds himself increasingly alienated from his bitter, authoritarian father, his religious faith, and his community. Baldwin treats the young man's battle with Manichaean choices—flesh or spirit, community or individualism, conversion or heresy—with masterful sensitivity and insight.

The book is divided into three parts: In part one, we share John's terror as he becomes aware that his desires and goals lie outside of the narrow expectations of his family and community. In the second part, we learn of the sorrowful experiences back South and up North that forever scarred John's father, Gabriel, and his mother, Elizabeth, even though they hoped their union would wash away the sins of their past. In part three, John surrenders himself to religious ecstasy, still seeking a way out of his dilemma.

Go Tell It on the Mountain is filled with biblical references that evoke the spirit of the black church and a realism that brings to life the Harlem of the 1930s, a northern ghetto whose inhabitants were still struggling with southern demons. Baldwin, in a 1984 interview with the *Paris Review*, captured what he was trying to say in the novel about all of us and about his own life: "[Writing *Go Tell It on the Mountain*] was an attempt to exorcise something, to find out what happened to my father, what happened to all of us, what had happened to me and how we were to move from one place to another." Its brilliant style and sophisticated portrait of a young man struggling with complex issues made this one of the landmark novels of the postwar period.

Things Fall Apart (1958)

Chinua Achebe
Novel

*T*hings Fall Apart is one of the most widely read African novels ever published. It is written by one of Nigeria's leading novelists, Chinua Achebe. Set in the Ibo village of Umuofia, *Things Fall Apart* recounts a stunning moment in African history—its colonization by Britain. The novel, first published in 1958, has by today sold over 8 million copies, been translated into at least forty-five languages, and earned Achebe the somewhat misleading and patronizing title of "the man who invented African literature." It carefully re-creates tribal life before the arrival of Europeans in Africa, and then details the jarring changes brought on by the advent of colonialism and Christianity.

The book is a parable that examines the colonial experience from an African perspective, through Okonkwo, who was "a strong individual and an Igbo hero struggling to maintain the cultural integrity of his people against the overwhelming power of colonial rule." Okonkwo is banished from the community for accidentally killing a clansman and is forced to live seven years in exile. He returns to his home village, only to witness its disintegration as it abandons tradition for European ways. The book describes the simultaneous disintegration of Okonkwo and his village, as his pleas to his people not to exchange their culture for that of the English fall on deaf ears.

The brilliance of *Things Fall Apart* is that it addresses the imposition of colonization and the crisis in African culture caused by the collapse of colonial rule. Achebe prophetically argued that colonial domination and the culture it left in Africa had such a stranglehold on African peoples that its consequences would haunt African society long after colonizers had left the continent.

The arrival of the missionaries had caused a considerable stir.
There were six of them and one was a white man. The white man
began to speak to them through an interpreter who was an Ibo
man, though his dialect was different and harsh to the ears, but
who said he was one of them, as they could see from his color
and his language. "We have been sent by God to ask you to leave
your wicked ways and false gods," he told them.

—from *Things Fall Apart*

A Raisin in the Sun (1959)

Lorraine Hansberry
Play

A *Raisin in the Sun,* written by the then twenty-nine-year-old Hansberry, was the "movin' on up" morality play of the 1960s. Martin had mesmerized millions, and integration was seen as the stairway to heaven. *Raisin* had something for everyone, and for this reason it was the recipient of the prestigious New York Drama Critics Circle Award.

The place: a tenement flat in Southside, Chicago. The time: post–World War II. Lena Younger, the strong-willed matriarch, is the glue that holds together the Younger family. Walter Lee is her married, thirty-something son who, along with his wife and sister, lives in his mother's apartment. He is short on meeting responsibilities but long on dreams. Beneatha (that's right, Beneatha) is Walter's sister—an upwardly mobile college student who plans to attend medical school.

Mama Lena is due a check from her late husband's insurance, and Walter Lee is ready to invest it in a liquor store. The money represents his opportunity to assert his manhood. It will bring the jump start he needs to set his life right. Beneatha tells him that it's "mama's money to do with as she pleases," and that she doesn't really expect any for her schooling. However, Mama wants to use her new money for a new beginning—in a new house, in a new neighborhood (white).

Walter cries, and Mama relents. She refrains from paying cash for the house and places a deposit instead, giving Walter the difference to share equally between his investment and Beneatha's college fund. Walter squanders the entire amount. Meanwhile, Mama receives a call from the neighborhood "welcome committee" hoping to dissuade the family from moving in.

While roundly criticized for being politically accommodating to whites, *Raisin* accurately reflected the aspirations of a newly nascent black middle class.

Blues People: Negro Music in White America (1963)

LeRoi Jones
Criticism

During the early 1960s as the civil rights movement was gaining intensity, American society—particularly its young—was also experiencing an upheaval. One of its many reflections was a new interest in black music, especially the blues: Social and political countercurrents of the era led many of the sixties generation to embrace the blues as an honest, direct, and earthy people's alternative to establishment culture. Contemporaneous with that movement, in 1963 poet/playwright LeRoi Jones (now Amiri Baraka) published a collection of essays that has since become pivotal to any discussion of African American music and culture: "*Blues People,*" commented *Library Journal* at the time, "is American musical history; it is also American culture, economic, and even emotional history. It traces not only the development of the Negro music which affected white America, but also the Negro values which affected America."

Blues People takes the major African American contributions to American music—jazz, the blues, spirituals, and rock and roll—and describes them in the context of the wider story of African American history and culture. Jones carefully draws out the connections between the social and political frustrations of black folks in America and their incredible musical expressiveness and invention. He identifies the source of this musical genius as the "blues impulse" and traces its evolution from the spirituals and work songs of enslaved Africans to the twentieth-century explosions of blues, jazz, and rock and roll.

This is far from a dry sociological study; Baraka infuses his discussion with his obvious love of the subject and writes with the

78

same sharp intelligence, insight, and playful wit that he brings to his poetry, drama, and prose. This book provides a crucial understanding of the dark and difficult wellsprings of African American popular music.

The Negro slave is one thing. The Negro as American is quite another. But the path the slave took to "citizenship" is what I want to look at. And I make my analogy through the slave citizen's music—through the music that is closely associated with him: blues and a later, but parallel development, jazz. And it seems to me that if the Negro represents, or is symbolic of, something in and about the nature of American culture, this certainly should be revealed by his characteristic music.

—from *Blues People*

Jubilee (1966)

Margaret Walker
Novel

When Margaret Walker's grandmother used to tell her stories about her mother's life as a slave on a southern plantation, Walker vowed that she would one day share those stories with the world. *Jubilee* is not only the fictional recounting of Dr. Walker's great-grandmother's life, it is also a black woman's view of the political, economic, and social structure of the plantation system before the Civil War—a powerful response to the gilded images of plantation life found in novels such as *Gone with the Wind*. Through the story of Vyry Brown, a fierce and fearless black woman, daughter of a slave and a slave owner, *Jubilee* focuses on the sounds and textures of everyday life on a plantation for a black woman. It is also among the first books to describe the tricky relationship between black women and white women, a relationship whose intimate roots in slavery are discussed here.

The novel is divided into three sections: The first, "Sis Hetta's Child—the Ante-Bellum Years," covers Vyry's childhood and first encounters with the sorrows of love under the slave system. It ends with a failed escape attempt. The second section, "My Eyes Have Seen the Glory," examines Vyry's life as a nurse during the Civil War. The final section, "Forty Years in the Wilderness—Reconstruction and Reaction," covers the period after emancipation, when Vyry and her family face new troubles—natural disasters, the Ku Klux Klan, and the abounding racism of the South after the Civil War. In every phase of life, Vyry meets her challenges with grit, intelligence, grace, and strength.

Jubilee was lauded for its warm, engaging prose and its authenticity. In fact, it took Walker thirty years to research and write the book. The research shows itself in the way she is able to re-create the most intimate details of Vyry's life—her everyday routine, the language she used, the foods she ate, her pastimes and passions. The book is also noteworthy for its presentation of a heroic African American woman born in slavery. It is astounding that anyone could think that black women survived the abuse and exploitation of slavery without immense reserves of strength, wits, and courage, but America had chosen happy, hysterical, and mindless mammies and pickaninnies as the popular image of antebellum black womanhood. Smart, tough Vyry was a wonderful correction to those stereotypes. First published in 1966, the book's first edition went through nineteen printings.

Black Skin, White Masks (1967)

Frantz Fanon
Nonfiction

That the writing of the Martinique-born psychiatrist, intellectual, and revolutionary Frantz Fanon should become seminal to African Americans during the tumultuous black power period is not surprising. As biographer Peter Geismar has written:

> Fanon's writings were first fully appreciated within the Western civilization that he attacked so violently: His books have become required reading for the black revolutionaries in the United States who consider their people as part of the Third World—a term commonly used to designate the whole of the undeveloped world.

The accuracy of Fanon's analysis of the psychological situation of the oppressed arose from firsthand experience, from his own early encounter with Western civilization during his student days in France. He has recorded that encounter in his first book, *Black Skin, White Masks* (originally published in 1952). Through a systematic psychological analysis, Fanon attempts to articulate (and perhaps to also exorcise) the psychic trauma of the colonized.

Published in America in 1967, *Black Skin, White Masks* investigates "the warping of the Negro psyche by a 'superior' white culture." Fanon describes his reasons for writing the book as follows: "My consciousness is not illuminated with ultimate radiances. Nevertheless . . . I think it would be good if certain things were said. These things I am going to say, not shout. For it is a long time since shouting has gone out of my life . . . Why write this book? . . . I reply quite calmly that there are too many idiots in this world. And having said it, I have the burden of proving it."

And he does. In his inimitable straightforward style, Fanon pokes fun, but in all seriousness, at what he saw as empty rhetoric regarding relationships between blacks and whites. If you have not yet read Fanon, start here with his first book, which is filled with his sharp observances and piercing humor. "This book should have been written three years ago . . . but these truths were fire in me then. Now I can tell them without being burned. These truths are not intended to be hurled in men's faces. They are not intended to ignite fervor. I do not trust fervor."

Even if you do not appreciate Fanon's arguments, you will be struck by the clarity of his tone and the magnitude of his vision.

The Crisis of the Negro Intellectual
(1967)

Harold Cruse
Nonfiction

Harold Cruse's *The Crisis of the Negro Intellectual* was one of the most controversial and influential books written during the late 1960s Black Power period. In it, Cruse makes a spirited, polemical argument about the failure of the black bourgeoisie, artists, and intellectuals to create autonomous black cultural institutions and scholarship and criticizes their dependence on white institutions and ideologies. The book landed like a bomb in academic and cultural circles, and its influence continues to be felt today.

Cruse traced the recent history of African American intellectual life to highlight the patterns of failure at each juncture. The Harlem Renaissance, a much-vaunted flowering of black intellectual and artistic life, failed because its leaders allowed, and even encouraged, white patronage to be its lifeblood. Black intellectuals in subsequent decades allowed themselves to be controlled by communists, who while encouraging blacks to integrate with them, maintained their own ethnic institutions. Cruse argued that black intellectuals who failed to create a paradigm for looking at the world based on black sensibilities and viewpoints were abdicating their responsibility to their less-educated brothers and sisters. By allowing ostensibly sympathetic white intellectuals to frame the American discussion of race, these black intellectuals removed themselves, and their constituency by extension, from that vital debate.

Cruse's book has had wide-reaching ramifications in black scholarship since its publication. It has been criticized by scholars across the ideological spectrum, including Afrocentrists, whom Cruse derided as "ceremonial nationalists." But whether they agreed or disagreed, his powerful and impassioned plea for a black cultural nationalism influenced a generation of intellectuals to reassess the relevance of their work.

We a BaddDDD People (1970)

Sonia Sanchez
Poetry

S onia Sanchez is one of the most admired and enduring poets to come out of the Black Arts Movement in the late 1960s and early 1970s. *We a BaddDDD People* is a classic from that period, a collection of poems that spoke to the revolutionary yearnings of the black masses in their native tongue. The revolution she espoused was one of self-love and self-knowledge in the face of racist hate; the African rhythms she created in her poetry (especially when she read it aloud) and her use of black vernacular were poetic manifestations of that drive toward communal self-love.

Characterizing Sanchez's poetry of that period, critic Gloria Wade-Gayles says,

> [Sanchez] used the language of the people rather than the polished language of the academy, mixing images of the ghetto, lower-case letters, dashes, slashes, hyphenated lines, abbreviations, unorthodox spelling, and other experiments with language and form to redefine what a poem is, what it does, and for whom it is written.

As Sanchez herself explains it, "I see myself helping to bring forth the truth about the world. I cannot tell the truth about anything unless I confess to being a student, growing and learning something new everyday. The more I learn, the clearer my view of the world becomes. To gain that clarity . . . I had to wash my ego in the needs/aspirations of my people." *We a BaddDDD People* is a lyrical tribute to the revolutionary aspiration of black people to discover and love themselves despite the hostility of the world around them.

The Hero and the Blues (1973)

Albert Murray
Nonfiction

According to Murray in *The Hero and the Blues,* in literature "storybook images are indispensable to the basic human processes of world comprehension and self-definition. . . . the most delicately wrought short stories and the most elaborately textured novels, along with the homespun anecdotes, parables, fables, tales, legends, and sagas, are as strongly motivated by immediate educational objectives as are signs, labels . . . and directives. . . . To make the telling more effective is to make the tale more to the point, more meaningful, and in consequence, if not coincidentally, more useful. Nor is the painter or the musician any less concerned than the writer with achieving a telling effect."

So begins Murray's three-part essay to writers, editors, educators, publishers, reviewers, and teachers, scolding them for having forgotten that "fiction of its very nature is most germane and useful not when it restricts itself to . . . social and political agitation and propaganda . . . but when it performs the fundamental and universal functions of literature." Murray, an academician and historian, believed that literature established the context for social and political action. And that the writer, who created stories or narrated incidents that embodied aspects of human nature, not only described them but also suggested possibilities that could contribute most to people's welfare.

Calling on Dostoyevsky, Hemingway, Thomas Mann, Marx, Freud, Malcolm X, Eldridge Cleaver, Count Basie, Duke Ellington, and many others to support his premise, Murray's slim but sweeping narrative praises the artist, writer, and musician as social commentator and educator, as long as he doesn't venture far from his storytelling roots.

Song of Solomon (1977)

Toni Morrison
Novel

Song of Solomon, Toni Morrison's lyrical third novel, begins with an arresting scene—a man on a roof threatening to jump, a woman standing on the ground, singing, and another woman entering labor. The child born of that labor is Macon "Milkman" Dead III; *Song of Solomon* is the epic story of his lifetime journey toward an understanding of his own identity and ancestry. Milkman is born burdened with the materialistic values of his father and the weight of a racist society; over the course of his odyssey he reconnects to his deeper family values and history, rids himself of the burden of his father's expectations and society's limitations, and literally learns to fly.

When the novel opens, Milkman is clearly a man with little or no concern for others. Like his father, he is driven only by his immediate sensual needs; he is spoiled and self-centered and pursues money and sexual gratification at all costs. The novel centers around his search for a lost bag of gold that was allegedly taken from a man involved in his grandfather's murder and then abandoned by his Aunt Pilate. The search for gold takes Milkman and his friend Guitar, a young black militant, to Shalimar, a town named for his great-grandfather Solomon, who according to local legend escaped slavery by taking flight back to Africa on the wind. On his journey, under the influence of his Aunt Pilate, a strong, fearless, natural woman whose values are the opposite of Milkman's father's, Milkman begins to come to terms with his family history, his role as a man, and the possibilities of his life apart from a cycle of physical lust and satisfaction.

In telling the story of Milkman's quest to discover the hidden history of the Deads, Morrison expertly weaves together elements

As fleet and bright as a lodestar he wheeled toward Guitar and
it did not matter which of them would give up his ghost in the
killing arms of his brother. For now he knew what Shalimar
knew: If you surrendered to the air, you could *ride* it.

—from *Song of Solomon*

of myth, magic, and folklore. She grapples with fundamental
issues of class and race, ancestry and identity, while never losing
sight of Milkman's compelling story. The language in *Song of
Solomon,* Morrison's only novel with a male protagonist, is earthy
and poetic, the characters eccentric, and the detail vivid and convincing. The result is a novel that is at once emotionally intense,
provocative, and inspiring in its description of how one man
rediscovered the latent power within him.

Song of Solomon is considered to be Toni Morrison's masterpiece and is in the top echelon of literary works produced by any
American writer. It is also her breakthrough novel in both critical
and commercial success: It was the first African American novel
since *Native Son* to be a main selection of the Book of the Month
club and it won the prestigious National Book Critics Circle
Award among others. The book received a second life, and bestseller status, twenty years after its initial publication when talk
show host Oprah Winfrey announced it as a selection for her on-
air book club.

Elbow Room (1981)

James Alan McPherson
Short Stories

J ames Alan McPherson is one of the best American short story writers to come out of the 1960s and 1970s. His first volume of short stories, *Hue and Cry*, was published in the same year he graduated from Harvard Law School at the age of 25. His second collection, *Elbow Room*, won him the Pulitzer Prize for fiction in 1981.

McPherson's prime gift as a writer is his ability to draw utterly believable, and sympathetic, characters. The men and women brought to life in the stories of *Elbow Room* are folks you already know from the barbershops, trains, and backrooms of black communities North and South. Their words are easy to recognize, and their situations all too familiar. But the familiarity we feel with the characters only heightens the sense of melancholy that pervades these stories. The stories center around the differences between people—differences in race, outlook, beliefs—that more often than not prove to be irreconcilable. Sometimes, those differences are treated to gently comic effect, as in the poignant remembrances of "Why I Love Square Dancing." Other times, the stories evoke rousing black folktales of "bad men," as in "The Story of a Dead Man." And sometimes McPherson, in spite of himself, offers hope, as in the title story, whose main character, Virginia, makes "elbow room" in her head for the differences among people.

This collection offers a wide range of compelling writing, finely drawn characters, and provocative situations. Even when McPherson's stories center on relations between the races, his characters express universal truths about humanity and how we interact in the spaces we share.

Damballah (1984)

John Edgar Wideman
Novel

John Edgar Wideman grew up in the Homewood section of Pittsburgh, a setting he has used for a number of his award-winning novels and stories. *Damballah,* Wideman's collection of stories about the fictionalized black community of Homewood, is the first in a trilogy consisting of *Damballah, Hiding Place,* and *Sent for You Yesterday.* Somewhat autobiographical, the books are linked by shared characters, events, and locales. Like much of Wideman's writing, the stories in *Damballah* are intense and lyrical examinations of the intense psychological experience of black people in urban America.

The first story, "Orion," is about an African brought to an American plantation who wants to teach "the old ways" to a young slave. Knowing that only in death can he do so, he sets out to get it. "One scream that night. Like a bull when they cut off his maleness. . . . A bull screaming once that night and torches burning in the barn and Master and the men coming out and no Ryan. . . Mistress crying behind a locked door and Master messing with Patty down the quarters."

"Hazel" is the story of a young girl accidentally crippled by her brother and who is now trapped by her mother's good intentions. "When I look at you sitting in that chair . . . I can't tell you what a trial it is. Then I think . . . there's a whole lot she'll never have to suffer. . . . The lies of men, their nasty hands . . . having their way, having their babies."

Wideman's writing is powerfully visceral, not tempered with sentiment or poetic prose, which is one reason it is not more widely read than it is. His intelligent and inventive use of language and his concern with the psychological issues that affect African Americans, however, make his work essential. *Damballah* is pure Wideman, and if you have not yet read him, it is a good place to start.

A Hard Road to Glory: A History of the African American Athlete (1993: Vol. 1, 1619 to 1918; Vol. 2, 1919 to 1945; Vol. 3, Since 1946)

Arthur Ashe
Nonfiction

A *Hard Road to Glory* is, in three volumes, the definitive history of black athletics in America. A work of monumental importance to African American history, it traces the development of African American athletes from Africa in the seventeenth century to today. The book took Ashe over six years to compile, requiring the assistance of a professional research staff and the advice of several world-famous scholars. So committed was Ashe to this project that the majority of the staggering costs of research came out of his own pocket. The book that was ultimately produced puts the iconic image of the African American athlete back into the context of black cultural and social life over the centuries.

"The 1920s was known as the 'Golden Decade of Sports' . . . Of course it should have been more appropriately called 'The Golden Decade of (White) Sports,' for black athletes were shut out of major league baseball, eased out of professional football, not allowed to join a fledgling professional basketball league, barred from Forest Hills in tennis, and unlawfully kept out of contention for the heavyweight boxing crown."

Ashe thought that by drawing attention to the historical barring of blacks from the opportunities available through professional sports, he could help aspiring black sports enthusiasts. "Today, thousands of young African Americans continue to seek their places in the sun through athletics. . . . Perhaps this history will ease the journey with sober reflections of how difficult and improbable the hard road really is."

In his twenty-year tennis career, Ashe won some of the most coveted tennis championships in the game. An eloquent statesman and gifted writer, he was also the author of *Off the Court* and *Days of Grace*.

Krik? Krak! (1995)

Edwidge Danticat
Short Stories

When Haitian storytellers get ready to tell a story, they say *"Krik?"* Their eager listeners respond, *"Krak!"* With *Krik? Krak!* Edwidge Danticat established herself as a superior storyteller within and without Haiti's narrative tradition. *Krik? Krak!* reveals the wonder, terror, and pain of Danticat's native Haiti and the enduring strength of Haitian women. Danticat writes about the terrorism of the Tonton Macoutes; the death of hope and the resiliency of love; the Haitians who fled to America to give their children a better life, as her parents did; and the bridge to the past through the tradition of storytelling.

The first seven stories are about chaotic life under political oppression and poverty in Haiti, and the imaginative strategies devised by Haitians to maintain their ideals and hopes in the face of unfathomable hardship. The powerful first story, "Children of the Sea," sets the tone for the Haitian stories. It is a moving series of diary entries from alternating narrators: a young man fleeing Haiti on a dilapidated boat and his girlfriend back on the island, who is living in fear of her life and of his. The last two stories, based in New York City, demonstrate how even after leaving their homeland, Danticat's Haitian characters cling to their heritage while trying to adapt to a new land and a new set of opportunities.

The stories are about people who embrace mythic powers and rites of passage and people who long for peace and happiness for themselves and their country. Danticat captured readers and reviewers with her passion and lyrical writing in what she refers to as her distant third language. A finalist for the National Book Award and Danticat's second book, *Krik? Krak!* is full of vibrant imagery and grace that bear witness to the Haitian people's suffering and courage.

Politics, Nationalism, and Revolution

Commentary

by Arthur Flowers

The Destruction of Black Civilization made me cry. Sure did. I had just read it, back in the 70s I think, and was biking down 125th Street thinking about how far we've traveled and how far we've fallen and was suddenly just crying, vowing never again. I'll never forget that moment. Encounters with books are as responsible as anything for my own still-evolving understanding and lifelong commitment to the struggle.

Works of struggle have pride of place in black literature. A culture's literature is that culture's communal voice. As such, the literature inevitably reflects the traumas that culture is going through at any given time, its burning survival issues. Since the beginning of our journey in the West, it can be argued that the Struggle has been a primary trope of black people in America and around the modern world. Which way freedom? Black literature has consistently reflected the ongoing struggle for survival and empowerment waged by the black people of America and the world. It would be difficult to overestimate the importance of the revolutionary impulse in black literature.

The earliest of our literature, the slave narratives, struggled with the critical questions of the time—freedom and slavery, assimilation and resistance. With the transformation of black America from a rural peasantry to an urban people during the great migration, the burning questions became those of urbanization and cultural survival in an increasingly complex society. The Black Arts Movement, along with the concurrent civil rights and Black Power movements, was fundamentally concerned with issues of identity and empowerment. It was during this period that the literature, and black America as a whole, turned its primary energies from protest addressed to white audiences to a more internal focus. A healing thing.

The literature reflects back to us who we are and passes the word on to future generations. It is a primary tool of cultural retention and orchestration, of the process by which a culture selects the trends and impulses it decides are pertinent to its survival and prosperity. It is the literature that records and defines ideas and values, that forges the visions by which we live and strive, by which we dream. Literature opens minds and passes on ideas, allowing folks to see themselves and their lives in new perspectives, what Julie Dash calls "rupturing their reality."

Marcus Garvey was highly influenced by the book *Ethiopia Unbound* by Casely Hayford, from which he took, among others, the phrase "One God, One People, One Destiny." In turn, Marcus Garvey influenced not only thousands and thousands of black folks, he also influenced the historical dynamics of his times and therefore the future. It can be argued that he has influenced millions of black folks through his writings in *Africa for the Africans.* This happens to some degree every time a reader is touched by a work.

As the voices of a culture that has from its inception felt itself under mortal siege, black people in America and around the world have always valued the voices of struggle. This is, in part, a cultural legacy. The griotic impulse is strong in our literature. Africa's oral tradition and art have been both sacred and functional. Black literature is working literature, and black writers have never been afraid to speak truth to power.

There is something endearing about the willingness of black writers to speak when called, no matter the cost. Martin Luther King had to speak up for his movement, even from the cold floor of a jail cell in *Letter from a Birmingham Jail.* David Walker wrote his *Appeal* and was soon after found dead in the streets of Boston. And what was on the mind of Malcolm when he knew criticism of the Nation, as found in his posthumous *Autobiography of Malcolm X,* could cost him his life. Or on the minds of slaves like Frederick Douglass, who risked torture and death to learn how to read and write, who instinctively understood that the word was a magic that would literally free them from bondage?

Why do tyrants quake when writers speak? Because the Word means something. Because the people trust true writers to care for them and to speak when they need a voice, because the world listens when writers of conscience speak.

That's why Wole Soyinka had to flee Nigeria in the dead of the night for daring to say the generals had no clothes. At least he got away; his fellow writer Ken Saro Wiwa didn't. "If they treat me like this with my international rep," said Saro Wiwa at his show trial, "imagine how they treat those who have no voice." He left last words before they hanged him: "I give my soul to God, but the struggle continues."

The Struggle. It is the Struggle that shapes us, it is the Struggle we must shape. These works of struggle are works that are essential reading for those who aspire to be truly self-determinant in an increasingly complex world that severely marginalizes the unsophisticated and the uninformed. They are essential reading for those who care about the destiny of our people. They are shield and spear.

Today, our problems seem sometimes insurmountable. But they have always seemed insurmountable. Slavery, southern peonage, urban sojourners—our problems have always been epic and we have always overcome. But first there must be vision. What exactly are the issues that we must address, what are the ideological instruments that must be forged to finesse the problems of our generation? What is the long game? What is the vision that guides us?

Once again, we are standing at a crossroads. Who shall show the way? It is in the works of struggle that the answers will be found. It is in the works of struggle that we will find the visions that shape our destiny. *A luta continua.*

Arthur Flowers is the author of De Mojo Blues *and* Another Good-Loving Blues. *He teaches creative writing at Syracuse University.*

David Walker's Appeal in Four Articles, Together with a Preamble, to the Coloured Citizens of the World (1829)

David Walker

Essay

Self-published in 1829 and distributed to slaves throughout southern plantations through ingenious methods, Walker's *Appeal* caused a firestorm reaction among southern slaveholders. The subversive intent of *Appeal,* which called for violent resistance against slavery, made Walker a marked man. His appeal to resistance was not rooted solely in retribution. Walker based his arguments on biblical and historical examples of resistance. He was truly committed to social change but keenly aware of the radical means required to achieve it. Walker's *Appeal* can be said to be an early African American precursor to Malcolm's *By Any Means Necessary* or *The Ballot or the Bullet*—a fearless cry for freedom, by any means necessary.

But while *Appeal*'s fame rests on its militancy, Walker was not a simple bomb-throwing revolutionary. Like Frederick Douglass, Martin Luther King, and innumerable other African American activists who would follow, Walker firmly believed in and based his arguments on the same principles that white Americans so righteously claimed: those found in the Bible and in the U.S. Constitution. But Walker was a realist; he held out faint hope that white Americans would, on their own, ever hold to the principles of their sacred and civic scriptures. Walker also showed his thoughtfulness by providing in his *Appeal* a program for the development of his people after the abolition of slavery.

Unfortunately, what "appealed" most to the authorities of the time was Walker's death. A price was put on his head and he was found dead in June of 1830, an apparent victim of poison. Still, upon reading Walker's *Appeal,* the white aristocracy was put on notice—the days of the slaver were numbered. Less than a year and a half after the publication of Walker's work, Nat Turner's rebellion demonstrated in action the commitment to liberation that Walker articulated with such fire in his *Appeal.*

Are we MEN!!—I ask you, O my brethren! are we MEN? . . .
The whites have always been an unjust, jealous, unmerciful, avaricious and blood-thirsty set of beings, always seeking after power and authority.—We view them all over the confederacy of Greece, where they were first known to be anything, (in consequence of education) we see them there, cutting each other's throats—trying to subject each other to wretchedness and misery—to effect which, they used all kinds of deceitful, unfair, and unmerciful means. . . . Now suppose God were to give them more sense, what would they do? If it were possible, would they not *dethrone* Jehovah and seat themselves upon his throne?

—from *David Walker's Appeal*

The Philosophy and Opinions of Marcus Garvey; or Africa for the Africans (1923)

Marcus Garvey
Nonfiction

Marcus Mosiah Garvey, a Jamaican by birth, was the founder of international back-to-Africa movements for the racial emancipation of blacks—the United Negro Improvement Association (UNIA) and African Communities League (ACL).

After World War I, Garvey emerged as the militant voice of "Africa for the Africans." His message of racial unity (and segregation) was welcomed by blacks and confirmed by other nationalist movements of the day. On this tidal wave of support, Garvey was able to raise several million dollars and establish Harlem's thirty or so square blocks, where UNIA was headquartered, as the capital of the black world. But as quickly as Garvey rose, he was toppled. He went from obscurity to messiah to convicted felon within five years. He was arrested by federal authorities in 1922 and charged with misusing funds intended to establish Black Star, an African American steamship company whose intended purpose was the repatriation of African Americans to Africa. He was sent to a federal penitentiary in February 1925. After serving two years of his five-year sentence, he was deported back to Jamaica, never to return.

These speeches and articles are Garvey's thoughts on everything from education to miscegenation, to prejudice, radicalism, government, power, poverty, slavery, propaganda, war, and ideals. Amy Jacques-Garvey, Garvey's second wife, published *Philosophy and Opinions* "to keep a personal record of the opinions and sayings of my husband. . . . In order to give to the public an opportunity of studying and forming an opinion of him; not from inflated and misleading newspaper and magazine articles, but from expressions of thoughts enunciated by him in defense of his oppressed and struggling race; so that by his own words he may be judged. . . ."

Black Bourgeoisie (1957)

E. Franklin Frazier
Nonfiction

When it was first published in 1957, *Black Bourgeoisie* was simultaneously revered and reviled because it cast a critical eye on one of the cornerstones of the black American community—its middle class. In the 1950s, before the recent burgeoning of the black middle class, Frazier identified the problems that occur in the aftermath of "black-flight" from the inner cities and black communities of the rural South. The book's relevance has only increased as over the years the divide between increasingly prosperous middle-class blacks and their increasingly desperate "underclass" brethren has grown into an almost uncrossable chasm.

By tracing the evolution of the black bourgeoisie, from the segregated South to the integrated North, Frazier shows how the blacks who comprised the middle class have lost their cohesion by moving out of black communities and attempting to integrate white communities. The result of this integration "is an anomalous bourgeois class with no identity, built on self-sustaining myths of black business and society, silently undermined by a collective, debilitating inferiority complex." Frazier hoped to dispel the image of blacks as having thrown off the psychological and economical ravages of slavery to become economically powerful, because according to Frazier, it was a lie that was damaging the community.

Frazier, chairman of the Department of Sociology at Howard University and president of the International Society for the Scientific Study of Race Relations, hoped that *Black Bourgeoisie* would impel blacks to make changes that would empower their community. For the most part, those hoped-for changes have not occurred. Nevertheless, today, as many black people are calling into question the very existence and relevance of an autonomous "black community," his book offers a fascinating perspective on the costs of that community's dissolution.

Since Emancipation, Negroes had been outsiders in American society. Negroes were not only at the bottom of the economic ladder but all the pretended economic gains which Negroes were supposed to have made had not changed fundamentally their relative economic position in American life. The new Negro middle-class was comprised entirely of wage earners and salaried professionals and the so-called Negro business enterprises amounted to practically nothing in the American economy.

—from *Black Bourgeoisie*

The Fire Next Time (1963)

James Baldwin
Essays

"God gave Noah the rainbow sign, No more water, the fire next time!"

S o opens James Baldwin's *The Fire Next Time*. It comprises two previously published essays in the form of personal letters. The first is a letter to his nephew written on the hundredth anniversary of the Emancipation Proclamation that attacks the idea that blacks are inferior to whites. The second, a much longer letter addressed to all Americans, recounts Baldwin's coming-of-age in Harlem, appraises black nationalism, and discusses in detail the connection between racism and Christianity. Written in the heat of the civil rights era, the book reflects Baldwin's passion for justice and his iconoclastic ideas about the revolutionary power of love in the battle for America's survival.

Baldwin spares neither blacks, whites, Muslims, nor Christians from his hard analysis. He condemns the role Christianity has had in fostering white Americans' sense of superiority and disconnection from reality. Baldwin sees Christianity as an obstacle rather than a conduit to better relations between the races. The black church, too, is guilty for encouraging self-hatred and despair among its followers. In Baldwin's view, the Nation of Islam's literally black-and-white theology, wherein the god-sanctioned racism of whites is reversed, merely appropriates the self-destructive tendencies of white Christianity. His frustration with racism is that it is a needless impediment to the true purpose of life: to explore the possibilities of existence with courage, to search for enlightenment that can be passed on to posterity. Willingly containing ourselves in the rigid, artificial box of race serves only to prevent

The only thing white people have that black people need, or
should want, is power—and no one holds power forever.

—from *The Fire Next Time*

us from finding real meaning in our lives and increases the amount
of needless suffering in the world.

The Fire Next Time is probably Baldwin's finest and fiercest
book. As a child, Baldwin was a preacher in an evangelistic store-
front church in Harlem; in *The Fire Next Time,* he draws on the
language and imagery of the Old Testament prophets to paint an
almost apocalyptic picture of American race relations. With equal
fervor, he paints a courageous picture of his unique vision of an
ideal American society, one rid of racial barriers and premised on
love and respect. The book captured the attention of Americans
in the throes of the civil rights era, and was an immediate bestseller when it was published. It is now regarded as one of the
most brilliant and important books to come out of that era, and
Baldwin's fiery plea for love in the face of hatred retains its power
for readers today.

The Black Jacobins (1963)

C. L. R. James
History

Haiti's revolution has always been a point of pride for people of African descent around the world. It was in Haiti that slaveholding European colonizers were finally driven away at the hands of the island's black population. *The Black Jacobins* dramatically and powerfully recounts the events that led up to the bloody and history-altering Haitian revolution of 1791–1803.

The revolution began in the wake of the Bastille and ended in the French colony of Santo Domingo, one of the wealthiest colonies in the world due to its rich natural resources and its importing of cotton, indigo, and coffee. Forever tied with the revolution is Toussaint-Louverture, a barely literate slave who united the slaves and mulattos of Santo Domingo and led them against the ruling population of the colony, as well as French, Spanish, and English forces, to alter the fate of millions of people and shift the economic currents of three continents.

"In 1789 the French West Indian colony of Santo Domingo supplied two-thirds of the overseas trade of France and was the greatest individual market for the European slave-trade. . . . The whole structure rested on the labour of half-a-million slaves." In 1791, after decades of inhumane and savage treatment by their "masters," the slaves revolted—led by one man, Toussaint-Louverture. "One of the most remarkable men of a period rich in remarkable men. The history of the Santo Domingo revolution will therefore largely be a record of his achievements and his political personality. . . . Between 1789–1815, with the single exception of Bonaparte himself, no single figure appeared on the historical stage more greatly gifted than this Negro, a slave till he was 45 [sic]. Yet Toussaint did not make the revolution. It was the revolution that made Toussaint."

The Wretched of the Earth (1963)

Frantz Fanon
Nonfiction

F rantz Fanon's influence on the thinking of the proponents of black power has been enormous. One finds references to his ideas in the works of authors such as Maulana Karenga, James H. Cone, and James Forman. An explanation for this can be found in the timeliness of his seminal work, *The Wretched of the Earth*.

According to William L. Van Deburg,

> . . . the ideological underpinnings of the Black Power movement owed a great deal to the conceptualizations of Frantz Fanon, a black psychiatrist from Martinique who had joined a career as physician/scholar with that of a political militant in service of the Algerian revolution. Fanon, whose work, *The Wretched of the Earth* was published (just before his death) provided black American activists with a compelling analysis of the consciousness and situation of "colonized" peoples everywhere. Chief among his teachings was that violence in support of political and cultural liberation was a positive force, one that was both psychologically empowering and tactically sound. Forceful opposition to an oppressive regime was said to reaffirm the humanity of the oppressed, allowing them to "experience themselves as men."

Armed with this wisdom, mid-sixties activist intellectuals began to speak of African America as an internal colony at war with the forces of cultural degradation and assimilation. By adopting variants of Fanon's concepts, rank-and-file Black Power militants were able to identify with the colonized of the Third World even as they affirmed the notion that violent acts could lead to both mental catharsis and meaningful political change.

112

Africa Must Unite (1963)

Dr. Kwame Nkrumah
Essay

Dr. Nkrumah begins *Africa Must Unite* with the words *freedom, hedsole, sawaba, uhuru*: the slogans of what he calls "the greatest political phenomenon of the latter part of the twentieth century—African nationalism." The book reflects the optimism and energy of the 1950s and 1960s, when many African nations were, at last, throwing off their European colonial rulers, and black people throughout the world were engaged in movements of liberation.

The former president of Ghana, Dr. Nkrumah wrote *Africa Must Unite* right after the country had gained its independence, and he based his arguments and direction on the new perspectives that opened up for Ghana at that momentous time. "The survival of free Africa, the extending independence of this continent, and the development towards that bright future on which our hopes and endeavours are pinned, depend upon political unity. In this century there have already been two world wars fought on the slogans of the preservation of democracy; on the right of peoples to determine the form of government under which they want to live."

"Africa unite" was the chant repeated throughout Africa in the late 1960s and used to bind all black and brown peoples together. "The great millions of Africa, and of Asia, have grown impatient of being hewers of wood and drawers of water, and are rebelling against the false belief that providence created some to be the menials of others." Dr. Nkrumah believed that Africa must unite because all of Africa, no matter the enslavers, are enslaved for much the same reasons: forced labor and subjugation for the enrichment of other peoples. It was Dr. Nkrumah's belief that the twentieth century, a century of emancipation and revolution, would finally eradicate colonial rule and imperialist exploitation. His broad, Pan-Africanist vision, while still not a reality, remains an inspiration.

The River Between (1965)

Ngugi Wa Thiongo
Novel

A s has been the case for many of his fellow African writers, Kenya-born Ngugi Wa Thiongo has been at various times imprisoned, persecuted, and exiled for his writing and political activism. *The River Between* was Ngugi's first written, but not his first published, novel (*Weep Not, Child* was published in 1964). It powerfully tells the story of the inevitable conflicts faced by African society as it attempts to reconcile its traditional beliefs with the imperatives of colonialism.

The novel is set in the 1930s and 1940s in rural Kenya and focuses on the conflict between Christian and traditional beliefs. The story is set among the Gikuyu people living on two adjoining ridges, Kameno and Makuyu, which are divided by a river. The people of Kameno follow a land-based religion; the people of Makuyu are led by the Christian convert Joshua. The young and charismatic Waiyaki is sent from Kameno to the mission school to learn the ways of the colonialists so as to resist their claims to the Kameno lands. The conflict centers around the initiation rites of the Gikuyu people. Muthoni, daughter of the cleric Joshua, defies her father's wishes and participates in the ritual. She dies when her wounds fail to heal, and the rift between the two factions becomes irreparable. Politically, the Kiama, a militant antigovernment, anti-Christian movement, continues to agitate successfully. When Waiyaki falls in love with Nyambura, Muthoni's sister and Joshua's daughter, the stage is set for a tragic confrontation.

The River Between is a powerful and gripping retelling of the passing of the African traditional life.

Black Power (1967)

Stokely Carmichael and Charles V. Hamilton
Nonfiction

In the late 1960s, as the struggle for civil rights—both between blacks and the nation and within the civil rights organizations themselves—escalated, activist Stokely Carmichael uttered a rallying cry that would signal a significant shift in the philosophy and tactics of some black groups involved in the struggle. Carmichael was the newly elected chairman of the Student Non-Violent Coordinating Committee (SNCC) and just released from jail for activities surrounding James Meredith's march. In announcing the expulsion of all whites from the SNCC, Carmichael declared, "The only way we gonna stop them white men from whuppn' us is to take over. . . . We been saying freedom for six years and we ain't got nothin'. What we gonna start saying now is 'Black Power!'"

That was in 1966. A year later, Carmichael, together with political scientist Charles V. Hamilton, coauthored the book *Black Power*, which presented what at the time was thought to be the definitive statement of a new "racial philosophy" and attempted to formulate a new approach that would enable blacks to solve the problems associated with their oppression on their own, without relying on the generosity and guidance of whites. Black Power was not, at least in theory, designed as a threat to white people. It was, in a sense, merely the latest incarnation of Booker T. Washington's gospel of self-help. Black Power was designed to allow black people, through their own institutions and organizations, to achieve economic and political liberation. The phrase itself was a brilliant use of language: the two short, punchy words together formed a vision of a radically different future for black people, who more often than not found themselves disenfranchised and on the wrong end of policemen's swinging clubs.

The authors were also internationalist in their view: ". . . Black Power means that black people see themselves as part of a new force, sometimes called the 'Third World'; that we see our struggle as closely related to liberation struggles around the world. We must hook up with these struggles." In the book's eight essays, Carmichael and Hamilton critique the political significance of various existing institutions with a consistent eye to their relevance to black struggle.

Black Power was one of the clearest manifestations of the movement's change of direction in the late 1960s. The change was significant: the language of militant black liberation soon replaced, and even discredited for a time, the language of nonviolent protests. While the value of that transformation is still being debated, the influence, and power, of Carmichael's hard-charging polemic is still being felt.

This book is about why, where, and in what manner black people in America must get themselves together. It is about black people taking care of business—the business of and for black people. The stakes are really very simple: if we fail to do this, we face continued subjection to a white society that has no intention of giving up willingly or easily its position of priority and authority. If we succeed, we will exercise control over our lives, politically, economically, and physically. We will also contribute to the development of a viable larger society; in terms of ultimate social benefit, there is nothing unilateral about the movement to free black people.

—from *Black Power*

Soul on Ice (1968)

Eldridge Cleaver
Memoir

Soul on Ice, written in 1954 when Cleaver was eighteen and serving time in prison for marijuana charges and rape, is a searing, groundbreaking autobiography of a life lived on the edge and without remorse. His story became one of America's great literary and sociological discoveries. With it, Cleaver triumphed as a cultural critic, a social commentator, a sociologist, and a writer.

After a series of religious experiences in prison, Cleaver became a Muslim convert, then a Muslim preacher of extraordinary eloquence and conviction, and then a firm follower of Malcolm X. He described his transformation through reading: "Through reading I was amazed to discover how confused people were. I had thought that, out there beyond the horizon of my own ignorance, unanimity existed, that even though I myself didn't know what was happening in the universe, other people certainly did."

Much of Cleaver's commentary was on target because he'd walked the road and he knew the signs, and he was a man who, if nothing else, called things like he saw them. "It may be that I harm myself by speaking frankly and directly, but I do not care about that at all. . . . I know that by following the course which I have charted I will find my salvation. If I had followed the path laid down for me by the officials, I'd undoubtedly have long since been out of prison—but I'd be less than a man. I'd be weaker and less certain of where I want to go, what I want to do, and how to get there. . . ."

Soledad Brother: The Prison Letters of George Jackson (1970)

George Jackson
Epistolary

That prisons have long been a means of containing black male self-assertiveness and anger is a self-evident truth to a large number of African Americans. George Jackson's *Soledad Brother* gives testament to this, as well as to the reality of the enormous power, talent, and intelligence being restrained behind bars. A collection of Jackson's letters from prison, *Soledad Brother* is an outspoken condemnation of the racism of white America and a powerful appraisal of the prison system that failed to break his spirit but eventually took his life.

At eighteen, Jackson was given a one-year-to-life sentence for stealing $70 from a gas station. In prison Jackson became radicalized and, together with another prisoner, started a Marxist revolutionary cell. Through a series of events, Jackson would be charged with the murder of a white prison guard and would subsequently be killed while allegedly trying to escape—despite the fact that all charges against him had been dropped. At Jackson's death, he was thirty years old. Twelve of those thirty years had been spent in prison, seven and one-half of those years in solitary confinement.

Jackson's letters make palpable the intense feelings of anger and rebellion that filled black men in America's prisons in the 1960s. But even removed from the social and political firestorms of the 1960s, Jackson's story still resonates for its portrait of a man taking a stand even while locked down. Although he was a naïve petty thief when he was first arrested, Jackson, like men from Malcolm X to Nathan McCall, found redemption behind bars. *Soledad Brother* was published in 1970; Jackson was killed the following year.

If I leave here alive, I'll leave nothing behind. They'll never count me among the broken men, but I can't say that I'm normal either. I've been hungry too long, I've gotten angry too often. I've been lied to and insulted too many times. They've pushed me over the line from which there can be no retreat. I know that they will not be satisfied until they've pushed me out of this existence altogether. I've been the victim of so many racist attacks that I could never relax again . . . I can still smile now, after ten years of blocking knife thrusts, and the pick handles of faceless sadistic pigs, of anticipating and reacting for ten years, seven of them in solitary. I can still smile sometimes, but by the time this thing is over I may not be a nice person. And I just lit my seventy-seventh cigarette of this twenty-one hour day. I'm going to lay down for two or three hours, perhaps I'll sleep.

—from *Soledad Brother*

Seize the Time: The Story of the Black Panther Party (1970)

Bobby Seale
Nonfiction

The demand for black power in the late 1960s meant different things to different groups within the black community. For the mildest of its mouthers, the slogan was a call for black economic self-sufficiency and political power within the American system. For others, it meant complete racial separatism and cultural nationalism. For still others, it meant a complete anticapitalist revolution in the Marxist model, except that where Marx thought the revolutionary vanguard would emerge from the industrial working class, Marxist black revolutionaries saw the revolution emerging from the black ghetto underclass. The Black Panthers, who were believed by many to be the most aggressively militant and revolutionary of the black organizations of the period, embraced the latter position.

Seize the Time was written by Bobby Seale, then chairman of the Black Panther Party, to clear up misunderstandings on the part of the public by thoroughly explaining the organization's origin, activities, and goals. The Black Panther Party began in Oakland, California, in October 1966, founded by Seale and the late Huey P. Newton, who would go on to be its most visible and controversial leader. In contrast to the nonviolent methods being advocated by other activist groups of the time, the Panthers openly advocated the use of violence to achieve their goals, putting into action their interpretation of Malcolm X's "by any means necessary" philosophy. Starting from the theory that the police—the arm of the suppressive white establishment in the ghetto—must be monitored by blacks, they took to the streets with loaded cameras and guns, thus claiming for themselves and the black youths of the ghetto the respect and due process they felt was lacking. It also unleashed an era of increasingly violent activity by revolutionaries of all colors that was met with a fierce backlash on the part of the government.

Seize the Time was written while Seale was in San Francisco State Prison, during a period when nearly every black activist organization was under attack by government agencies. Seale's book is written in a language and style that reflect the urgency, passion, and justifiable paranoia of that turbulent era. While the Panthers were undermined by forces without and within, *Seize the Time,* with its urgent call for black self-defense and black pride, remains a compelling account of one manifestation of an oppressed people's continuing struggle for liberation.

The life and existence of the Black Panther Party, the ideology of the Party in motion, is a biography of oppressed America, black and white, that no news report, TV documentary, book, or magazine has yet expressed. To do so, the media would let the people know what's really going on, how things have happened, and how we're struggling for our freedom. So before the power structure, through its pigs, attempts to murder any more of us, or take more political prisoners in its age-old attempt to keep us "niggers" as they like to say, "in our place," I have put together the true story of the Black Panther Party.

—from *Seize the Time*

The Destruction of Black Civilization: Great Issues of a Race from 4500 B.C. to 2000 A.D. (1971)

Chancellor Williams
History

*T*he *Destruction of Black Civilization* took Chancellor Williams sixteen years of research and field study to compile. The book, which was to serve as a reinterpretation of the history of the African race, was intended to be "a general rebellion against the subtle message from even the most 'liberal' white authors (and their Negro disciples): 'You belong to a race of nobodies. You have no worthwhile history to point to with pride.'" The book was written at a time when many black students, educators, and scholars were starting to piece together the connection between the way their history was taught and the way they were perceived by others and by themselves. They began to question assumptions made about their history and took it upon themselves to create a new body of historical research.

The book is premised on the question: "If the Blacks were among the very first builders of civilization and their land the birthplace of civilization, what has happened to them that has left them since then, at the bottom of world society, *precisely what happened?* The Caucasian answer is simple and well-known: The Blacks have always been at the bottom." Williams instead contends that many elements—nature, imperialism, and stolen legacies—have aided in the destruction of the black civilization.

The Destruction of Black Civilization is revelatory and revolutionary because it offers a new approach to the research, teaching, and study of African history by shifting the main focus from the history of Arabs and Europeans in Africa to the Africans themselves, offering instead "a history of blacks *that is a history of blacks.* Because only from history can we learn what our strengths were and, especially, in what particular aspect we are weak and vulnerable. Our history can then become at once the foundation and guiding light for united efforts in serious[ly] planning what we should be about now." It was part of the evolution of the black revolution that took place in the 1970s, as the focus shifted from politics to matters of the mind.

The Spook Who Sat by the Door (1973)

Sam Greenlee
Novel

The Spook Who Sat by the Door was originally brought into print by a small publisher, Richard Baron Press, and quickly became an underground favorite. Published in the near aftermath of the Black Power movement, *The Spook* fictionalized the urban-based war for liberation that never quite manifested.

Senator Gilbert Hennington is in a close race for reelection and needs an issue with which to galvanize the Negro vote. His answer: a public call for the integration of the heretofore lily-white Central Intelligence Agency (at its Field Operatives level). Of the hundreds who applied, twenty-three are chosen for training under express orders that no one successfully complete the course. With the exception of one, Dan Freeman, they are eliminated. Exasperated at Freeman's tenacity, Calhoun, the agency's judo instructor, tells him, "I'm going to give you a chance. You just walk up to the head office and resign and that will be it. Otherwise, we fight until you do. And you will not leave this room until I have whipped you and you walk out of here, or crawl out of here, or are carried out of here and resign. Do I make myself clear?" Midway through the fight, "Freeman wondered if he could keep from killing this white man. No, he thought, he's not worth it. . . . But he does have an ass-kicking coming and he can't handle it. This cat can't believe a nigger can whip him. Well, he'll believe it when I'm through. . . ."

Freeman is never assigned to the field, but is given a glass-enclosed office where he sits in display. But he has a plan and soon resigns, returning to Chicago to organize the Cobras, a street gang, into an armed and skilled insurgency unit. On a hot Chicago night, a police killing sparks the riot that becomes the war led by Freeman and the Cobras, now dubbed Uncle Tom and the Freedom Fighters. Fast-paced, well written, entertaining, memorable.

Notes of a Hanging Judge (1990)

Stanley Crouch

Essays

Provocative is the word most frequently attached to the writings of Stanley Crouch, one of America's finest cultural critics. Crouch's essays are written with cool assurance and precision, but they always pack a punch for his favorite targets, from "racial hustlers" and cheap media products to knee-jerk identity politicians and historic revisionists. No matter what the topic—jazz, media, literature, film, history, politics—Crouch's biting, iconoclastic essays land with metronomic regularity on the same fundamental issue: the importance of black people taking their rightful and hard-earned place at the table of American culture and democracy, instead of insisting on a contrived outsider pose and wallowing in unnecessary martyrdom.

The essays in *Notes of a Hanging Judge* were written between 1979 and 1988—years when many of the gains of the civil rights era were being overturned by the Reagan administration and the so-called Culture Wars were just starting to heat up. Crouch's essays capture the intellectual ferment of the era, offering trenchant criticism on emerging cultural trends and milestone moments in film, literature, and politics. One of his most memorable essays, "Nationalism of Fools," is a biting profile of a 1985 Nation of Islam rally led by Minister Louis Farrakhan at Madison Square Garden. Typical of Crouch's approach, he mocks what he considers Farrakhan and the Nation's "muddled" ideology and senseless anti-Semitism, but also thoughtfully considers why such a message and messenger could attract 25,000 people at that historical juncture.

Other essays attach other black cultural totems of the 1980s: "Aunt Medea" argues that Toni Morrison's much-praised *Beloved* "explains black behavior in terms of social conditioning, as if listing atrocities solves the mystery of human motive and behavior." In "Do the Race Thing," he derides Spike Lee's film *Do the Right Thing* as "the convention of a new black exploitation film." And in "Man in the Mirror," he takes the unusual stance of defending Michael Jackson's extensive plastic surgery by placing it within the context of the American and African American tradition of improvisation: "The American dream is actually the idea that an identity can be improvised and can function socially if it doesn't intrude upon the freedom of anyone else."

It will be hard to find many people who agree with Crouch on every point; his ideas can raise the hackles of conservatives and liberals alike. And his essays can sometimes seem unnecessarily curmudgeonly—sometimes almost mean-spirited. Nevertheless, his often surprising essays, argued in lively and enjoyably rich prose in this collection, are essential to anyone who values serious ideas.

Race Matters (1993)

Cornel West
Nonfiction

C ornel West is one of the most recognized of American
public intellectuals. His message of social liberation, rooted
deeply in the black Baptist tradition, strikes a chord among an
audience of lay readers and academics because it is equally intellectual and accessible. And because of its inherent humanism, it
crosses racial and cultural lines as well.

In *Race Matters,* West asks for a renewed engagement on the
question of race and presents a bracing call to action to establish
a new framework from which to discuss the issue. West believes
race represents a dire paradox for the nation: either America recognizes the comon humanity of all of its citizens, acknowledges
its spiritual impoverishment, and overturns a political environment dominated by image rather than substance, or it risks the
unmaking of the democratic order.

Ours is a crisis, contends West, that evolves in large measure
from the predominantly market-driven American way of life. The
attendant emphasis on individuality and competition renders traditional black communal life ineffective and leads to the denigra-
tion of black people. This situation, West explains, creates not
just a social and political crisis in the black community, but a deep
existential crisis as well:

> Under these circumstances black existential angst derives from
> the lived experience of ontological wounds and emotional scars
> inflicted by white supremacist beliefs and images permeating
> U.S. society and culture. These beliefs and images attack black
> intelligence, black ability, black beauty, and black character daily
> in subtle and not-so-subtle ways. . . . The accumulated effect
> of the black wounds and scars suffered in a white-dominated

society is a deep-seated anger, a boiling sense of rage, and a passionate pessimism regarding America's will to justice.

Thus, centuries into the African American experience, more than one hundred years after the abolition of slavery, and decades after the major battles of the civil rights movement, race, contends West, still matters.

God's Bits of Wood (1996)

Sembene Ousmane
Novel

S embene Ousmane, the author of several novels written in France, is Senegalese by birth. *God's Bits of Wood* tells the story of the bloody and tragic workers' strike on the Dakar-Niger railway in 1947.

Ousmane captures the spirit of the West African people in their conflict with the colonial powers. Their mistreatment at the hands of their employer is cast in both race and class terms: "We are being robbed. We do the same work the white men do. Why then should they be paid more? In what way is a white worker better than a black worker? Only the engines we run tell the truth—and they don't know the difference between a white man and a black. If we want to live decently we must fight!"

Ousmane's writing is crisp and textural, as you would expect from an author who is also one of Africa's best-known film-makers: "The last rays of the sun filtered through a shredded lacework of clouds. To the west, waves of mist spun slowly away, and at the very center of the vast mauve and indigo arch of sky the great crimson orb grew steadily larger. The roofs, the thorny minarets of the mosques, the trees—silk-cotton, flame, and mahogany—the wall, the ochered ground; all caught fire."

God's Bits of Wood honestly portrays the ambivalence between the Africans and the encroaching French and between the Africans themselves. "Among my people, no one speaks the white man's language, and no one has died of it! Ever since I was born—and God knows that was a long time ago—I have never heard of a white man who had learned to speak Bambara, or any other language of this country. But you rootless people think only of learning his, while our language dies." Although this particular pitched battle between the forces of colonialism and the forces of revolution comes to a disappointing end, Ousmane's depiction of the spirit of the people makes it clear that the fight to reclaim their language, land, and labor is far from over.

Soul and Spirit

Commentary
by Hazel Reid

I have a dream today . . . I have a dream that one day all
God's children, black men and white men, Jews and Gentiles,
Protestants and Catholics, will be able to join hands and sing in
the words of the old Negro spiritual, "Free at last! Free at last!
Thank God Almighty, we are free at last!"
—The Rev. Dr. Martin Luther King Jr.

The twentieth century has ended, leaving behind its monumental symbols of achievements in material progress—its icons of industrial, scientific, and technological advancement. It is also leaving a legacy of wars, a highly polluted earth and atmosphere, systems of serious economic and social inequalities and related problems that hinder the progress of human development, and an increasing human loss of a sense of connectedness with the spiritual source of life. In this period of millennium transition, the question is: What will be the major achievements of this next era? Responses to this question include predictions such as unimaginable progress in technology; the replacement of money with electronic systems of economic exchange; major medical developments, especially the uncovering of the complete genetic makeup of humans and other species; the production of more sophisticated weapons of war; and successful communication with extraterrestrial beings. However, the twenty-first century also holds out the possibility of significant progress in the spiritual evolution and liberation of the human species.

In the face of the troubled state of the world in which we live and of predictions for deteriorating human relationships and even the earth's destruction—this is a magnificent promise. It prompts the further question: Who would be the most likely to want to serve as agents of this spiritual approach to human liberation? It

135

would not likely be those who have profited most from the tangible material advancements of the last several centuries and place greatest value on material goods. The people who would be most likely to grasp at hope in a spiritual model for liberation would have to be those who have suffered the greatest exploitation during the past centuries of scientific and technological advancements. From this point of view, peoples in the Pan-African world should be among the most likely to see hope in this prophecy. For us, as for other oppressed peoples, the spiritual approach is not new. We have established a substantial track record in using spirit as a means to endure, survive, and achieve extraordinary accomplishments.

Scientists and other skeptics tend to approach the idea of spirit as superstition, since they cannot see it, cannot touch it, and cannot examine it under available microscopes. However, logic suggests that the universal attempt to use spirit to explain human problems and direct human destiny is far too significant to be dismissed as mere superstition and ignorance. Those attempts are often captured in our greatest literature on the spirit.

The track record we have established in using the spirit to solve human problems includes the following examples:

• *African spiritual tradition*   In Pan-African cultures, we have developed models of holy spaces where we can go for healing—both physical and spiritual. Such models have been developed by people who practice the traditional African religions, as well as modifications of them such as Santeria, voodoo, and obeah.

• *Christian churches*   The African models of spirituality have been carried over to the black church as well, those holy grounds for healing and sustenance where the faithful congregate for prayers, singing, dancing, laying on of hands, and testifying. Churches have played a major role in the liberation of African peoples in the Western world from slavery to the present. James Cone's *A Black Theology of Liberation* and Samuel Dewitt Proctor's *The Substance of Things Hoped For* describe the varieties of ways that church can work to sustain and liberate.

• *Prayers and meditation* As a spiritual practice, meditation is most prevalent among Asian peoples, but it has also played a role in the lives of African people around the world. For many people, including the Hindus in India, meditation is a major means of uniting with the Divine Spirit, increasing spiritual consciousness, and seeking liberation from the human condition. Prayer has served the same function within the framework of African American religious practices. Two wonderful examples of how this has been done are James Melvin Washington's comprehensive *Conversations with God* and Marian Wright Edelman's *Guide My Feet.*

• *Affirmations* A phenomenal example of the use of affirmation is found in the works of Iyanla Vanzant, including her best-selling *Acts of Faith.* Her self-affirming and self-loving vision of the world is also found in her first book, *Tapping the Power Within.*

These examples are only a few of the many models that exist that can be examined with the goal to develop models of physical and spiritual healing of the world. Martin Luther King Jr. proclaimed that he had "seen the Promised Land," and even though he knew he "might not get there" with us, he died believing in its possibility. We certainly may not get there—at least not in physical form. But the least we can do is to think and act in creative and spiritual ways that will move humanity in quantum leaps toward a more just and more harmonious society. It is only in this way that we will be able to speed up the prophecy of Dr. King.

The books in this section that address the issue of the spirit as a means of liberation take different angles, all of which provide different perspectives that we can integrate in our search for freedom.

Hazel Reid is an educator and anthropologist. She is the author of Ritual for a New Liberation Covenant *and teaches English at the City University of New York.*

Jesus and the Disinherited (1949)

Howard Thurman
Nonfiction

P ublished in 1949, Howard Thurman's *Jesus and the Disinherited* delivers a masterful interpretation of how God works in our lives. Thurman was one of the foremost preachers and theologians of the twentieth century, and much of his work centered on the relevance of the Christian message to the contemporary struggles of black people. In this, Thurman's masterwork, he argues that the Gospel of Jesus Christ is not just a map for getting to the next world, but a guidebook for the empowerment of the poor and disenfranchised in this world. Thurman was one of the leading preachers of this new Social Gospel that eventually flowered in the form of the church-centered civil rights movement.

Thurman identified the central spiritual problems faced by black folks as the overwhelming stresses of poverty, racism, and a sense of spiritual disconnectedness. He then turned to the life of Jesus as a primary example of the power of love to drive the spiritual regeneration required to sustain a vision of God and self in modern society. The life of Jesus serves as a guidepost to the kind of love that is a hallmark of human spirit, success, and personal salvation. But Thurman doesn't believe that the Gospel only applies to the individual search for salvation: He also challenges our unconscious submission to the philosophies of individualism and insists that the Gospel is a manual of resistance for the poor and disenfranchised.

He interprets the life of Jesus within a context of the oppressed and offers incisive and liberating thoughts on man's most egregious of sins: fear, deception, and hate. Of fear, he says: "He who fears is literally delivered to destruction. . . . There are some things that are worse than death. To deny one's own integrity of personality in the presence of the human challenge is one of those things."

While *Jesus and the Disinherited* was influential in shaping the philosophies of the early civil rights movement, it remains topical and deeply relevant even today.

Letter from a Birmingham Jail (1963)

Martin Luther King Jr.

Nonfiction

Martin Luther King's *Letter from a Birmingham Jail* was written while the civil rights leader was serving a sentence for spearheading the mass protest demonstrations of 1963 in Birmingham, Alabama. In it, King responds to a group of white Alabama religious leaders who had publicly urged him to limit his activities to local and federal courts. The religious leaders accused King and his Southern Christian Leadership Council of being "outside agitators" whose peaceful resistance could serve to incite further civil disturbance and rioting. King's letter from prison, which incisively laid out his brilliant counterargument, was one of the definitive writings of the civil rights era: It codified the methods of direct-action civil disobedience and offered a vigorous defense of its theological and moral foundations.

King's letter first laid to rest the idea that he was ever an "outside agitator"; how could anyone be an outsider to the cause of humanity? He framed the civil rights struggle as the vital struggle for human rights and godly justice on earth. He drew on biblical parallels and the writings of Christian thinkers, especially St. Thomas Aquinas, to make the point that not all laws enacted by humans are just by a divine standard. King was particularly harsh on these religious leaders for their desire to quiet him and others in order to preserve a facade of peace and civil tranquillity at the expense of true social justice. King could not imagine a Christianity that sanctioned, through inaction, oppression and prejudice against any of God's human creations.

Like the epistles of the Christian apostle Paul, the moral urgency of King's letter was only increased by the circumstances of its composition: In an author's note to the published edition

We know through painful experience that freedom is never voluntarily given by the oppressor; it must be demanded by the oppressed. Frankly, I have yet to engage in a direct-action campaign that was "well-timed" in the view of those who have not suffered duly from the disease of segregation. For years now I have heard the word "Wait!" It rings in the ear of every Negro with piercing familiarity. This "Wait" has almost always meant "Never." We must come to see, with one of our distinguished jurists, that "justice too long delayed is justice denied."

—from *Letter from a Birmingham Jail*

of his letter, King wrote: "This response to a published statement . . . was composed under somewhat constricting circumstances. Begun on the margins of the newspaper in which the statement appeared while I was in jail, the letter was continued on scraps of writing paper supplied by a friendly Negro trustee, and concluded on a pad my attorneys were eventually permitted to leave me."

The publication of *Letter from a Birmingham Jail* was pivotal in influencing public opinion in favor of the civil rights movement, and it caused the movement to receive both greater participation and greater financial support. Today, it is a reminder of the moral and religious imperatives that drove the 1960s civil rights movement and its brilliant leader.

A Black Theology of Liberation (1970)

James H. Cone

Essays

W hen *A Black Theology of Liberation* was first published in 1970, it was revolutionary because it claimed that white theology had no relevance as Christ's message because it was "not related to the liberation of the poor." It also asserted that "racism. . . . is found not only in American society and its churches but particularly in the discipline in theology, affecting its nature and purpose." Cone was among the leaders in the establishment of a black theology movement that reinterpreted Christianity as a tool for the liberation of the black community.

His message was the Christian response to the Black Power movement that emerged in the late 1970s. Like Martin Luther King in his *Letter from a Birmingham Jail,* Cone rejected any form of Christianity that defended the oppressive status quo, and he argued persuasively that the God of the Bible is first of all a God of the poor and of those seeking liberation from oppression. Cone felt that what was needed was a "fresh start" in theology that would arise out of the black struggle for justice and be in no way dependent upon the approval of white academics or religious leaders. "I knew that racism was a heresy, and I did not need to have white theologians tell me so. Indeed, the exploitation of persons of color was the central theological problem of our time. 'The problem of the twentieth century,' wrote W. E. B. Du Bois in 1906, 'is the problem of the color line.' Just as whites had not listened to Du Bois, I did not expect white theologians to take black theology seriously."

A Black Theology of Liberation laid the groundwork and sets the standard for that "fresh start." Cone's revolutionary work has been immensely influential among black ministers throughout the United States and the liberation theology movement around the world.

Theology is to put into ordered speech the meaning of God's activity in the world, so that the community of the oppressed will recognize that its inner thrust for liberation is not only *consistent with* the gospel but *is* the gospel of Jesus Christ.

—from *A Black Theology of Liberation*

Mumbo Jumbo (1972)

Ishmael Reed
Novel

Ishmael Reed is a *different* kind of writer, and *Mumbo Jumbo*, a mystery, gives the reader a glimpse into his kaleidoscopic imagination. Papa La Bas, the founder and head of the Mumbo Jumbo Kathedral, is on a holy quest to find the sacred and ancient text of the Jes Grew movement. The Jes Grew believers are black, honor the life of the body and spirit, and praise through dance. Their philosophical nemesis, the Wallflowers, are firmly rooted in a Judeo-Christian belief system. Hinckle Von Vampton, a white man and member of the Wallflower Order, hopes to find the holy text as well, but to destroy it.

Central to the enjoyment of this intriguing and quirky novel is Reed's revision of religious history, slanted to a black point of view. The history of religion begins in Egypt with the black prince Osiris. His principal praise form was dance. His main adversary was his brother, Set (the original Evil). In form, Set manifests as conformity, rules, and censorship. Moses, a direct descendent of Set, surreptitiously acquires a written record of Osiris's ancient mysteries of nature, but does so during the wrong phase of the moon—that is, with malicious intent. He knows, then, only the opposite sides of the teaching. Reed postulates that the teachings of Moses, his Commandments, its "thou shalt not's," and the Bible are distortions of the text. Moses, and those who follow historically from him—Christ, the Apostles, and others—are impostors.

Reed's *Mumbo Jumbo* is irreverent, incisive, crisp, and trenchant.

Faith and the Good Thing (1974)

Charles Johnson
Novel

Faith Cross, a beautiful young black woman from the Georgia back country, was left little to live by. Her mother, Lavidia, left her with only this: Faith must find herself a "Good Thing." Faith does not know what this Good Thing is, but she knows it is what she needs to find the peace and happiness she so fervently desires. Before her mother dies, Faith is "saved," and at first, God appears to fulfill her need. But the satisfaction she derives from that episode pales in comparison to the expectations of the mysterious Good Thing. Dissatisfied with her first shot at salvation, Faith follows the advice of a seer, the Swamp Woman, and goes to Chicago to continue her search.

In Chicago, Faith falls prey to rape and gets heavily involved in prostitution, drugs, and alcohol. Her quest for the Good Thing leads her into doomed romances, childbirth, and a haunting relationship with a philosopher named Dr. Richard M. Barrett, who also searches in vain for the Good Thing. Faith's journey magically leads her back to the land of her youth and a realization of the Good Thing.

Charles Johnson, only the second African American author to win the National Book Award (in 1991 for *The Middle Passage*), is a philosopher at heart. In *The Good Thing*, Faith's journey represents our individual search for self. Unlike Richard Wright, concerned as he was with the external conditions that affect existence—physical salvation—Johnson, in *Faith and the Good Thing*, searches for salvation of the spirit. This seminal work, structured as a folktale, precedes by twenty-five years the queries and answers offered by "new age" African American self-help authors.

The Famished Road (1991)

Ben Okri
Novel

"To be born is to come to the world weighed down with strange gifts of the soul, with enigmas and an inextinguishable sense of exile."

Azaro, or Lazarus, is among a group of spirit-children reluctant to be born, tired of the constant cycle of birth and death, and the banality of the lives in between. Eventually, Azaro decides to once more allow himself to be born, reneging on his pact with his fellow spirits, but then lives his life straddling the physical and spiritual worlds, outwitting spirits who wish to reclaim him and dodging the pitfalls of his teeming Nigerian village compound on the eve of independence. Ben Okri's startlingly inventive writing is richly lyrical and filled with hallucinatory images of both the magical spirit world and the equally bizarre, and often grotesque, physical world.

Azaro is born into a village stricken with poverty, disease, and disaster and filled with political intrigue. *The Famished Road* is a series of tales that captures Azaro's enchanted world: the corrupt politicians, his besieged family, encircling malevolent and benevolent spirits, and the daily goings-on of his neighbor, all of which he recounts in florid language. This celebration, held at the local bar, is viewed through the eyes of the young Azaro: "The men danced tightly with the women. Everyone sweated profusely. The women twisted and thrust their hips at the men. . . . One of the women was practically cross-eyed with drunkenness. A man grabbed her around the waist and squeezed her buttocks. She wriggled excitedly. The man proceeded to grind his hips against hers as if he didn't want the slightest space between them. The woman's breasts were wet against her blouse." What follows is a hilarious and masterful use of denouement, as pandemonium ensues, dampening both the evening and libidos.

About halfway through, readers may be startled, finding themselves no longer reading *The Famished Road* but listening to it . . . even watching it. And Azaro's father, the Black Tyger, is an event unto himself. Ben Okri, recipient of Great Britain's prestigious Booker Prize for his work in *The Famished Road,* creates an allegory of life whereby a river becomes a road that swallows its travelers, as life, voracious and unsated in its hunger, overwhelms and swallows those who travel its road. Life, proposes Okri, is a famished road.

Tapping the Power Within (1992)

Iyanla Vanzant
Nonfiction

*T*apping the Power Within was the first book by Yoruba priestess and lawyer Iyanla Vanzant, author of the best-selling self-empowerment books *Acts of Faith* and *The Value in the Valley*. *Tapping the Power Within* established Vanzant's deep spiritual and emotional connection with black women everywhere.

The book, which summarizes Vanzant's twelve years of study and training, is part autobiography, part self-help, and part diary. Vanzant uses her life experiences to illustrate and explore the core issues of a black woman's life: redefining the ideals of beauty, friendship, self-love, empowerment, and forgiveness. With these stories drawn from her life, she attempts to imbue readers with knowledge of their own inherent strength and the faith to believe in a higher power.

Vanzant's voice is personable and warm, and the power of her work lies in the fact that she is the embodiment of someone who has already tapped the power within. Her own troubled life reads like a catalog of everything that can go wrong in the life of a late-twentieth-century black woman: "At age 17, I had my first child. At age 19, I entered an abusive marriage. At 22, I had my first nervous breakdown. . . . At age 23, I began receiving public assistance. At age 25, I was virtually homeless. At age 29, I was in therapy. When I was 30, my husband broke my jaw, I had my second breakdown." Yet after all of that drama, she found the spiritual resources within herself to overcome it.

Her books broke new ground in some key areas and set the tone for many inspirational and spiritual books—both fiction and nonfiction—that followed in the 1990s. She was among the first authors to reach a wide audience espousing African-based spirituality as a source of wisdom and guidance, as opposed to the traditional black church. She also directed readers to go inside themselves to heal their own torn psyches, instead of directing her readers toward outward political and community action. And Vanzant talked to black women about their experiences with familiarity, candor, and love that readers have responded to in the millions. Her vast readership understands that she teaches by example, that she has triumphed and has reached back to her sisters to offer the wisdom of her experiences.

Conversations with God: Two Centuries of Prayers by African Americans (1995)

James Melvin Washington, Ph.D.

Anthology

These 190 prayers, which span 235 years of African American faith in God, the church, and their fellowman, provide revelatory insights into the hearts and minds of African Americans. These pieces were culled from the work of historical and literary figures such as W. E. B. Du Bois, Countee Cullen, Martin Luther King Jr., James Baldwin, Sojourner Truth, and Alice Walker and from letters, journals, and newspapers from more obscure sources. Presented together, they form an undeniable documentation of the resolute and sustaining faith of African Americans.

Conversations with God is a glimpse into the divine because it illuminates the powers of spiritual perseverance while giving insight into the oratory and rhetoric of personal prayer. Washington explained the coherence religion brought to black life as follows: "The absurdities of racism insinuate themselves in conscious and unconscious ways in the lives of black people. Religion has been a central way for us to maintain our sanity." By presenting this collection of moving and powerful sermons, poems, and oratory, Dr. Washington also answers the perplexing question of faith: "Why do people who suffer continue to believe in a God who supposedly has the power to prevent and alleviate suffering?"

Dr. Washington, professor of church history at Union Theological Seminary and adjunct professor of religion at Columbia

University, has been an ordained Baptist minister for more than twenty-five years. Here he has given us an exhaustive and uplifting source of information and inspiration, complete with a glossary, a bibliography, and a contributors' page that is also an invaluable biographical resource.

Guide My Feet: Prayers and Meditation on Loving and Working for Children
(1995)

Marian Wright Edelman
Nonfiction

> *Guide my feet while I run this race. Guide my feet while I run this race. Guide my feet while I run this race, for I don't want to run this race in vain.*
>
> —Negro spiritual

With *Guide My Feet,* Marian Wright Edelman hoped to enrich the lives of children by educating the adults around them. "I set out to write a different book—a policy book—but out tumbled prayers instead." And who could blame her? Edelman has made it her life's work to advocate the enrichment of the lives of America's children, to ensure America's future. A longtime civil rights lawyer and founder and president of the Children's Defense Fund, she has taken as her mission the education of all Americans about the needs of children.

She states at the outset: "As I have grown older and wearier trying to help get our nation to put our children first and become more worried about my own children growing up in an America where morals and common sense and family and community values are disintegrating, I pray more and more." This small treasure of a book is intended as a spiritual reference of prayers, meditations, and personal faith in hopes that the rituals that precede and bolster these daily affirmations of people, family, and self will give black Americans and all Americans the strength to take active roles in their children's lives and, subsequently, in their own.

The quest to put children first has required climbing mountain after mountain, with no end in sight. It will require climbing many more mountains and endless work. . . . It will require personal and collective transformation and commitment by you and me to build a safe and loving world for every child—however long it takes.

—from *Guide My Feet*

My Soul Is a Witness: African American Women's Spirituality (1995)

Gloria Wade-Gayles, ed.

Anthology

My Soul Is a Witness is a wonderful collection that speaks to the importance of religion and spirituality in the lives of African American women. Wade-Gayles frames the evolution of African American religion by showing the historical and contemporary ways that black women have expressed their spiritual beliefs. It is this powerful connection to the spiritual that has guided and protected black people, both individually and communally, through the most difficult of times.

Employing essays, poetry, and excerpts from works by various authors, the opening section, "Boarding the Old Ship of Zion: Witnessing for Our Mothers' Faith," sets the tone of this soul-satisfying anthology. Maya Angelou's "Our Grandmothers," Mari Evans's "The Elders," and Rita Dove's "Gospel" are poignant poems that help lay the foundation for our many manifestations of faith.

In "Testifying: The Spiritual Anchor in African American Culture," Wade-Gayles brings together, among others, the voices of Toni Morrison (an excerpt from *Beloved*), Carolyn M. Rodgers ("how I got ovah II/It Is Deep"), and an essay ("Sing Oh Barren One") from Bernice Reagon Johnson of Sweet Honey in the Rock. The unifying theme is the various ways that women have responded to a call from the Spirit.

Wade-Gayles explores every stone, every aspect of African American culture to show where and how spirit manifests. Margo V. Perkins's "The Church of Aretha" offers Aretha Franklin's ability to suffuse her melodies with the power of spirit as testimony to spirit in our everyday lives. The anthology also follows the

155

evolution of African American spiritual expression: "Challenging Traditions" speaks of a woman's self-discovery and empowerment; "Praying at Different Altars" reveals manifestations of Spirit in the Catholic, Islamic, and Yoruba religions. "The Healing Power of Affirmations and Rituals" introduces a newer, more modernistic approach to spirit. Iyanla Vanzant, Susan Taylor, Marita Golden, and bell hooks offer deeply insightful prescriptives.

The *Women's Review of Books* called *Witness* "a jewel which belongs in libraries, churches, classrooms and homes of women and men of all colors, cultures and religions." Let the church say . . . Amen.

The Substance of Things Hoped For: A Memoir of African American Faith

(1995)

Samuel DeWitt Proctor

Memoir

S amuel Proctor, pastor emeritus of the Abyssinian Baptist Church in Harlem, is one of the preeminent theologian orators and educators in the country. *The Substance of Things Hoped For* is the story of not only his personal and spiritual journey but that of many African Americans.

Proctor begins his tale with his grandparents Hattie and George Proctor, who were born into slavery, because he credits their hard work and determination with instilling the morals and values that enabled his family, although very poor, to flourish and succeed. "Faith put steel in their spines to endure physical bondage, and zeal in their souls to prevail against evil; it illumined their minds to keep the vision of a better day. . . . Faith gave them a sense of eternity, a mystical transcendence that transposed their pain into song and their agony into a durable, resilient quest for complete humanity, the substance of things hoped for." For his grandparents, "faith was a way out from the day to day drudgery and toil, an absolvement, a destination." His grandmother often told him: "No use fretting and crying. If you do your part, God will do the rest."

The Substance of Things Hoped For shows how faith has nurtured and guided many African Americans who hail from similar backgrounds. "The spiritual resilience derived from their faith allowed most enslaved African Americans to come through their degrading experience whole, without losing their humanity. . . . With nothing but faith they *imagined* the future. They fixed their trust in God and began their journey up the road to equality."

Sisters' Stories

Commentary

by Eisa Nefertari Ulen

Imagine the power of a woman born and raised in the midst of blackness, surrounded by blackness—breathing, living, spitting back—in blackness. Imagine that woman loving herself enough to love her own people. Imagine her strong, unattached, so free. Imagine her studying ways to study herself, to study us—using that knowledge to think and know herself, and us. She takes that back to the rich black earth, sucking the solos of people—a folk rich in blackness. Then imagine that woman writing. Mama Zora first gave us the glory of a life fully lived with her *Their Eyes Were Watching God*. That classic saw into the future of our very souls. It guides our feet by casting the footsteps Hurston's fictional Janie took as she strode into her life. Vital storytelling, talk that teaches, is just one signifier of the genre coursing its way through *Their Eyes Were Watching God*. Other signifiers strengthen the power of the tale. When the tale celebrates the cherished *i*, we learn the power of a selfhood that includes us all. Meaning is conveyed through color, context through aesthetics, and definition through beauty. Dusky spiritual power cloaks the soul in our stories, protecting sisters, enabling survival. And those women characters almost always connect to the natural world, as Janie discovers her emergent self in a budding pear tree. These are the signs that the writer is working from the particular perspective of black womanhood. These signs were first crafted with precision by Hurston, and her *Eyes* rightfully heads the list of essential Sisters' Stories.

It is this unmatched excellence that sent Alice Walker *Looking for Zora*. It is this same creative power that will strengthen your spirit as you read all the other women whose voices sound for you. Acknowledge the power of the word and decode the messages these women have created for you. Tap the meaning and substance of voices resisting silence. If a book is a window to the world, then a black woman's book is a window to your self. Open it, read it, find for yourself, as Janie discovers, "There's two things people got to do for theyselves. They got to go to God, and they got to find out about livin' for theyselves." Live your life more fully because of the lessons learned in black women's fiction. The chants and spells, the whispers and sighs, the crafted precision, the bodacious war cry that *insists,* honey—tap into this essential power.

The spirit song generated by black women's writing in the United States, the Caribbean, and Africa has actually sounded for centuries. For the written word is rooted in spoken sonance, and women have been speaking in tongues since whenever. A collective unconsciousness crossing cultures and time feeds the muse that inspires the black woman writer. We can trace ourselves back to a Yemaya and know that virtue and sensuality are one. We can understand Ayizan and imagine the souk, the bazaar, the marketplace, the vegetable stand gracing a Sea Island road. Remembering that the continent gave birth to monotheistic faith, we believe in the magic that makes a virgin belly swell with life and push a son into the world. We feel the pain of a woman looking back, remembering the horror of a place where other women were ravaged mercilessly by fevered men, and, in looking back, turned to salt. We can believe one woman's body would be that deeply affected by her sisters' pain. No, we are not Lot. We wouldn't have left her on that mountainside, so close to the top. Because we know Isis could rescue her own child, seek out his scattered self, and bring him back together. Ah, yes, that's how we keep our New World families connected. We know the women of Zimbabwe; their name is Nzinga. We know the women of the Delta; their name is Hatshepsut. The golden calf of the wandering people, the sacred cow among the people of the caste; she is Hathor.

Islamic pilgrims still bathe in the waters the Creator sent to support a single mother.

It is in her richness of experience and heritage that lies the black woman writer's ability to transcend stereotype, to reconfigure archetype. This is her birthright. There lies her might. The essential sisters' voices are her fieldnotes, for she has traveled the world. And so shall you, reading the sacred word.

Too many of us are already young adults or even older when we first read about our very own selves. Too many of us remember our very first encounter with a book written by a black woman because, for too many, that moment took place in an age when clear memories form. For a little black girl to have always had these words around her, to have grown up in a place where black women writers were accessible, has been a weirdly twisted special privilege for far too long. "Sisters' Voices" spreads the word. If you've never known these names and titles, tap into the kitchen talk that has sustained you thus far. The black woman author has sat at the plastic tablecloth, too. If you've read these books before, read them again. Marvel at your new self as you bring recent experience to a page anxious to give you something fresh in return.

Sisters' voices soothe with the signs of a life worth loving. From sisters' voices glean the glory of a love worth living. Sisters' voices check the spirit and align the elements of selfhood. Feel a bound collection of black female imagination. Feel her weight. Now, listen closely. Fly through the lyrics of her song.

Eisa Nefertari Ulen is the author of the novel Spirit's Returning Eye *and a contributor to* Am I the Last Virgin: Ten African American Reflections on Sex and Love *and* Letters of Intent: Women Cross the Generations to Talk About Family, Work, Sex, Love, and the Future of Feminism. *She teaches English composition at Hunter College, City University of New York.*

Their Eyes Were Watching God (1937)

Zora Neale Hurston
Novel

In *Their Eyes Were Watching God*, Zora Neale Hurston draws a sharp portrait of a proud, independent black woman looking for her own identity and resolving not to live lost in sorrow, bitterness, fear, or romantic dreams. Like most lives of black women of the early twentieth century (or any time for that matter), Janie Crawford's life, told here in her own sure voice, is not without its frustrations, terrors, and tragedies—in fact, it is full of them. But the power of her story comes from her life-affirming attitude: Through all the changes she goes through—once divorced, twice widowed (once by her own gun-wielding hand)—she kept a death-grip commitment to live on her own terms, relying only on her own guts, creativity, strength, and passion, and the power she drew from her community, to pull her through. In Janie, Hurston created a character that reflected her own strong belief that the most important mission we have is to discover ourselves.

Janie Crawford was raised in the household of her grandmother, Nanny Crawford, a maid and a former slave. Janie, like her mother before her, was born of rape, and Nanny is committed to protecting her from the sexual and racial violence she and her daughter endured. She pushes Janie into marriage with an older man named Logan Killicks, a farmer with some property. Her life with Killicks is full of boredom and hard labor, so she runs off with Joe Starks, a handsome and well-off storekeeper who moves her to the all-black town of Eatonville, Florida. Even with the prestige and security this new marriage brings, she is bored and unfulfilled by her stunted life with Starks. When Starks dies, Janie begins to live with Tea Cake Woods, a man who cannot provide her with the stability that her Nanny taught her to value, but who finally gives her the passion and satisfaction she'd been looking for all along. Even when further tragedy greets her, she maintains a staunchly positive view of the future.

Hurston, an anthropologist and folklorist, fills this novel with shotgun rhythms and the poetic language of her native south. Language in this novel is crucial; it is through the beautiful self-made idiosyncrasies of southern speech and storytelling that Janie expresses her own will toward self-definition. *Their Eyes Were Watching God* has been called the first African American feminist novel because of its portrayal of a strong black woman rebelling against society's restrictions—and the received wisdom of her Nanny, no less—to seek out her own destiny. But ultimately, this is not a novel that looks out to the world to make political protest or social commentary; it concerns itself with describing the power that lies within us to define ourselves and our lives as we see fit, unbound and unfettered by society's limitations and prejudices. As Alice Walker once wrote, "There is enough self-love in that one book—love of community, culture, traditions—to restore a world."

"Come to yo' Grandma, honey. Set in her lap lak yo' used tuh. Yo' Nanny wouldn't harm a hair uh yo' head. She don't want nobody else to do it neither if she kin help it. Honey de white man is de ruler of everything as fur as I been able tuh find out. Maybe it's some place way off in de ocean where de black man is in power, but we don't know nothin' but what we see. So de' white man throw down de load and tell de nigger man tuh pick it up. He pick it up because he have to, but he don't tote it. He hand it to his womenfolks. De nigger woman is de mule uh de world so fur as Ah can see. Ah been prayin' fuh it tuh be different wid you. Lawd, Lawd, Lawd!"

—from *Their Eyes Were Watching God*

The Street (1946)

Ann Petry
Novel

Ann Petry's best-selling first novel, *The Street*, is the tragic story of Lutie Johnson, a young black woman, and her struggle to live decently and raise her son amidst the violence, poverty, desperation, and racial discord of Harlem in the late 1940s.

Lutie's marriage falls apart after she takes a job as a live-in nanny and maid in Connecticut, leaving her husband, Jim, and her son behind. When Lutie finds out that Jim "has taken up with another woman," she packs up her son and her things and moves out. She eventually ends up on 116th Street, signing the lease on the only apartment she can afford: three rooms in a building with narrow dark halls and prying, noisy neighbors.

Often compared to Richard Wright's *Native Son* for its stark despair, *The Street* was the first book by an African American female writer to sell over one million copies.

As for the street . . . she wasn't afraid of its influence, for she would fight against it. Streets like 116th Street or being colored . . . had turned Pop into a sly old man who drank too much; had killed Mom off when she was in her prime. In that very apartment house in which she was now living, the same combination of circumstances had evidently made the Mrs. Hedges who sat in the street-floor window turn to running a fairly well-kept whorehouse . . . and the superintendent of the building—well, the street had pushed him into basements away from light and air until he was being eaten up by some horrible obsession. None of those things would happen to her, Lutie decided, because she would fight back and never stop fighting back.

—from *The Street*

Annie Allen (1949)

Gwendolyn Brooks
Poetry

None other than the poet laureate of African America, Langston Hughes, declared Gwendolyn Brooks to be the most important literary treasure in America. He was not alone in his regard for this singularly vital American poet: In 1950, Brooks became the first African American to win the Pulitzer Prize for poetry, for her remarkable second book of poems, *Annie Allen*. Dominated by several long poems, *Annie Allen* is an epic cycle that describes from within the changes in a young woman as she moves from effervescent youthful dreams of romance, marriage, and happiness to the concrete reality of adulthood in the inner city's circle of black women. Like all of Brooks's poetry, it is steeped in the black world that she loved, but it addresses a theme with universal resonance: the struggle of growing into womanhood in a tough, uncompromising world.

The book is divided into three sections: "Notes from the Childhood and Girlhood," "The Anniad," and "The Womanhood." The sections trace the mythic journey of Annie from a child whose young worldview is heavily influenced by naïve romantic dreams to an adult woman whose sense of herself and the realities of her world have expanded and deepened. Annie, our epic hero, finds her dreams unfulfilled and her life constricted but strives to successfully complete the journey with dignity intact.

Brooks did not marry herself to any one school of poetry. Her writing style in *Annie Allen* was her own unique mix of traditional poetic forms and unconventional, intensely lyrical language that she drew from her black urban environment. And even though the poems in the cycle work as a cautionary tale about the dangers lurking in the path of young girls journeying to womanhood in the inner city, she never compromises the complexities of Annie's life and emotions to make easy political points. *Annie Allen* is a masterpiece because of Brooks's commitment to authentically rendering the feelings of her heroine and the hazards and rewards of the world she navigated.

What shall I give my children? Who are poor,
Who are ajudged the leastwise of the land,
Who are my sweetest lepers, who demand
No velvet and no velvety velour;
But who have begged me for a brisk contour,
Crying that they are quasi, contraband
Because unfinished, graven by a hand
Less than angelic, admirable or sure.
My hand is stuffed with mode, design, device.
But I lack access to my proper stone.
And plentiful of plan shall not suffice
Nor grief nor love shall be enough alone
To ratify my little halves who bear
Across an autumn freezing everywhere.

—"Children of the Poor," from *Annie Allen*

Maud Martha (1953)

Gwendolyn Brooks
Novel

*M*aud Martha was the first novel by world-class poet Gwendolyn Brooks. It is the story of a woman with doubts about herself and her place in an indifferent world. It is also a story of triumph, the triumph of the lowly. Through Brooks's straightforward and honest portrayal of the novel's heroine, the reader is forced to come face-to-face with Maud Martha and recognize that her essence resides deep within every one of us. Within this honest and intimate story of one woman's struggles and failures, Brooks's incandescent poetic language shines through.

The book is not driven by any specific plot, but collects thirty-four vignettes from Martha's life, taking her from age seven to the time of her second pregnancy. Brooks focuses on Martha's domestic life, first as a child, then a wife, then a mother. Through the seemingly small but poetically described incidents of Martha's life, we see how her childhood dreams meet with disappointing results because she is crippled by her own poor self-worth and the incompatibility of her desires and her reach.

Critic David Littlejohn said of the book: "[Maud Martha] is a striking human experiment . . . a powerful, dagger of a book, as generous as it can possibly be. It teaches more . . . than a thousand pages of protest." Brooks herself has said that much of *Maud Martha* is autobiographical. She "didn't want to write about somebody who turned out to be a star 'cause most people don't turn out to be stars. And yet their lives are just as sweet and just as rich as any others and often they are richer and sweeter."

I Know Why the Caged Bird Sings (1970)

Maya Angelou
Memoir

"I am human, and nothing human is alien to me."

This statement as much as any other defines the uniquely expansive and knowing vision of Maya Angelou. In her works of poetry, drama, and memoir, she describes the imperfections and perversions of humanity—men, women, black, white—with an unrelenting and sometimes jarring candor. But that candor is leavened by an unusually strong desire to comprehend the worst acts of the people around her and find a way for hope and love to survive in spite of it all. *I Know Why the Caged Bird Sings* is the beautifully written and brutally honest chronicle of Angelou's life from her arrival in Stamp, Arkansas, at age three to the birth of her only child in San Francisco, at age sixteen. In between those two events, Angelou provides an unforgettable memoir of growing up black in the 1930s and 1940s in a tiny southern town in Arkansas.

Angelou vividly describes the everyday indignities pressed on blacks in her small town, whether by the condescending white women who shortened her name to Mary because her real name, Marguerite, took too long to say, or by the cruel white dentist who refused to treat her because ". . . my policy is I'd rather stick my hand in a dog's mouth than a nigger's." She also faced horror and brutality at the hands of her own people—she was raped by her mother's boyfriend when she was eight years old and later witnessed his murder at the hands of her uncles, a trauma that sent her into a shell of silence for years. Nevertheless, she emphasizes the positive things she learned from the "rainbows" in the black community of her youth that helped her survive and keep her hopes alive: her grandmother, Momma, who owned a

"It was the best of times and the worst of times . . ." Her voice slid in and curved down through and over the words. She was nearly singing. I wanted to look at the pages. Were they the same that I had read? Or were there notes, music, lined on the pages, as in a hymn book? Her sounds began cascading gently. I knew from listening to a thousand preachers that she was nearing the end of her reading, and I hadn't really heard, heard to understand, a single word.

"How do you like that?"

It occurred to me that she expected a response. The sweet vanilla flavor was still on my tongue and her reading was a wonder to my ears. I had to speak.

I said, "Yes, ma'am." It was the least I could do, but it was the most also.

"There's one more thing. Take this book of poems and memorize one for me. Next time you pay me a visit, I want you to recite."

"I have tried often to search behind the sophistication of years for the enchantment I so easily found in those gifts. The essence escapes but its aura remains. To be allowed, no, invited, into the private lives of strangers, and to share their joys and fears, was a chance to exchange the Southern bitter wormwood for a cup of mead with Beowulf or a hot cup of tea and milk with Oliver Twist. When I said aloud, "It is a far, far better thing that I do, than I have ever done . . ." tears of love filled my eyes at my selflessness.

—from *I Know Why the Caged Bird Sings*

general store and remained a pillar despite the struggles of being a black woman in a segregated and racist southern town; the Holy Rollers of the revivalist black church, who used coded language to attack the racist system they lived under; and Mrs. Bertha Flowers, the aristocratic black woman who brought her back from her shell of silence by introducing her to a love of literature, language, and recitation.

Her mastery of language and storytelling allows Angelou to record the incidents that shaped and troubled her, while also giving insight into the larger social and political tensions of the 1930s. She explains both the worst aspects of her youth and the frequent moments of exhilaration with drama and vigor; it's in the carefully described details and minor incidents that her childhood world is brought to life. *I Know Why the Caged Bird Sings* was nominated for the National Book Award in 1970 and remains an immensely popular book among people worldwide to this day for its honest and hopeful portrait of a woman finding the strength to overcome any adversity, of a caged bird who found the means to fly. Angelou has written four follow-up autobiographical works: *Gather Together in My Name, Singin' Swingin' and Getting Merry Like Christmas, All God's Children Need Traveling Shoes,* and *Heart of a Woman.*

The Autobiography of Miss Jane Pittman
(1971)

Ernest Gaines
Novel

Miss Jane Pittman's American journey spanned over one hundred years, from the 1860s to the 1960s, and took her from picking cotton on a Louisiana plantation to taking part in dismantling the walls of segregation in her southern town. *The Autobiography of Miss Jane Pittman* is her story, told in her own words (although the narrator is putatively a high school teacher who comes to interview her for a school project but soon fades to the background). In Miss Jane, Ernest Gaines created one of the most memorable women in all of American literature. Although she witnessed firsthand the wrenching transition of a people from slavery to freedom, Gaines makes her more than a vehicle for that epic story. Miss Jane is a fully realized, three-dimensional character with her own loves and hates, strengths and weaknesses, which makes her observations on the incredible events around her all the more authentic and compelling. Gaines's skill in giving her a distinct and memorable voice with which to tell her story amplifies the humanity of Miss Jane.

When her story begins, Jane is a slave girl named Ticey, still working on a plantation in Louisiana as the Civil War winds down. She changes her name to Jane at the instigation of a Confederate soldier, a minor rebellion against her owners that costs her a severe beating. After emancipation, she leaves the plantation and joins up with a group of ex-slaves on their way to Ohio. The group is massacred by former Confederate soldiers, with only Jane and Ned, a young boy who Jane unofficially adopts, surviving. Jane then settles in Louisiana and serves as an influence for several black men who work hard to achieve dignity and economic and political equality: first Ned, who changes his name to Ned Douglass after his hero Frederick and becomes a campaigner for the most basic civil rights for blacks, but who is eventually lynched by whites; Joe Pittman, Jane's common-law husband and breaker of wild horses, who is killed by a black stallion; and Jimmy Aaron, a young civil rights worker born on a plantation in Louisiana, who becomes one of the movement's martyrs.

Miss Jane is a complex character, by turns superstitious and sensible, a survivor and a risk-taker. Through the story of her life, she speaks of tolerance and human understanding, commitment and sacrifice, human dignity and its price. With *The Autobiography of Miss Jane Pittman,* Gaines makes the small truths, the everyday pains, and the hard choices of this woman add up to moments of illumination. The book was a bestseller and was later made into a popular television movie, which won nine Emmy Awards.

for colored girls who have considered suicide/when the rainbow is enuf (1975)

Ntozake Shange
Choreopoem

*f*or colored girls who have considered suicide/when the rainbow is enuf is a dauntlessly provocative and forceful play about the difficulties of being black and female in the twentieth century. It is a "choreopoem," a form invented by its author, Ntozake Shange. It consists of a series of twenty poems spoken by seven women, each of whom is dressed in a different color: red, orange, yellow, green, purple, and blue—the six colors of the rainbow—and brown, a neutral color that represents the earth and flesh. The women speak the poems as monologues and occasionally as a chorus; they also sing and dance. Through their poems, the women share stories of the joy, pain, suffering, strength, and resilience of black women from an exclusively feminist perspective. Their poems use potent and often profane language to throw a spotlight on destructive relationships with black men and on the healing power that women find among one another.

The play opens with three poems about childhood and love, including "dark phases," a poem about the difficulties of growing up as a black girl outside the black urban centers of America. The second group of poems includes the lady-in-red's "latent rapist," a disturbing poem about the sexual betrayal of rape by a friend. The next group features the lady-in-brown's "toussaint" about her childhood fascination with Haitian revolutionary Toussaint-Louverture and her subsequent crush on a young boy named Toussaint Jones. Also in this group is a poem about three women who are seduced and then deceived by the same man, but who find solace in their friendship. The fourth group consists of four

"i had convinced myself colored girls had no right to sorrow /
& I lived // & loved that way & kept sorrow on the curb /
allegedly // for you / but I know I did it for myself // I cdnt
stand it // I cdnt stand bein sorry & colored at the same time
// it's so redundant in the modern world"

—from *for colored girls who have considered suicide/when the
rainbow is enuf*

poems entitled "no more love poems, #1–4," where the ladies
share with each other the pain and heartbreak of unrequited love.
The final group of poems includes the dramatic "a nite with beau
willie brown," about an abusive, drunken Vietnam vet who takes
his children from their mother and drops them to their deaths
from a fifth-floor window. The final poem in the piece is entitled
"laying on of the hands," a poem that affirms life despite the
losses, abuses, and rejection they've experienced: the poem ends
with the lady-in-red's memorable line: "i found god in myself &
I loved her fiercely."

Shange's work has been criticized for its stark, unsympathetic
portrayals of black men and its use of profanity, but it has moved
and electrified audiences from its first performances in a women's
bar in California to its award-winning run on Broadway precisely
because of its uncompromising point of view. Her combination of
strong language, imaginative staging, and decisively pro-woman
stance was revolutionary when this play first ran, and continues to
influence black women's drama and literature today.

Black Macho and the Myth of the Superwoman (1979)

Michele Wallace
Nonfiction

At just twenty-six, after working at *Newsweek* and teaching writing, Michele Wallace thrust herself into the literary and feminist spotlight with her first book, *Black Macho and the Myth of the Superwoman.*

In *Black Macho,* Ms. Wallace analyzes, from a feminist perspective, the sexual dynamic of the transition from civil rights to black liberation. "There is a profound distrust, even hatred, between black men and black women. It has been nursed along not only by racism on the part of whites but also by an almost deliberate ignorance on the part of blacks about the sexual politics of their experience in this country."

Wallace suggests that in the seventies the black man was feeling put off and put upon by the black woman's successes and began to believe in the myth of the black superwoman. He started to view her backbone, strength, responsibility to the family, success at finding and keeping work and generally getting ahead as her battling him "for his male prerogative as head of the household. And that she was as much to blame for the assault on black manhood as the white man."

Black Macho is bolstered by passages from the work of James Baldwin, Sojourner Truth, Norman Mailer, Daniel Moynihan, Eldridge Cleaver, Donald Bogle, Richard Wright, Susan Brownmiller, Tom Wolfe, and LeRoi Jones, as well as from historical documents on slavery. The book is so exhaustively researched and engaging that even if you don't fully agree with Wallace's argument, you will appreciate the passion with which she delivers it.

The Women of Brewster Place (1980)

Gloria Naylor
Novel

The Women of Brewster Place chronicles the communal strength of seven black women living in decrepit rented houses on a walled-off street in an urban neighborhood. Mattie Michael, the matriarch of the group, is a source of comfort and strength for the other women. Etta Mae Johnson is a free spirit who repeatedly gets involved with men who disappoint her. Kiswana Browne embraces racial pride and eventually accepts her mother's middle-class values. Lorraine and Theresa are lovers; when Lorraine is gang-raped, she is deeply troubled by the attack and murders Ben, who is one of her few supporters and the janitor of Brewster Place. Cora Lee loves her babies, while Ciel is on a path of self-destruction, having suffered a series of personal disasters.

The Women of Brewster Place is a moving portrait of the strengths, struggles, and hopes of black women. At the end of the novel, the women demolish the wall that separates them from the rest of the city. Gloria Naylor weaves together the truths and myths of the women's lives, creating characters who are free to determine the course of their lives, embodying the self-actualization tradition of the Harlem Renaissance.

Naylor's other books are *Bailey's Cafe, Linden Hills, Mama Day,* and *The Men of Brewster Place. The Women of Brewster Place,* her first novel, won the American Book Award for Best First Novel in 1983.

The Color Purple (1982)

Alice Walker
Novel

A lice Walker once told an interviewer, "The black woman is one of America's greatest heroes. . . . She has been oppressed beyond recognition." *The Color Purple* is the story of how one of those American heroes came to recognize *herself*, recovering her identity and rescuing her life in spite of the disfiguring effects of a particularly dreadful and personal sort of oppression. The novel focuses on Celie, a woman lashed by waves of deep trouble—abandonment, incest, physical and emotional abuse—and tracks her triumphant journey to self-discovery, womanhood, and independence. Celie's story is a pointed indictment of the men in her life—men who betrayed and abused her, worked her like a mule and suppressed her independence—but it is also a moving portrait of the psychic bonds that exist between women and the indestructible nature of the human spirit.

The story of Celie is told through letters: Celie's letters to God and her sister Nettie, who is in Africa, and Nettie's letters to Celie. Celie's letters are a poignant attempt to understand her own out-of-control life. Her difficulties begin when, at the age of fourteen, she is raped by her stepfather, who then apparently sells away the two children born of that rape. Her sister Nettie runs away to escape the abuse, but Celie is married off to Albert, an older man that she refers to simply as "Mr." for most of the novel. He subjects her to tough work on his farm and beats her at his whim. But Celie finds the path to redemption in two key female role models: Sophia, an independent woman who refuses to be taken advantage of by her husband or any man, and Shug, a sassy, independent singer whom Albert loves. It is Shug who first offers Celie love, friendship, and a radically new way of looking at

Well, us talk and talk bout God, but I'm still adrift. Trying to chase that old white man out of my head. I been so busy thinking bout him I never truly notice nothing God make. Not a blade of corn (how it do that?) not the color purple (where it come from?). Not the little wildflowers. Nothing.

Now that my eyes opening, I feels like a fool. Next to any little scrub of a bush in my yard, Mr. _____'s evil sort of shrink. But not altogether. Still, it is like Shug say, You have to git man off your eyeball, before you can see anything a'tall.

Man corrupt everything, say Shug. He on your box of grits, in your head, and all over the radio. He try to make you think he everywhere. Soon as you think he everywhere, you think he God. But he ain't. Whenever you trying to pray, and man plop himself on the other end of it, tell him to git lost, say Shug. Conjure up flowers, wind, water, a big rock.

But this hard work, let me tell you. He been there so long, he don't want to budge. He threaten lightning, floods, and earthquakes. Us fight. I hardly pray at all. Every time I conjure up a rock, I throw it.

Amen

—from *The Color Purple*

men, herself, and God. Finally, Celie leaves Albert to follow her own desires and discover her own talents and abilities. The novel ends in celebration: Celie is reunited with her sister and even the demonic Albert gets a shot at redemption.

The Color Purple is one of the most successful and controversial books ever written by a black woman. It was an international bestseller, won both the American Book Award and the Pulitzer Prize, and in 1985 was made into a much-discussed movie directed by Steven Spielberg. The movie and novel provoked controversy about Walker's portrayal of black men, which many found offensive and one-dimensional. Of course, Walker's book has out-lived both the movie and its critics; its no-holds-barred portrayal of black male-female relations broadened the trail blazed by her hero, Zora Neale Hurston. The novel is a wonderful fulfillment of its author's mission: to tell the untold stories of those black American heroes who withstood the gaudiest abuse a racist, sexist society could offer and emerged triumphant.

Praisesong for the Widow (1983)

Paule Marshall
Novel

*P**raisesong for the Widow* is a novel full of music and dancing; it describes the sickness that occurs when we disconnect from our heritage and the healing power that comes from reclaiming the music and rhythms of the ancestors. Its hero, Avatar "Avey" Johnson, was a new character in black literature: an affluent middle-aged black woman, a mother, a grandmother, and a widow. Avey and her late husband worked hard to climb from the slums of Harlem to the comforts of suburban White Plains. But that material comfort brought with it a spiritual disease—a hard-to-diagnose but impossible-to-ignore malaise that eventually erupted into violent illness during a Caribbean vacation. In this novel, Paule Marshall traces Avey's journey from sickness to strength, from the soulless suburbs to the African roots of her identity.

The novel opens with a curious scene: a woman throwing clothes into a suitcase. Since her husband passed away, Avey had been going on cruises with her friends from work, Thomasina and Clarice. It is on a Carribean vacation that she finds herself in distress and decides to abandon the cruise. She finds herself dreaming of childhood summers spent in South Carolina with her Aunt Cuney. Aunt Cuney used to take her to Ibo Landing to do the Ring Shout, a ritual dance in honor of the Africans who were brought to the Landing to be sold as slaves. Later she dreams of her late husband who, in his drive for material success in a white world, shut their lives off from the passion and sense of community they had once shared.

The next day she runs into Lebert Joseph, an old man who listens to her concerns, diagnoses her problem, and prescribes a cure: a trip to the island of Carricacou, where she undergoes a reunion with that part of her African heritage and traditions that she has allowed to lie dormant within her for so many years. On the island of Carricacou, Avey observes and eventually participates in rituals with the islanders. In one of their rituals, prayers and songs are followed by dances. Each nation is called on to dance, but Avey cannot join until they begin to dance the Carricacou Tramp, a dance she recognizes as the same Ring Shout she did as a child in South Carolina. With that, she is reunited with the roots of her own identity and that of her people. It is through the rituals on the island that she realizes the connective thread between the Ring Shout danced by church members, the neighborhood picnics and jazz music in Harlem, and the African origins of her people.

Praisesong for the Widow takes on a decidedly contemporary problem: the rootlessness of a generation of black women—and men—who forsook the traditions of the ancestors and the warmth of the community for a sterile and materialistic version of the American dream. In this novel, Marshall takes a character suffering from this modern dilemma and cures her by immersing her in a world of history, myth, and ritual. The novel is written so vividly and lyrically, one can almost see Avey dancing the Ring Shout and hear the drums in tribute to the islander's ancestors. The book won the American Book Award in 1984.

Sister Outsider: Essays and Speeches
(1984)

Audre Lorde
Essays

"The work of the poet within each one of us is to envision what has not yet been and to work with every fiber of who we are to make the reality pursuit of those visions irresistible."

Audre Lorde writes from the fabric of her life: black woman, lesbian, feminist, activist, daughter of immigrant parents, mother of a biracial child, cancer survivor. *Sister Outsider: Essays and Speeches* explores ways of increasing empowerment among minority women and the need for women to candidly deal with racism, sexism, and classism. It also promotes the unity of difference. Lorde explores the fear and hatred that exists between black men and women, lesbians and heterosexuals, and black women and white women and insists that we all must find common ground.

Lorde had an abiding belief in the unity of all peoples and the crucial role of communication in bridging the divisions that separate us. Rather than turning a blind eye to our different identities, she insisted that through the process of naming those differences and honestly and justly dealing with them, divergent perspectives could be brought together. Lorde's own identity crosses so many racial, sexual, and physical lines that in a sense she belongs to no one group and was thus able to see us all with a unique, unprejudiced clarity.

Sister Outsider covers almost a decade of Lorde's work. Nine of the pieces were written after she discovered that she had cancer. In the process of her coming to terms with her disease, she discovered universal lessons that we can all take with us in our struggles, whatever they be. Lorde finally lost her battle with cancer in 1992, but she has left behind a stirring legacy for us all.

Waiting to Exhale (1992)

Terry McMillan
Novel

Terry McMillan, in her way, has been among the most influential African American writers of the past twenty years. Her novels are accessible, realistic, and often hilarious accounts of the exotic rituals of modern, urban African American men and women looking for love and happiness—a theme not commonly found in African American fiction before her successful second novel, *Disappearing Acts*.

In *Waiting to Exhale,* her blockbuster best-selling third novel, four vibrant professional women console and support one another in a nurturing friendship that helps each of them deal with troubled relationships with men. *Waiting to Exhale* demonstrates that no matter how hard we search, sometimes Mr. Right just doesn't show up, but that life goes on without him.

Even as the book was dismissed by some critics as popular fluff or anti-male, millions of readers of all colors identified with the struggles and the enduring sisterhood of Robin, Savannah, Bernadine, and Gloria. *Waiting to Exhale* became a publishing sensation, proving for once and for all that there is a substantial audience of readers for popular, well-written African American novels. The book also became a successful movie starring Whitney Houston and inspired a flurry of knock-off books of lesser quality.

Your Blues Ain't Like Mine (1992)

Bebe Moore Campbell
Novel

Set in the 1950s in Mississippi, *Your Blues Ain't Like Mine* begins with the murder of Armstrong Todd, a Chicago youth living with his grandmother until his mother can get on her feet financially. Mississippi is no place for Armstrong. Raised in the North under the illusion that blacks were free from racial intolerance, and showing off to a group of black men in a pool hall, he inadvertently speaks French to Lily Cox, a poor white woman whose husband, Floyd, owns the place. Egged on by Jake McKenzie, the black man who runs Floyd's pool hall, Floyd is forced by the code of the South to exact revenge. At the insistence of Floyd's father, Lester, and older brother, John Earl, Floyd has a fatal confrontation with Armstrong in his grandmother's backyard.

While this thoughtful and suspenseful novel appears based on the true story of Emmett Till, the fourteen-year-old boy brutally murdered in Mississippi in 1955 for allegedly whistling at a white woman, Campbell puts a keenly personal face—black and white—on the human toll of racism. Jake McKenzie, in his jealousy over Armstrong's northern mannerisms and in his own diminished sense of self, virtually assures Armstrong's death. Floyd is the reluctant captive of a racial code of conduct that demands an exact retribution. This is a deeply moving novel.

Kehinde (1994)

Buchi Emecheta
Novel

After almost twenty years living in London, Albert Okolos is forcing his wife, Kehinde, to return to their native land, Nigeria. Albert is tired of the democratic nature of London, "Stupid country, where you need your wife's money to make ends meet." He longs for the status and prosperity he will obtain in Nigeria and is determined to move his family back to the "home" neither he nor Kehinde remembers clearly and their two children know not at all. "After eighteen years, he pined for sunshine, freedom, easy friendship, warmth. He wanted to go home to show off his new life style, his material success."

Kehinde begins a journey of self-discovery when she leaves her successful career and her London home to follow Albert to Nigeria, where he has been for a year. She arrives to find that she has been relegated to a marginal position in his life, that he has taken a second wife who is already pregnant by him. Kehinde must pull herself and her life together and learn about independence and strength from the least likely of sources—herself.

Like Kehinde, Emecheta was born in Nigeria. At seventeen, she married, had a child, and moved with her husband to London. At twenty-two, she left him and finished a sociology degree while supporting her five children. Part fiction, part autobiography, *Kehinde* is a clever and insightful story about family, country, roles, and responsibility that clearly illustrates how things are rarely valued until they are lost.

The Daughters of Africa: An International Anthology of Words and Writings by Women of African Descent from the Ancient Egyptian to the Present (1994)

Margaret Busby, ed.
Anthology

*D*aughters of Africa is a monumental achievement because it is the most comprehensive international anthology of oral and written literature by women of African descent ever attempted.

The anthology is exhaustive in scope and expansive in voice because it encompasses authors from the Caribbean, North America, Latin America, Europe, and Asia and translations from African, French, German, Dutch, Russian, and Turkish languages. Each story, whether fiction, nonfiction, memoir, or poem, is a singular experience. Here, together, is the clear, concise voice of Gwendolyn Brooks; the forceful presence of Sojourner Truth; the rhythmicality of Nikki Giovanni; the sly, taunting voice of Toni Cade Bambara; the straight talk of Terry McMillan; the commanding presence of Angela Davis; the rhythmic dialect of Una Marson; the jazzy vernacular of Sonia Sanchez; the vision of Octavia E. Butler; and the careful, direct prose of Billie Holliday. Each story is enhanced by a succinctly informative history of the author's life and work.

The success of the collection is that it clearly illustrates why all women of African descent are connected by showing how closely related are the obstacles, the chasms of cultural indifference, and the disheartening racial and sexual dilemmas they faced. In so doing, the collection captures the range of their singular and combined accomplishments.

Daughters of Africa's accomplishment lies in its glorious portrayal of the richness and magnitude of the spiritual well from which we've all drawn inspiration and to where we've all gone for sustenance, and as such, it is a stunning literary masterpiece.

Sojourner Truth: A Life, a Symbol (1994)

Nell Irvin Painter

Biography

Sojourner Truth was one of the most notable and highly regarded African American women in the nineteenth century. Named Isabella, she was born a slave in 1797 in Ulster County, New York, the second youngest of twelve children of James and Elizabeth. By the time she was sixteen, she was almost six feet tall. Isabella changed names twice in her lifetime, not wishing to be known by the name of her previous slaveholders. In 1843 she became Sojourner Truth, a woman whose proclaimed mission was to "sojourn" the land and speak God's "truth."

In this recently published biography, *Sojourner Truth: A Life, a Symbol,* historian Nell Irvin Painter gives us incisive information about Sojourner's life; she also deals with fascinating issues relating to this woman's life—issues such as child abuse (that of Truth toward her daughters), sexual abuse (that of her slave mistress toward Truth), as well as the psychological consequences for women from these kinds of behaviors.

A woman of remarkable intelligence despite her illiteracy, Truth had great presence. Her voice was low, so low that listeners sometimes termed it masculine, and her singing voice was beautifully powerful. Whenever she spoke in public, she also sang. No one ever forgot the power and pathos of Sojourner Truth's singing, just as her wit and originality of phrasing were also of lasting remembrance. As an abolitionist and feminist, she put her body and her mind to a unique task, that of physically representing women who had been enslaved. At a time when most Americans thought of slaves as male and women as white, Truth embodied a fact that still bears repeating: Among the blacks are women; among the women, there are blacks.

With *Sojourner Truth*, Painter, a renowned writer and Edwards Professor of American History at Princeton University, has written a biography that is much like Truth herself: fiery, eloquent, illuminating, and succinct. Perhaps most compelling is Painter's demystification of the "Ar'nt I a Woman" speech that has come to be associated with Truth and with the image of her as an invincible black female.

Brothers' Lives

Commentary

by S. E. Anderson

True black manhood is not about projecting the myths of hyper-black masculinity or black hypermasculinity. It's about resisting white male supremacy's relentless attempts to humiliate our humanity and emasculate our manhood. Black manhood is not about accepting the myth that women are intellectually and physically inferior to men and therefore should stand and/or walk behind "their man." It's about recognizing our feminine equals, who have proven themselves as some of the fiercest freedom fighters, leaders, and thinkers over centuries of struggle for black liberation. Black manhood is not about smooth seductions and a perpetual readiness to "score" or "conquer" *any* woman. It's about recognizing mutual sensuality and respect.

Our existence as black people in the United States and in the modern world has always been at risk. The one thing that each one of the books profiled in this chapter shows us is that at the very foundation of black manhood is sacrifice. Sacrifice of the individual for the sake of saving the whole, for the sake of helping us all reach a higher understanding of a revolutionary morality—a morality that opposes the racist and sexist hypocrisy of a male-centered culture of rapacious plunder, narcissistic conquest, and bestial submission.

True black manhood is what you will find struggling to be in the books recommended here. This is by no means an exhaustive and definitive selection on black manhood, but the books do reflect—very powerfully—the realities, past and present, of growing up a black man in North America. Especially is that the case in the comprehensive and now classic *Brotherman* anthology. Some of these selections show us that if you take the American

Dream seriously, it can become an eternal nightmare in which you become the visibly invisible black male monster overflowing with sexual drive and criminal intent (see Richard Wright's *Native Son* or Wideman's *Brothers and Keepers*).

Other books, like *The Autobiography of Malcolm X* or Earnest J. Gaines's *A Lesson Before Dying,* show us how our ancestral strengths and intelligence help us overpower the racist drive to submit our manhood and maleness to the pale dictates of The System. Still others expose our deep loving side, our profound love for family no matter that the odds are against our survival. Valuable books not included here include Sister Louise Merriwether's *Fragments of the Ark,* which beautifully and powerfully depicts the maintenance and transformation of black manhood and family during the time of the searing Civil War. She captures the heroic dimensions of the brothers involved and also shows us the complex "sheroics" of enslaved black women determined to live in freedom with their families. Also, as an essential complementary reading, one should pick up *The Black Civil War Soldiers of Illinois* by Edward A. Miller Jr. This is just one source that documents the racist and degrading treatment of black Civil War troops as well as the oftentimes superhuman heroics of brothers fighting to free their brethren and sisteren—and themselves—from the white enemy: North or South.

True black manhood finds its roots in the horrendous experiences of the enslavement process. We can find insight and inspiration from works about slavery produced by our sisters; for example, the works of Toni Morrison (*Beloved* and *Song of Solomon*) and Margaret Walker (*Jubilee*). We are becoming more and more aware of the heroics of Cinque (Sengbe Pieh of the Mende People) and the *Amistad* 53. These proud young men and women were filled with fierce determination not to be slaves but to return home to Africa free. We are just relearning about brother John Malvin, a "free"-born African of early nineteenth-century Virginia, and his battle to remain free in pre–Civil War America.

Or what of another Virginian—brother Anthony Burns (*The Trials of Anthony Burns*)—born enslaved and escaped to "freedom," winding up in 1854 in Boston on trial as a fugitive from slavery? What kept them sane? What allowed them to laugh and joke? To have space in their souls for love and desire?

These were powerful men. Part of their power and determination to survive and fight for freedom came from that powerful African inner urge to be FREE and at one with nature. Their power also flowed from their acknowledging and respecting black women's power and determination to survive and fight for freedom. They understood not only the material basis of the African spirit-will, but also why our sisters were the guides and preservers of black futures.

We, too, can be powerful men today at the dawn of the Third Millennium . . . if we follow the simple yet profound dictates of these elders and ancestors: Respect and embrace our sisters as equal soldiers in the war for humanity.

S. E. Anderson is the editor of In Defense of Mumia *and author of* Black Holocaust for Beginners.

Native Son (1940)

Richard Wright
Novel

Richard Wright was born in 1908, the first of two sons of a sharecropper. After publishing his first novel, *Uncle Tom's Children*, in 1938, Wright discovered to his alarm that "he had written a book which even bankers' daughters could read and feel good about." He swore that his next novel would be different. That book was *Native Son*, the story of Bigger Thomas's short and tragic life, which plumbs the blackest depths of human experience.

Native Son is told in three parts—Fear, Flight, and Fate—which sum up, perfectly, Bigger Thomas's life. Badly in need of a job to help support his family, the ne'er-do-well Bigger goes to work as a driver for the Daltons, a rich white family. As he is pulled every which way by his mother, "who wanted him to do the things *she* wanted him to do"; by Mrs. Dalton, "who wanted him to do the things she felt that *he* should have wanted to do"; by Mary Dalton, the young mistress of the house, "who challenged him to stand up for things he didn't understand"; and by his need for independence and autonomy in the midst of a dependent situation—he missteps, accidentally killing Mary.

Native Son is not an uplifting book with a happy Hollywood resolution. It has been criticized for its cardboard portrayal of black pathology and heavy-handed Marxist message. But the book is an absolutely gripping potboiler that is also intellectually provocative. It is on one level a seedy, simple story of an unsympathetic character meeting his fate at his own hands, and on another an illuminating drama of an individual consciousness that challenges traditional definitions of heroism, character, and integrity. Bigger was less a character caught in a specific criminal activity than he was a crime waiting to happen.

If He Hollers Let Him Go (1945)

Chester B. Himes
Novel

W ith his first novel, Chester B. Himes secured his place in the vanguard of the emerging young black writers of his time who were honestly detailing the rigors of black life in America. Unlike his contemporaries Richard Wright and Ralph Ellison, Himes was not a writer with overt political concerns. His novel does, however, delve into the existential cost that black men had to pay for the racism around them: that they had to live constantly, absurdly aware of the color of their skin.

Bob Jones's story is a simple one told in clear, direct prose. All Bob wants is "to be accepted as a man—without ambition, without distinction, either of race, creed, or color." But in the 1940s and 1950s, nothing was simple between blacks and whites. Bob quickly finds himself losing his hopes and ambitions as he is crushed beneath the weight of racism and discrimination. His life spins out of control until he hates everyone around him: the blacks for being powerless to change their lives; the whites for taking advantage of them. Bob Jones is every black man at that time, who was, every day, walking a tightrope of racial tension, except Bob falls, pushed by "a loose blonde who kissed him, then framed him on a rape charge."

If He Hollers Let Him Go is a masterpiece for its bitter and honest portrayal of the life of a normal black man in America, and it speaks to any person who has felt, at some time or other, that he or she has had enough abuse on account of the color of their skin. Himes demonstrated in the person of Bob Jones that one of the most critical rights that black people have been denied is the right to just live their lives unbothered and unmolested and to follow their impulses and desires with no greater reward or punishment than nature's laws of cause and effect.

The indignity of it, the gutting of my pride, what a nigger had to take just to keep on living in this goddamned world. The cold scared feeling started clamping down on me; it nailed me to my seat, weak and black and powerless.

—from *If He Hollers Let Him Go*

The Autobiography of Malcolm X (1965)

As told to Alex Haley

Memoir

*T*he *Autobiography of Malcolm X* is the story of one of the remarkable lives of the twentieth century. Malcolm X, as presented in this as-told-to autobiography, is a figure of almost mythic proportions; a man who sunk to the greatest depths of depravity and rose to become a man whose life's mission was to lead his people to freedom and strength. It provides a searing depiction of the deeply rooted issues of race and class in America and remains relevant and inspiring today. Malcolm X's story would inspire Alex Haley to write *Roots,* a novel that would, in turn, define the saga of a people.

Malcolm Little was born in Nebraska in 1925, the seventh child of Reverend Earl Little, a Baptist minister, and Louise Little, a mulatto born in Grenada to a black mother and a white father. Malcolm X quickly grew to hate the society he'd grown up in. After his father was killed, his mother was unfairly denied insurance coverage and his family fell apart. Young Malcolm went from a foster home to a reformatory, to shining shoes in the speak-easies and dance halls of Boston. After getting work as a Pullman porter, he went to New York and fell in love with Harlem. His stint as a drug dealer and petty crook landed him in jail, where he became a devout student of the Nation of Islam and Elijah Muhammad. That was when he figured out that "he could beat the white man better with his mind than he ever could with a club." Malcolm X's subsequent quest for knowledge and equality for blacks led to his unreserved commitment to the liberation of blacks in American society.

What makes this book extraordinary is the honesty with which Malcolm presents his life: Even as he regrets the mistakes he made as a young man, he brings his zoot-suited, swing-dancing, conk-haired Harlem youth to vivid life; even though he later turns away from the Nation of Islam, the strong faith he at one time had in that sect's beliefs, a faith that redeemed him from prison and a life of crime, comes through. What made the man so extraordinary was his courageous insistence on finding the true path to his personal salvation and to the salvation of the people he loved, even when to stay on that path meant danger, alienation, and death.

Manchild in the Promised Land (1965)

Claude Brown
Memoir

Manchild in the Promised Land is the story of the first generation of blacks who had left the South in search of a northern "promised land" of equality, abundance, and prosperity but found instead a vastly overcrowded and violent urban ghetto—a generation that went "from the fire into the frying pan."

"There was a tremendous difference in the way life was lived up North. There were too many people full of hate and bitterness crowded into a dirty, stinky, uncared-for, closet-sized section of a great city. The children of these disillusioned colored pioneers inherited the total lot of their parents—the disappointments, the anger. To add to their misery, they had little hope of deliverance. For where does one run to when he's already in the promised land?" So begins Claude Brown's literary masterwork.

Claude (Sonny boy) Brown wrote his extraordinary autobiography in his late twenties. At nine, he was a member of two notorious gangs who thrived on bullying and stealing. At eleven, he was sent to a school for "emotionally disturbed and deprived boys," where he stayed for two years; at fourteen, he was sent to a reformatory for the first of three times. In his mid-twenties, he would graduate from Howard University, and at thirty, he would start law school. *Manchild in the Promised Land* is the story of his life growing up in Harlem, to him a wondrous place where if you were quick, smart, and tough enough you could live, for a while, like a king or die like a pauper.

Brothers and Keepers (1985)

John Edgar Wideman
Nonfiction

Sometimes you *can* go back home. Of *Brothers and Keepers* John Edgar Wideman has said, "If I had a dime for every person who has come up to me and said 'I have a brother, or a sister, or a cousin in the same situation as you and your brother,' I would never have to write for a living again."

A collection of autobiographical essays, *Brothers and Keepers* is a story of a modern-day prodigal son. It is a story found all too often within a community in transition: two brothers sharing similar backgrounds, one remaining in the 'hood, the other leaving to travel the wider world. In doing so, however, the latter not only escapes the harmful influences of an economically impoverished environment but also alienates himself from the family, friends, and culture that fostered him. John Edgar Wideman holds the distinction of being only the second African American, after Alain Locke, the Father of the Harlem Renaissance, to receive a Rhodes Scholarship. However, it was the incarceration of Wideman's brother, Robby, that prompted him to relink his past by reconnecting with his imprisoned brother.

In *Brothers and Keepers,* Wideman tells of life in Homewood, Pennsylvania; of his conversations with his incarcerated brother; of his explorations of his guilt at having escaped; of his acceptance of the humanity of those he left behind; and finally, in his return, of the acceptance of his own humanity.

More so than any other writer, Wideman's public angst over his feelings of alienation with the black community, as well as his ability to resurrect the ties that nurtured him, brings the promise of hope and salvation to an African American community in turmoil. The price of the ticket may well be high, but you *can* go home.

Fences (1985)

August Wilson
Play

"There are only fences."

Troy Maxson is an angry man. He is an embittered ex-con who has built inner fences around his emotions that no one—neither his son Cory, his wife, Rosa Lee, nor his best friend, Jim—can cross. A proud and bitter man who was prevented by racism from playing major league baseball, Maxson is at fifty-three years of age a garbage collector. While his job allows him to successfully provide for his family, handling garbage represents for him a grim metaphor of his life. As he did during a bit in prison, he once again feels confined, and those who love him most, who depend on him most, suffer most for it.

Through Troy Maxson, playwright August Wilson personifies the man who grew up during the heat of Jim Crow: first proud, hopeful, and passionate in expectation; then emotionally withdrawn and disillusioned from incessant battles with life. Wilson also masterfully illuminates both the strength that lies within community and the adverse impact of a psychology of inequality that devastates the African American male and, in turn, his family and relationships, potentially disintegrating that same community.

Wilson's Pulitzer Prize–winning play offers a bleak picture of what happens to black males when their aspirations go beyond the fences within which they are confined. The fences of a racist society are compounded by the fences black men have often created to ward off loved ones who remind them of their failures. These fences only harbor pain and hasten an inevitable asphyxiation. *Fences* is a gripping portrait of a black man dying.

The Man Who Cried I Am (1985)

John Alfred Williams
Novel

Max Reddick, who is a talented "black writer" in America but a literary *genius* in Europe, is trying to come to terms with his dilemma. Max is tired of having to accept that being black will always be the primary definition of his life—despite his marriage to a white woman, despite his literary talent and aspirations, despite his intellectual and social relations, and despite his "escape" to the European cities of Paris and Amsterdam. At the end of his life, cut short by cancer, Max decides to question all the things that brought him to where he is today.

Reddick faced the familiar problem of spiritual homelessness that has often plagued black artists and intellectuals. "I'm the way I am, the kind of writer I am because I am a black man. I've been in rebellion, and a writer, ever since I discovered that even colored folks wanted to keep me away from books so I could never learn just how bad it all was. Maybe, too, to keep me from laughing at them. For taking it. My folks had a deathly fear of books."

Novelist, poet, and journalist John Alfred Williams has created in Max Reddick an unforgettable character: irascible, fiercely intelligent, irredeemable, and honorable. *The Man Who Cried I Am* is a stunning chronicle of not only Williams's life but the lives of all black people who have refused to be victims: blacks who have had to leave their country to claim their individuality, intellectual independence, and rightful recognition, and who have always yearned to be "home" but struggled to find such a place.

The Life of Langston Hughes (1986: Volume I, *1902–1941, I, Too, Sing America;* 1988: Volume II, *1941–1967, I Dream a World*)

Arnold Rampersad
Biography

This two-volume set is the definitive biography of Langston Hughes, the poet laureate of the Harlem Renaissance. Beginning with a family history linked to abolitionists, the Underground Railroad, John Brown's attack on Harper's Ferry, and the anti-slavery settlement of Lawrence, Kansas, author Rampersad delves deeply into the context of Hughes's life. From his tumultuous relationship with his father to his travels to the South and abroad, to the largesse and patronage he received from admirers of his work, to his life as a Harlem literary cognoscenti.

That Hughes spoke eloquently for the black masses is well known. Less known are the interesting turns and connections that brought him to recognition. In *The Life of Langston Hughes,* the stories abound. While on a tour of the South, and as the riveting Scottsboro case exploded onto the international scene, Hughes visited the University of North Carolina at Chapel Hill. "Although UNC was probably the most progressive white university in the South, for a black speaker to be featured there was extraordinary." In advance of his visit, he forwarded an essay about Scottsboro: "Let the Alabama mill-owners pay white women decent wages so they won't need to be prostitutes, he urged. And let the sensible citizens of Alabama (if there are any) supply schools for the black populace of their state, (and for the half-black, too—the mulatto children of the Southern gentlemen. [I reckon they're gentlemen]) so the Negroes won't be so dumb again. As for the jailed men—if blacks didn't howl in protest (and

I don't mean a polite howl, either) then let Dixie justice (blind syphilitic as it may be) take its course." Langston "slipped in and out of Chapel Hill" before the response to the essay erupted.

This is a great biography of a complex man who lived fully in defiance of stereotypes of brutish and illiterate black manhood. His life was one of courage, adventure, and amazing creativity. Rampersad captures that life with memorable success.

Miles: The Autobiography (1990)

Miles Davis (with Quincy Troupe)
Autobiography

Universally acclaimed as a musical genius, Miles Davis was one of the most influential musicians in the world. He was also famous for not talking, or for talking only in barely audible, cryptic, and ill-tempered riddles. But his silence only added to the mystique created by his genius with a trumpet. Miles was an embodiment of the arrogant, hedonistic, and immensely talented jazzman; he was also one of the icons of twentieth-century black life. His autobiography, written in energetic prose, is a brilliant telling of a one-of-a-kind life lived furiously.

Miles was born in Illinois in 1926 but grew up in St. Louis, where his father had a dental practice and where he first learned to play trumpet in high school. Miles Dewey Davis III was named after his father, who was named after his father. Miles's parents (his mother was an organ teacher) were married in Arkansas. "My mother was a beautiful woman. She had a whole lot of style, with an East Indian, Carmen McRae look, and dark, nut-brown, smooth skin. High cheekbones and Indian-like hair . . . I got my looks from my mother and also my love of clothes and sense of style . . . I got whatever artistic talent I have from her also."

Miles eventually became one of the premier jazz musicians of all time. The subject of several biographies, Miles here speaks frankly about himself and his extraordinary life: his drug problem, the places he's been, the people in his life, as well as the racism he encountered as a black man and as a musician. Never one to bite his tongue, he fills the autobiography with candid statements on everything from race to musicianship (and when he talks about the two together, as when he states that white men cannot play the guitar, look out). Quincy Troupe, a poet, journalist, and teacher who won the 1980 American Book Award for poetry, perfectly captures Miles's voice, imbuing the book with a crisp, clear, and melodious narrative. Davis may not come across as the most pleasant man on earth, but with his riveting anecdotes of jazz life in the 1950s and 1960s and his outspoken opinions, he is an undeniably fascinating character.

A Lesson Before Dying (1991)

Ernest Gaines
Novel

A *Lesson Before Dying* is a coming-of-age story set in a small Louisiana town in the late 1940s. Jefferson, a young black man involved in a shoot-out during a robbery, is convicted of murder and sentenced to the electric chair. Says the defending attorney to the jury, "What justice would there be to take this life? Justice, gentlemen? Why, I would just as soon put a hog in the electric chair as this."

Grant Wiggins, the hope of the community, has returned to teach school after having left for a university education. He fights internal demons, his aunt, and his guilt-ridden sense of community in deciding whether to escape the small town (and the small-town mentality) or to stay. He receives a visit from his aunt, Jefferson's godmother. With the pain of history on her face, the godmother spoke. "Called him a hog . . . I don't want them to kill no hog," she said. "I want a man to go to that chair, on his own two feet."

Grant's mandate was to instill in Jefferson a firm sense of self in the short time prior to his execution—a Herculean task, in that Grant had yet to come to terms with his own expectations of himself. In the end, and through their interaction, the two men come to realizations that allow each of them to successfully meet their demons.

In *A Lesson Before Dying*, Ernest Gaines personifies the angst of expectation that comes with being the first of a generation to succeed, the resolute power of community, and the importance of reciprocity—giving back to that which nurtured us.

W. E. B. Du Bois: Biography of a Race
(1994)

David Levering Lewis
Biography

It took renowned biographer David Levering Lewis eight years to research and write William Edward Burghardt Du Bois's monumental biography. And it stands as a testament to the hypnotic voice and compelling vision of the man who was known as the foremost constructor of the civil rights movement.

W. E. B. Du Bois, born in Massachusetts in 1868, was imbued with a mix of Dutch, black, and French blood. Although he was born three years after slavery was outlawed, Du Bois insisted that equal rights for blacks were still missing from American society. A man of staggering intellect and drive, Du Bois was the first black to hold a doctorate from Harvard University and was one of the founders of the NAACP. He wrote three historical works, two novels, two autobiographies, and sixteen pioneering books on sociology, history, politics, and race relations, including the monumental achievement *The Souls of Black Folk*. Du Bois also shaped the concept of a black intellectual elite, or a "Talented Tenth" of politicians, writers, and thinkers who would unite black America and foster the idea of blacks as a race of forceful and creative thinkers.

In 1963 on the day of the civil rights march in Washington, a speaker arrived with the news that Du Bois had died that momentous day at the age of 95. A hush descended over the huge crowd. A pall had settled because the man most responsible for the event would not be able to see it. Such was the power of Du Bois's personality, drive, intellect, and vision.

Black Betty (1994)

Walter Mosley
Novel

Black Betty is the fourth, and the strongest, installment in the Easy Rawlins mystery series. The time is the late 1940s, the place is Los Angeles, and the living is hard. Ezekial "Easy" Rawlins, a former soldier who is still hurting from the departure of his wife to Mississippi with another man, is facing pressure from his real estate dealings and from the challenges of raising two children. Desperate for work, he takes on an offer to find a woman, Elizabeth Eady, *a.k.a.* Black Betty, who has vanished into thin air. Her wealthy employer wants her back, and so the search begins. Add Mouse, Easy's sidekick, and murder and mayhem soon follow.

Mosley writes mystery, yes; but he also suffuses his stories with a deeply intimate knowledge of the black community and its struggles. This passage from *Black Betty* illustrates Mosley's skill at re-creating the surface and depth of life in the middle-class black communities of Los Angeles while at the same time addressing, in his two-fisted way, the existential issues that dog all African Americans:

> On the bus there were mainly old people and young mothers and teenagers coming in late to school. Most of them were black people. Dark-skinned with generous features. Women with eyes so deep that most men can never know them. Women like Betty who'd lost too much to be silly or kind. And there were the children, like Spider and Terry T once were, with futures so bleak it could make you cry just to hear them laugh. Because behind the music of their laughing you knew there was the rattle of chains. Chains we wore for no crime; chains we wore for so long that they melded with our bones. We all carry them

but nobody can see it—not even most of us. All the way home I thought about freedom coming for us at last. But what about all those centuries in chains? Where do they go when you get free?

All that and a mystery, too.

Mosley continues a tradition of African American detective fiction that uses this genre to explore issues of empowerment, a tradition begun by novelists like Chester Himes (*If He Hollers Let Him Go* and *A Rage in Harlem*), W. Adolphe Roberts (*The Haunting Hand*, 1926), and Rudolph Fisher (*The Conjure Man Dies*, 1932). Other books in the acclaimed Easy Rawlins series include *Gone Fishing, Devil in a Blue Dress, A Little Yellow Dog, A Red Death,* and *White Butterfly.*

Brotherman: The Odyssey of Black Men in America—An Anthology (1995)

Edited by Herb Boyd and Robert L. Allen
Anthology

"**B**rotherman" is a special greeting among black men. It is a verbal handshake, a shared mantra that expresses much more than a mere hello, that carries a number of meanings for black men no matter who they are. Their coded exchange of "brotherman" signals immediate recognition and rapport. It conveys a message that is at once an affirmation, an affectionate embrace, and a battle cry that proclaims "We have a common fate—what happens to one happens to all."

By creating "a living mosaic of essays and stories in which black men can view themselves, and be viewed without distortion," *Brotherman* opens a world that very few people get to see: "the world that the black man experiences as adolescents, lovers, husbands, fathers, workers, warriors, and elders."

Brotherman, the first collection of its kind, gives tribute to the resiliency of black men's creativity, intellect, and endurance by showcasing their greatest writers, public figures, and spokesmen: Howard Thurman, Amiri Baraka, Martin Luther King Jr., Nathan McCall, W. E. B. Du Bois, Malcolm X, Claude Brown, Alex Haley, Langston Hughes, James Baldwin, Marcus Garvey, Chester Himes, Ralph Ellison, John Edgar Wideman, Ishmael Reed, and many others.

Each piece is a unique experience because it presents a part of the puzzle that is the black man. Whether these parts add up to a whole is not the point; that the collection gives insight into the psyche of a lover, brother, friend, father, or neighbor is what secures its place in literary history.

Index of Books by Title

Index of Books by Author

Index of Books by Genre

Novels and Short Stories

Poetry

My Essential Books

Create your own list of essential books and forward them to QBR/ Sacred Fire, 625 Broadway, New York, NY 10012. We will publish them in QBR or post them on our web site (www.qbr.com). You may e-mail your list to: editor@qbr.com. Please include your name and address, including zip code.

This book may be kept

REALISTS
AND NOMINALISTS

REALISTS
AND NOMINALISTS

BY

MEYRICK H. CARRÉ
Lecturer in Philosophy, University of Bristol

OXFORD UNIVERSITY PRESS

Oxford University Press, Ely House, London W. 1

GLASGOW NEW YORK TORONTO MELBOURNE WELLINGTON
CAPE TOWN SALISBURY IBADAN NAIROBI LUSAKA ADDIS ABABA
BOMBAY CALCUTTA MADRAS KARACHI LAHORE DACCA
KUALA LUMPUR HONG KONG TOKYO

FIRST PUBLISHED MARCH 1946
SECOND IMPRESSION OCTOBER 1946
REPRINTED LITHOGRAPHICALLY IN GREAT BRITAIN
AT THE UNIVERSITY PRESS, OXFORD
FROM SHEETS OF THE SECOND IMPRESSION, 1950, 1961, 1967

PREFACE

THE brief studies that follow are intended to be an introduction to some of the great stages of thought that lie between the disruption of the Roman Empire in the West and the period of the Renaissance. I am well aware that the passages that have been selected for discussion are mere fractions torn from a vast and intricate history, but I hope they will serve some inquirers who wish to reconnoitre the frontiers of a new country. Students of philosophy are still apt to flit from the theories of classical Greece to the scientific assumptions of the seventeenth century without bestowing more than a hasty glance at the intervening eras of speculation. To say the least, this is an unhistorical procedure. The bond that unites the ancient outlook with the new is the persistence of Greek principles within the context of Christian doctrine. And the new conceptions, despite their loud rejection of Scholasticism, were deeply indebted to the medieval methods and are inexplicable without some appreciation of them.

Philosophers of the modern era concentrated their attention upon problems relating to the scope and validity of human knowledge. Such questions were assuredly not the primary concern of medieval thinkers. Yet in their immense and subtle inquiries into the rational order of existence they were necessarily led to investigate the nature of reason. It is this aspect of medieval thought that I have selected for description here. Although this approach is not the normal path to the understanding of the great scholastics, it allows the student to compare their treatment of questions that became prominent in later thought with modern discussions of these questions. And this aspect of Latin Christian philosophy brings us into touch with one of the central debates of the medieval era, the dispute over the status of general ideas, or universals.

In a limited survey simplification is inevitable. But instead of attempting to range over the vast field in a general manner I have sought to bring the reader close to the method and quality of scholastic argument by collecting the opinions of four representative figures. St. Augustine exercised a cardinal influence on all speculation from the earliest to the latest phase of medieval thought. From him, more than from any other authority, sprang the pronounced Realism that persisted into modern times. In the eleventh century there appeared a new view of knowledge that conflicted with the spiritual theory of Augustine and with his Neo-Platonic Realism. The first and most formidable critic of the older tradition was Peter Abaelard, and I have tried to show the substance of his attack on extreme Realism by following closely the argument of one of his works. The next great stage occurred in the thirteenth century, when St. Thomas Aquinas forged a new doctrine of experience founded upon an independent examination of the text of Aristotle, now for the first time made available in its authentic character. His theory of knowledge sought to combine the merits of the older and the newer outlooks, and his carefully balanced Realism united the claims of both the general and particular constituents of experience. But the fourteenth century saw novel and audacious theories in philosophy. One mark of the collapse of the great tradition was the appearance of Nominalism. The champion of this radical departure was William of Ockham. In him medieval reflection discovered its Hume. With him our brief illustrations of medieval accounts of knowledge must end.

Guided by recent expositors I have gone as far as I was able to the texts of my authorities. In the case of William of Ockham I have been compelled to rely on the copious quotations from his writings in the works of Abbagnano and of Tornay; for there are no modern editions of his main treatises. A list of books to which I am especially indebted is given at the end of the volume. There is one pre-eminent writer on medieval philosophy to whom every student must be gratefully obliged, whatever part of the field he explores, namely, Professor Etienne Gilson. At every point I have been aided by his incomparable learning and brilliant expositions. Professor C. C. J. Webb kindly read an early draft of the chapter on St. Augustine and sent me some instructive comments. The book was completed before the war; it has been revised, so far as circumstances permitted, during the war.

M. H. C.

CONTENTS

I

ST. AUGUSTINE

I

AUGUSTINE was born in the year 354 at Tagaste, a small town in
the Roman province of Numidia in north Africa. His father,
Patricius, held an official position in the town; he died when
Augustine was seventeen years old. His mother, Monica, was a
devout Christian, who exercised a profound influence on her extraordinary son. As a boy Augustine showed striking, though way-
ward, abilities, and at an early age was sent to continue his studies
at the University of Carthage. Here he distinguished himself in
rhetoric, though his fervent nature and the frivolity of student life
in Carthage often led him into dissipation. Carthage was a centre
of Manichæism, a creed which incongruously combined doctrines
drawn from Christianity and Zoroastrianism, and Augustine became for many years an adherent of the sect. A reading in his nineteenth year of a book by Cicero, *Hortensius*, kindled a passionate
interest in philosophy. Upon the completion of his University
course he taught rhetoric at Carthage. In the year 384, following a
brief visit to Rome, he was elected to a professorship at Milan.
Throughout these years at Carthage and Milan Augustine suffered

ABBREVIATIONS

C.S.E.L.	Corpus Scriptorum Ecclesiasticorum Latinorum. The figures refer to the volume and page.
P.L.	Patrologia Latina, edited Migne. The figures refer to the volume and column.
Confess.	Confessionum libri tredecim. The edition used is that edited by Gibb and Montgomery, Cambridge, 1927.
Contra Acad.	Contra Academicos.
De an.	De anima et ejus origine.
De civ. Dei	De civitate Dei.
De divers. Quaest.	De diversis quaestionibus octoginta tribus.
De Gen. ad litt.	De Genesi ad litteram.
De lib. arb.	De libero arbitrio.
De mag.	De magistro.
De mus.	De musica.
De ord.	De ordine.
De quant. an.	De quantitate animae.
De Trin.	De Trinitate.
De vera rel.	De vera religione.
Ep.	Epistolae.
Serm.	Sermones.
Solil.	Soliloquia.

acute mental conflict. He became increasingly dissatisfied with the tenets of the Manichees. The doctrines of Christianity deeply attracted him, but he found himself unable wholly to embrace its creed. Persistently he sought to free himself from the materialist theory of reality which he had learnt from the Manichæan philosophers.

'If I had been able to conceive a spiritual substance, all their specious arguments would have been destroyed at one blow, and cast out of my mind; but I could not. Yet so far as concerned the physical aspect of this world and the entire realm of nature apprehended by the bodily senses, I came to the conclusion, the further I gave myself to reflection and comparison, that the tenets of most of the philosophers were far more acceptable. Consequently, in the manner of the Academic School, as it is usually interpreted, doubting everything and wavering between all, I made up my mind to abandon the Manichees. For I felt that while I remained in a state of doubt I ought not to continue to belong to a sect to which I already preferred certain philosophers. Yet to these philosophers since they were without the saving name of Christ, I utterly refused to entrust the care of my sick soul.'[1]

The philosophers to whom he owed his liberation were the Platonists. Through the study of them he was led to accept as rationally legitimate an order of reality beyond the material world, an order for which his soul craved. The influence of these philosophers coincides with profound personal experience. The further steps in his conversion to the Christian Faith—the sermons of Ambrose, the conversation with Simplician, the scene in the garden —are touchingly described in the *Confessions*. He resigned his professorship and retired with a few intimate friends to a villa at Cassiacum in the neighbourhood of Milan. In the books written at this time, *Against the Academic Philosophers, On Order*, and *On the Blessed Life*, Augustine gives a charming picture of the little group of disciples who had gathered round him. He records the eager study of the classics; the long evening discussions under the spreading tree in the meadow; his own solitary vigils to the murmur of the little stream outside his room.

Shortly after his baptism, when the party were preparing to return to Africa, Augustine was overwhelmed with grief by the death of Monica. He returned to Rome and, in 388, to Africa. There at his native town of Tagaste he lived the life of an ascetic. To this period, from 386 to 391, belong the works which contain

---

[1] Confess. v. xiv. 25.

a large measure of his philosophical teaching, the treatises *On the Immortality of the Soul, On Music, On the Extensity of the Soul,* and *On Free Will.* His conversion marked not only a moral and religious change; it was also a turning away from literature and rhetoric to philosophy and theology. The first series of treatises directed against the doctrines of the Manichæans appeared also at this time. In his forty-first year, such was his reputation in the Christian community, he was consecrated Bishop.

For thirty-five years Augustine gave himself unremittingly to the welfare of his diocese, and far beyond its bounds dominated the councils of the Church in Africa. But in spite of his ecclesiastical care, in spite of ill health, he continued to pour out a vast range of works. He engaged the sects which threatened the Church, the Manichees, the Donatists, the Pelagians, the Arians, in detailed and tireless controversy. These controversial books alone number forty-four. He published fifteen commentaries on the Scriptures. Of his other writings two have made a general appeal throughout the ages. *The Confessions* were composed in order to check the flattery which was directed by Christians everywhere in the Empire towards the great Bishop. They contain a pathetic revelation of his early struggles for peace of mind, and disclose the humility of a saint. *The City of God* is a huge work upon which Augustine was engaged for fourteen years. In it he contrasts at length the kingdom of God with the secular state, describes the evolution of humanity, and ranges over the system of Christian beliefs. Of his other numerous works, those *On the Master* (a discussion on the principles of teaching), *On the Trinity,* and *On the Literal Interpretation of Genesis* include passages which are of philosophical interest.

The latter years of Augustine witnessed the ruin of the civilized world. The barbarians streamed through the defences of the Empire. Soon their hordes were devastating Italy. Armies revolted; usurpers appeared. Finally in 410 men heard with despair that the Eternal City had fallen. Africa was filled with fugitives from Rome. The broken Empire was further shattered by intrigues. At length the doom fell upon the African provinces. Boniface, Count of Africa, invited the Vandals to support his cause. Swiftly the Roman districts were overrun. Boniface was soon in flight before his recent allies and the remnants of his force were penned in Hippo. These disasters embittered the last days of Augustine.

Three months after the beginning of the siege he fell ill, and at the end of August in the year 430 he died. A year later Hippo was captured and given to the flames.

The vast intellectual activity of Augustine must be appreciated against the culture of the period. It was an age in which the standards of learning were in process of decay. Scientific and philosophical reflection had begun to wane before the Christian era, and the later phases of the Roman Empire saw a further decline in the standards and range of inquiry. What survived of Greek thought became suffused with morality and with theology. The mind of the Roman was practical and political, and Cicero praises his countrymen because, thanks to the gods, they were not like the Greeks, and knew how to limit the study of mathematics to useful purposes.[1] The compendia of natural knowledge that provided men with the science of the physical world were haphazard collections of curiosities and superstitions. There was little attempt to verify the tales handed down by tradition or to seek a coherent explanation of the facts. The guiding influence on Roman education was oratory. But even this was studied in an artificial and mechanical style. In the schools the attention of the pupils was concentrated upon formal rules of grammar and syntax and they were trained to classify topics in superficial divisions and subdivisions. The literary masterpieces of the past were dissected with little appreciation of their spirit. This pedantic education deeply affected thought, and its consequences can be noticed in the writings of Augustine. He is fond of verbal distinctions. The argument is often lacking in rigour, it rambles and loses sight of the point at issue. He had received the best education that his time could offer, but his knowledge of Greek is scanty, and he cites the Greek philosophers in Latin translations. Jerome remarks that hardly anyone in his day was reading Aristotle and few had heard so much as the name of Plato. This is exaggeration. But Augustine complains that his fellow students at Carthage could make nothing of Aristotle's *Categories*, in spite of the eloquence of their masters.[2] In reading Augustine it must not be forgotten that his training was in the school not of Greek philosophy, but of Cicero.[3]

Yet he did more than any other Christian teacher to bring Christian conceptions into touch with philosophical principles.

---

[1] *Tusculanae*, i. 2.   [2] Confess. IV. xvi. 28.
[3] H. I. Marrou, *St. Augustin et la fin de la Culture Antique*, Paris, 1938, investigates in detail Augustine's attainments.

Hostility to learning was general in the Church. 'The common herd', wrote Clement of Alexandria, of his flock, 'fear Greek philosophy as children fear goblins.' Nor was it only the common herd who rejected the heritage of thought in favour of simple faith. Some of the leaders were vehemently opposed to speculation. For Tertullian all the teaching of secular literature is foolishness and a Christian must ignore it. Philosophers make a trade of notoriety and set out to destroy virtue.[1] And dialectic, the invention of 'the wretched Aristotle', is the mother of heresy. 'Let those who profess a Christianity affected by the Stoic, Platonic, or Dialectical philosophy beware. We ourselves have no need for curiosity after Jesus Christ, nor for investigation, after the Gospel.'[2] Even Augustine's master, Ambrose, looked on philosophy with suspicion and asserted that all that was good in the Greeks had been borrowed from Scripture. The Faith gives men all that is necessary to know.

The searching and comprehensive inquiries of Augustine led the meditations of subsequent generations of churchmen to pass beyond this rule of pious ignorance. His writings invited men to examine the rational basis of their faith. He did not deny that it is necessary to believe in order to know; understanding is the reward of faith. But he declared also that Christian doctrine contains many things that we cannot believe unless we understand them. A man who thinks it is sufficient to hold fast to the Faith without aspiring to an understanding of it ignores the true end of faith.[3] No man of his age was better fitted to provide Christian beliefs with a metaphysical foundation. He had passed through the ferment of Oriental theosophy. He had wrestled with scepticism. He was steeped in the tenets of the most profound philosophy of his time. His speculations are stamped with the mark of his studies in Neoplatonism. The thinkers he cites in *De civitate Dei* as those to whom he owed his intellectual salvation are Plotinus, Jamblichus, Porphyry, and Apuleius. There is much, indeed, in Plotinus that he found lacking, and there were cardinal points in the system of the *Enneads* that he rejected. But it is principally through Augustine that the Hellenic tradition of thought was united with Western Catholic philosophy and theology. He adapted and inserted into a Christian context the Neoplatonic conceptions of reality. The low state of culture of his era affected his philosophical discussions. But his intellectual diligence was unparalleled; and he was endowed

---

[1] *Apologeticum*, 46. [2] *De Praescriptionibus Haereticorum*, 7.
[3] Ep. cxx.

with a disposition 'that longed not merely to believe the truth, but also to understand it'.[1]

His philosophical views as a whole are nowhere coherently set forth. At an early age of his career, as we have seen, his ethical and metaphysical inquiries were thrown aside for pressing doctrinal controversies. Discussions of purely philosophical interest are henceforth to be found embedded in the theological and exegetical treatises. They are scattered widely through the enormous compass of Augustine's works. But in truth this division between the philosophical and theological aspects of his thought is foreign to Augustine's intentions. Philosophy for him is intrinsically joined with theology. 'I desire to know God and the soul. Nothing besides? Nothing at all.'[2] The end of philosophy is not knowledge but wisdom. Knowledge is concerned with temporal events. Its field is, as we should say, science. Wisdom is the apprehension of eternal things. And wisdom is a part of the blessed life.[3]

Accordingly we do not find in Augustine the distinction between the realm of Reason and the realm of Faith which is seen in later scholastic writers. He reserves, indeed, certain spheres wherein Faith precedes Reason, namely those dogmas of the Christian religion which pertain to salvation.[4] Faith does not here exclude Reason. It is Reason informed with religious perception. 'Far be it', he says, 'that we should have faith without accepting or demanding reason for our faith.'[5] And he adds that faith is only possible to rational beings. But he held, too, that failure to understand the truths of faith is to be ascribed not wholly to intellectual defect, but also to moral obliquity.[6]

In spite, however, of the organic relation of philosophical discussions to the theological expositions in which they are set, a series of arguments concerning the nature and validity of knowledge that form a consistent scheme of metaphysical thought, may be detached from the writings of the great Bishop. His examination of the principles of thought are part of a vast proof for the existence of God; though from this aspect God is to be conceived as the ideal of knowledge implicit in all human endeavour after understanding, the ideal of an all-embracing coherent unity of experience.

We may now venture to describe, as closely as possible in his own terms, Augustine's theory of knowledge.

---

[1] Contra Acad. III. xx. 43; C.S.E.L. lxiii. 80. [2] Solil. I. ii. 7; P.L. xxxii. 872.
[2] De Trin. XII. xv. 25; P.L. xlii. 1018. [4] Ep. cxx. i. 3; C.S.E.L. xxxiv. 706.
[3] Ib. [6] De Trin. xv. xxvii. 50; P.L. xlii. 1097.

II

In a passage in the *Confessions* Augustine gives an epitome of his doctrine.

'And thus by degrees I passed from bodies to the bodily sensations of the mind. And from this stage I came next to the mind's inner faculty, to which the bodily senses refer external objects. And this is the limit of the intelligence of animals. Passing beyond this I proceeded next to the rational faculty to which all that is collected from the bodily senses is referred for judgement. And this faculty perceiving itself in me also to be unstable raised itself to its intellectual level, and turned the mind's reflections away from the tyranny of habit, withdrawing itself from the throngs of confusing images, in order that it might find the light by which it was suffused. For with complete conviction it proclaimed that what is unchangeable is to be preferred to what is changeable, and thus it had knowledge of the unchangeable itself. For unless it had in some way known to it, the mind would have had no ground for preferring it to the changeable. And so in one tremulous stroke of vision it arrived at that which is.'[1]

Bodies, sensation, inner sense, judgement, pure thought, intuition—such are the steps in Augustine's investigation of knowledge.[2] The prevailing purpose of the investigation is to prove the existence of a realm of absolute timeless reality. Each grade of knowledge is shown to rest on a more stable, more comprehensive, more fundamental mode of cognition. The chief defect which compels the mind to press on from the earlier to the later forms of apprehension, from the knowledge of physical objects to the contemplation of the Ideas, is the presence of impermanence. The intellect perceives above the flux of visible things and above human minds a system of unchangeable truths.[3] And the *res intelligibles* which are open to the grasp of intellectual insight are not merely formal propositions; they are the constitutive principles of things. Endowed with the power of 'illumination' the mind may descry beyond space and time the source of Ideas.

Augustine recurs to this ascent towards reality in many different forms. In a notable passage in *De quantitate animae*[4] seven steps of

---

[1] Confess. VII. xvii. 23.

[2] For Augustine thought (*mens*) embraces both reason (*ratio*) and intellectual understanding (*intellectus*). Reason is the distinctively human power of discovering relevant connexions by a process of analysis and synthesis. *Intellectus* apprehends those infallible truths which are clues to the nature of reality. In the exercise of this faculty man attains to some knowledge of purely spiritual substances. [3] De divers. Quaest. xlv. 1; P.L. xl. 28.

[4] Op. cit. xxxiii. 70 ff.; P.L. xxxii. 1073.

mental development are distinguished. In the first stage the mind appears, even in plants, as life preserving the unity of the physical structure and causing growth and reproduction. At the next level it perceives through the senses and exhibits the primary animal appetites. Next it shows itself in man as tradition and custom. Fourthly, the mind rises above the interests of the external world to the region of moral life. Next it reaches a state of joyful confidence and proceeds to the sixth stage, in which it strives to understand those things which truly and supremely exist. Finally it attains a vision of truth.

Often the movement of his thought is more direct. The human mind in considering visible things can recognize that it is itself superior to them. But since it falls short of wisdom and is still trying to reach it, it becomes aware that its own nature is transient and perceives beyond itself the unchanging truth.[1]

In the course of his numerous explorations of this ascent of the mind Augustine necessarily discusses the elements of which knowledge is composed. He analyses mental processes such as perception and judgement so as to exhibit the complex activities present in them. His views on these points, especially the account of the relation between physical impressions and sensations, profoundly affected the philosophy of the Middle Ages. But it is important to realize that psychological analysis is incidental to Augustine's main concern. He is preoccupied with the nature of reality which he finds disclosed in the spirit's search for truth. It is the metaphysical question concerning the status of various types of knowledge which interests him. He passes over, as we shall notice, important points in the psychology of knowledge in order to press the mind's recognition of the Ideas.

A further characteristic, which introduces the distinctive approach of medieval thought to these topics, must be mentioned. Throughout Augustine's discussions of logical and psychological questions an intimate relation with moral notions is maintained. The higher mental activity, for example, is also the better.

‘*Augustine*. Now to which of these three belongs all that the bodily sense perceives? . . . is it to be placed in that class which only exists or in that which also lives, or in that which also understands? *Evodius*. In that which only exists. *A*. Then in which class of these three do you suppose sense itself to fall? *E*. In that which lives. *A*. Which of these two then do you judge to be better? Sense itself or that which sense

---

[1] Cf. De divers. Quaest., passage cited above.

perceives? *E*. Sense, surely. *A*. Why? *E*. Because that which also lives is better than that which only exists.'[1]

The discussion is transferred from a classification in point of natural order to a classification in point of value. Always the discussions on knowledge press the moral superiority of one mode of experience over another. Mind is nobler than the body, reason higher than sense. The quest for the Ideas is the quest for spiritual value.

To detach from this concentration on truth conceived as a way to blessedness and salvation discussions of theoretical import offers some violence to Augustine's thought. As M. Gilson observes, it is difficult at any point to say with precision 'whether Saint Augustine is speaking as a theologian or as a philosopher, whether he is proving the existence of God or developing a theory of knowledge, whether the eternal truths of which he speaks are those of understanding or of morality, whether it is a doctrine of sensation which he is expounding or the consequences of original Sin'.[2] The rejection of the sensible order is a facet of the condemnation of the flesh. The independence of mind and body and the supremacy of the eternal Ideas are aspects of the ascendancy of spirit over matter.

With these considerations in mind let us now turn to the first stages of the mind's ascent to truth.

III

We have seen that a crucial stage in the development of Augustine's mind was the discovery of a reply to the challenge which the fashionable school of philosophy had brought against the validity of knowledge. The thought of the age was widely influenced by the tradition of Pyrrho, according to which all our knowledge is infected with subjectivity. The real nature of things is wholly unknown to us. Since nothing is certain, a suspension of judgement is the only prudent attitude to adopt. The heirs of Pyrrhonic scepticism were the philosophers of the New Academy whose opinions were elegantly represented for Augustine by the writings of Cicero. To find a positive basis for knowledge was for the young Augustine a task not of playful dialectics but of anxious moral concern. For he could advance no step towards the beliefs which his soul desired without establishing confidence in knowledge.

[1] De lib. arb. ii. v. 11 ; P.L. xxxii. 1245.
[2] *Introduction à l'étude de St. Augustin*, Paris, 1929, p. 294.

It was, as we have seen, the study of the Platonists which led him to a positive basis for knowledge; but the discovery is expressed in a form peculiarly his own. The argument is given in a number of passages throughout his works.[1] The substance of these passages is twofold. Firstly, it is argued that the process of doubting presumes the certain knowledge that something exists, namely the doubter and his mental activities. Secondly, the criticism of knowledge implies a criterion of truth.

The principles of nature are obscure. Men have disputed, for example, whether the energy of life is derived from air or from fire, whether the self is simple or complex. Philosophers have even impugned the evidence of our senses. Yet there is at least one fact which no one, however sceptical, can call in question, namely the existence of himself. Though I doubt, I am aware of myself as existing when I doubt. *Si fallor sum.* Even if I suppose my experience to be an illusion or a dream I must assume that I exist. And this conviction provides a ground for knowledge. Using less ambiguous terms than Descartes, whose famous argument these passages so fully anticipates,[2] Augustine maintains that the primary intuition of the self includes all the processes which can be abstractly distinguished within it. It includes desiring, remembering, willing, thinking, feeling. More summarily, it comprises a direct apprehension, a judgement, and a feeling. 'I am most certain that I am, and that I know this and enjoy it.'

This truth is immediately perceived. Whatever doubts philosophers have thrown on the reports of the senses concerning the external world, they have never been able to disprove truths of this character.[3] For (as we shall discover) Augustine thinks there are other truths of the same order.

Now the crucial question for Augustine, as for Descartes, is what is further implied by this intuition of the self as to the fundamental nature of knowledge. We are left in no doubt. In the passage in *De civitate Dei* it is said: 'We do not discern these ideas through some bodily sense as we apprehend colours, sounds, and tastes; but without any delusive representation (*ludificatoria imaginatione*) of spurious perception or of images (*phantasiarum vel phantasmatum*) I am most certain that I am and that I know this and enjoy it.' Elsewhere the mind is said to know this truth

[1] Cf. Solil. ii. 1, P.L. xxxii. 885; De Trin. x. x. 14, P.L. xlii. 981; De civ. Dei· xi. 26, C.S.E.L. xl. i. 551.
[2] Cf. Meditations, ii.   [3] De Trin. xv. xii. 21; P.L. xlii. 1073.

'of itself'. It knows itself through itself, because it is incorporeal.[1] It perceives itself 'not by a movement through space, but by an incorporeal reversion to itself'.[2] This knowledge, in a word, is detached from all contact with the data of sense-perception. The mind knows the external world indirectly. Awareness of the self as continuous and permanent—and the self without these characteristics vanishes from view—is derived not from the continuity and coherence of the objective world, but from a disembodied entity. In fact, as we shall see, Augustine believes that the mind produces its experience from its own resources.

Thus the ground of certitude points to a radical dualism in knowledge; and perceptual experience occupies from the outset a secondary position.

In the second line of attack upon scepticism which is found in Augustine's writings he is standing on firmer ground. He argues that scepticism assumes a criterion of truth. To be conscious that I am deceived presumes some awareness of what constitutes reality. And the cardinal principle which is thus revealed is the principle of non-contradiction or, in positive terms, of coherence. We may not know what quality a thing in reality possesses. But we know that it cannot both have a particular quality and not have it. The same mind cannot both perish and be immortal; if the world contains only four elements it cannot contain five.[3] This principle gives a positive guide to knowledge, a clue to its general nature. But again the question arises whether it gives any but a formal content to knowing apart from reference to sense-experience.

We meet at this point with a distinctive feature of Augustine's discussions on truth. He is 'the master of the inner life'. His powers of psychological introspection were exceptional, and his pages contain many valuable observations of mental processes.[4] But more than this, he is always bidding us look within ourselves to find the gateway to virtue and to knowledge. The moral law is written in our hearts; and the first step to truth is to be thoroughly acquainted with oneself. 'Go not outside thyself, but return within thyself; for truth resides in the inmost part of man.'[5] This subjective note, first and chiefly struck by Augustine, divides ancient

[1] De Trin. IX. iii. 3; P.L. xlii. 963.
[2] De Trin. XIV. vi. 8; P.L. xlii. 1042.
[3] Contra Acad. III. xiii. 29; C.S.E.L. lxiii. 68.
[4] See J. Morgan, *The Psychological Teaching of St. Augustine*, London, 1932.
[5] De vera rel. xxix. 72; P.L. xxxii. 154.

philosophy from medieval and modern speculation. Christianity
and the decay of civilization had transferred the direction of
intellectual endeavour from the outer world to the soul. The forms
of relation characteristic of mental life were raised to the status of
metaphysical principles; and the processes of will, of memory,
and of thought were applied to the operations of reality.

But the truth reached by the inner path is anything but subjective. If our ideas did not refer to an independent and objective
realm, no discussion would be possible between men. Everyone
would be confined to their own ideas, and *quot homines tot senten-
tiae.*[1] The region of reality is the world of Ideas, necessary, immutable, intelligible.

Augustine's main concern is this realm of Ideas, and he constantly seeks to show that they are integral to thought, even at the
lowest levels. Fundamentally knowledge is one. But it expresses
itself in two ways, which are distinguished as lower and higher
reason. The former is further termed *Scientia*. *Scientia* is defined
as the knowledge of temporal and changing things necessary for
prosecuting the activities of this life.[2] Its spring is practical.
The higher reason is *Sapientia*, wisdom. Its motive is contemplation and its objects the intelligible Ideas. Thus action is subordinate to contemplation.

Let us now trace the steps by which Augustine advances from
bare sensation to the knowledge of *intelligibiles res*.

IV

The interesting point about Augustine's account of perception
is the way in which the isolation of the mind from its objects is
preserved. This separation foreshadows the representative or indirect theory of perception, which in a scientific setting formed the
basis of theories of knowledge in the seventeenth and eighteenth
centuries.

The theory is determined by the nature of the mind and its
relation to the body. The mind is wholly different in substance
from the body. It is, in comparison with the body, simple, while
being present as a whole everywhere throughout the body.[3] The

---

[1] De lib. arb. ii. x. 28; P.L. xxxii. 1256.

[2] De Trin. xii. xii. 17; P.L. xlii. 1007. The chief value conceded to *Scientia* is
that it provides an opportunity by which the Faith may be supported and
defended. Cf. De Trin. xiv. i. 3; P.L. xlii. 1037.

[3] De Trin. vi. vi. 8; P.L. xlii. 929. Strictly speaking, *anima*, which is used
throughout this discussion, means the vital animating function of *animus*, the
substantial mind. *Animus* contains thought (*mens*) as well as life (*anima*).

body is regarded as belonging entirely to the physical order. Its parts change and decay, but (save for a certain spontaneity attributed to light) it is subject only to external influences. The principle upon which Augustine insists in contrasting the two substances is that mind is always active, body always passive. The notion underlying this contrast has nothing to do with the Cartesian dualism of mechanical extended substance and unextended thinking substance, though the outcome is similar. The principle is rooted in the Neoplatonic and theological view of the mind as a symbol and vehicle of the spiritual order; and it carries with it the consequences frequently dwelt on by Augustine. 'The idea that the body can make any impression on the spirit cannot be seriously maintained, as though the spirit were subject to the motions of the body in the same way as matter. For what acts is in every way more excellent than that which it acts on.'[1] The mind, ever active, animates a body ever passive; and the body has no influence on the mind's activity. How, then, are the processes of sensation and perception to be explained? The influences which play upon the body cannot be transmitted by way of the sense-organs to consciousness; for the sense-organs are as physical as any other portions of matter, and can only affect matter. Motions striking upon the ear, for example, do not produce impressions on the mind. 'When we hear, the rhythms which occur in the mind are not produced by those rhythms which we know to be in the sounds themselves.' We may postpone for the moment the problem how the rhythms in the sounds themselves are known. Let us first inquire how the sensory qualities are perceived.

Augustine's explanation, to which medieval theories of perception frequently recur, is given most clearly in the passage in *De musica* that follows the quotation which has been given above. Some extracts from this passage may be given:

'For my part I hold that the body is only animated by the mind in a directive manner (*intentione facientis*). . . . Any physical objects which penetrate or press on the body from outside, affect not the mind but the body only, so as to hinder or promote its functions. Accordingly, when it struggles against resistance, and experiences difficulty in controlling the material forces thrust against it, a heightened awareness results (*fit attentior*) owing to the difficulty of acting, and this attention to difficulty, when it reaches the level of consciousness, is sensation, and is

[1] De Gen. ad litt. xii. 16; C.S.E.L. xxviii. 1, 402: cf. De Musica, VI. v; P.L. xxxii. 1167. St. Augustine understands by *musica* not the art of singing or playing but the science of the laws which regulate harmony and rhythm.

described as pain or effort. . . . In a word it seems to me that the mind when it experiences sensation in the body receives no impression from it, but becomes more attentive to impressions on the body. These acts of attention appear to the mind as pleasant when the body's functions are promoted, disagreeable when they are frustrated. The total effect is what is known as sensation. But the apprehension which, even when we are aware of no sensation, is present in us, is the body's organ, and this is controlled by the mind, so that it becomes better prepared to deal with effects in the body, admitting what is appropriate and rejecting what is harmful. . . . Now when those influences occur which produce, so to speak, differences in the body, the mind exerts efforts of attention appropriate to each of its parts and organs, and is said to see, to hear, to smell, to taste, or to sense by touch. . . . These are the activities by which, in my view, the mind meets the impressions of the body when it experiences sensation. I do not believe it directly receives the impressions.'[1]

To grasp St. Augustine's meaning we must explore a little further the implications of the *intentione facientis*. For him the fundamental characteristic of mind is not cognitive but conative. A form of will precedes the expression of sensation. 'Prius enim quam visio fieret jam voluntas.' This fundamental teleological activity of the mind has a vegetative and an animal level which are described at length in *De quantitate animae*.[2] Its functions at these levels are to preserve the body's organic unity, to nourish it, to cause its growth and reproduction, to direct its movements and its perceptions. Sensation is thus related, as we should say, to biological function. Normally this level of mind acts without consciousness. It informs and directs the sense-organs. 'Vitali motu in silentio corpus aurium vegetebat.' The mind secretly sustains by its living activity the organ of hearing. When, owing to obstruction, there is enhancement of effort the sensation becomes conscious. But—and this is the essential feature of the theory— the independence of the two orders is strictly retained. The mind watches over and manages the body, observing the impressions which fall upon it. Some it ignores; a mass of them it reproduces from its own nature and informs with these elementary and barely conscious reproductions, the body's sense-organs; some it recreates as emotions and desires. The images or impressions of bodies are

---

[1] De mus. VI. v. 9, 10; P.L. xxxii. 1168–9. This passage should be compared with the account of vision in *De Trin.* XI. ii. 2–5, where the role of sense is described in more passive terms. But even here it is said that 'for him who sees there is the sense of sight and the intention of looking at and attending to the object'.

[2] Op. cit. xxxiii. 71; P.L. xxxii. 1074.

fashioned by the mind 'of its own substance'.[1] 'It is not the body
that feels but the mind through the body, which it uses as a
messenger. in order to produce within itself what is announced
outside.'[2] The mind can form images without the intervention of
the body.

The theory is striking. It recognizes in a remarkable way the
conative origin of consciousness to which modern psychology has
returned. Primitive awareness is traced to tensions set up by
physical obstructions. But the parallelism of body and mind is
preserved at some cost. It is difficult to grasp what 'being attentive to' and 'watching over' the body can mean unless the physical
accompaniment of such processes is illogically assumed. It will be
noticed, too, that in spite of the initial distinction between the
nature of mind and body, an independent activity is allowed to the
body. Further, from the point of view of the theory of knowledge
we may ask how far sensations, if they are made by the mind,
represent reality.

It is doubtful whether this question would have troubled
Augustine. Sometimes he leaps the difficulty by asserting that the
object and the similitude of it wrought in sensation are alike.[3] At
other times he assumes that the 'senses' of the mind reproduce the
'form', that is to say, the actual nature of the object. But his
essential reply is that the question of objectivity does not arise in
relation to *sensibilia*. The apprehensions of the senses are not themselves true or false. If we ask whether the object is as it appears to
be, whether the oar which appears broken in the water is in fact
broken, we appeal not to the senses but to the judgement. It is
precisely because the sceptics confine themselves to the witness of
the senses that knowledge becomes impossible for them.[4]

The sensory elements are not the primary entities of knowledge.
In *De libero arbitrio*[5] it is pointed out that in addition to the reports
of the separate senses which give us colour, sound, flavour, smooth-
ness, and so forth, there are other qualities pertaining to the form
of bodies, the qualities of being large, small, square, and round,
which we do not perceive by any one sense. These non-sensory
perceptions are referred in the Aristotelian manner to 'a certain
inner sense to which all things are reported from the familiar five

[1] De Trin. x. v. 7; P.L. xlii. 977.
[2] De Gen. ad litt. xii. 24; C.S.E.L. xxviii. 1, 416.
[3] De Trin. xi. iii. 6; P.L. xlii. 989.
[4] Contra Acad. iii. xi. 26; C.S.E.L. lxiii. 67.
[5] De lib. arb. ii. vii, viii; P.L. xxxii. 1249-53.

senses'. And this common interior sense is present in the minds of animals; in virtue of it they avoid what is displeasing and pursue what is pleasing to them. In modern terms its province is the instinctive life.

In an interesting discussion in *De quantitate animae*[1] various elements of perception which are not derived from sensation are traced. These elements are said to be 'presumed or inferred'. The discussion is in the form of a dialogue. Perception is first defined as bare apprehension by the mind of what affects the body. 'Sensum puto esse non latere animam quod patitur corpus.' But, it is pointed out, if this *non latere animam* means an isolated and immediate mental element, difficulties arise. In the first place, vision does not consist only of an immediate image in the sense-organ. Unless it were to include more than this we should see no more than our own eyes. Distance or spatial reference is implied in the act of seeing. In the second place we perceive more than that which sight alone gives, even when it is thus complicated. For example, we perceive fire, though our actual image is that of smoke. Already we are beginning to be aware that perception is a kind of knowledge through sensation. In addition to the image, which reproduces the impression on the organs of the body, something else is presumed or inferred. A further example of what is not known by sensation, taken literally, is the fact of growth. 'It is one thing to see nails longer, another to know that they grow.' Considerations such as these compel us to revise our definition. There is a *sensum*, we must say, which is an impression on the body of which the mind is barely (*per se*) aware without the intervention of any other factor. Every impression on the body of which the mind is barely aware is this *sensum*, but every *sensum* is not simply this. It may be complicated by perspective and by meaning, in the sense suggested above. Lastly, the current division between the minds of animals and of men is adduced. Surely, it is suggested, Odysseus' dog, which recognized him after twenty years, displayed more than 'bare perception'. Its recognition of its master is obviously more than this. What it lacked, however, was the human characteristic of knowing that it recognized its master. We must, in fact, distinguish two types of perception, perception *per rationem* and perception *per corpus*. But even the latter, which is common to men and animals, includes more than bare apprehension. And human perception points beyond, to *scientia*.

[1] Op. cit. xxiii–xxvi; P.L. xxxii. 1058–65.

To these considerations we may add passages in which retention as a factor in perception is discussed. It is observed, for example, that in hearing the briefest syllable, *a fortiori* a word of several syllables, unless the motion of the beginning of the syllable were retained in our mind when the ending is uttered, we should not hear it at all, still less understand it. Perceiving is more than sensing.

These suggestions are neither clearly nor fully worked out. They serve to indicate the mental and formal characteristics of elementary knowledge; and these characteristics lead Augustine quickly to the further stages of his ascent towards reality. But the next phase in the development of knowledge is still more summarily treated. For at this point the development of general ideas—man, colour, triangularity—naturally falls to be described. But the recognition of common qualities which enable us to think of objects and to predicate their qualities does not arise for Augustine through the process of generalizing the particular given elements. No account of the formation of concept by comparison and abstraction can be found in his writings. He speaks frequently of the way in which the images of things perceived by the senses are retained in the memory. Sensation reproduces the species of the corporeal thing; these images are formed in the memory, and the *visio cogitantis* is fashioned from the memory images.[1] But abstraction in the Aristotelian sense, by which general concepts are derived from sensory impressions, is foreign to his outlook. For the Aristotelian account is founded on the belief that the body and the physical world act upon the mind; and we have seen that Augustine does not admit this.

On the one hand, sensation is necessary for a knowledge of things. On the other hand, sensory perception implies, as we have seen, general notions 'inferred or assumed'. But beyond this it must be admitted that it is difficult to discover any further psychological account. We have pointed out above that psychological analysis is, for Augustine, incidental to the problem of truth. It is from this point of view that we must interpret his references to general ideas.

He is interested, not in the formation of concepts, but in the criteria of truth contained in them. To speak, for example, of the human mind *specialiter et generaliter*, that is of the generic human mind, is to refer to the truth. 'We do not gather a notion of the

---

[1] De Trin. xi. ix; P.L. xlii. 996. Cf. iii. 6 of the same book.

human mind in its general character by comparison, observing a number of minds with bodily eyes; we contemplate indestructible truth, by means of which we define precisely, as far as we can, not the nature of one particular man's mind, but the nature it ought to be according to the eternal reasons.'[1] It is assumed that general notions are entirely independent of sensible origin, in the same way as the notions of truth, coherence, equality, and number. Their content comes 'from above'. The mind refers the intelligible norms which it contemplates above it to the sensations and images derived from its commerce with the body and with physical objects. *Scientia* is rooted in perception, but it is not derived from the flux of sensations. And since *scientia*, the farther it advances, is increasingly concerned with the 'reasons', numbers, and forms of things, it does not require the process of abstraction from particular sensations. For these Ideas are discussed without reference to the sensible world. 'But that capacity of ours which is concerned with the treatment of corporeal and temporal things is, indeed, rational in that it is not common to us and the beasts, but is drawn, as it were, out of that rational substance of our mind by which we are in contact with the intelligible and immutable truth, and which is deputed to handle and direct the inferior things.'[2]

Thus the perception of the world depends on the activity of intellectual apprehension, and this in turn upon the eternal reasons. The analysis of knowledge is dominated everywhere by the Platonic Ideas. We are drawn quickly in all Augustine's discussions on knowledge to the sphere of timeless entities.

V

But before we enter on those conceptions which occupy the central interest of Augustine's thought we may glance at his general attitude to the 'rational knowledge of temporal things'. Many writers have made play with utterances in which he appears to deprecate scientific inquiry into the operations of nature. Some of these frequently quoted remarks demand to be read in their context. Thus the passage in the *Confessions*[3] about 'vain and curious desire, veiled under the name of knowledge' refers to magical and superstitious inquiries. And the saying in *The City of*

[1] De Trin. IX. vi. 9; P.L. xlii. 966, 955.
[2] De Trin. XII. iii. 3; P.L. xlii. 999.   [3] X. xxv. 54, 55.

God,[1] that the knowledge of temporal things with which devils are puffed up is contemptible to angels, must be connected with the preceding passage in which the defect in the knowledge possessed by devils is pointed out. What is wrong with devils' knowledge is not that it is concerned with temporal things, but that it lacks charity. Texts can indeed be cited in which empirical knowledge is slightingly spoken of;[2] but this is a different matter to disparaging a scientific understanding of Nature. For Augustine's view of natural knowledge was Platonic, and the empirical method was deemed subordinate to the mathematical. He emphatically warns Christians against the danger of clinging to crude beliefs about the natural world on the authority of Scripture.

'It frequently happens that there is some question about the earth, or the sky, or the other elements of this world, the movement, revolutions, or even the size and distance of the stars, the regular eclipses of the sun and the moon, the course of the years and seasons; the nature of the animals, vegetables, and minerals, and other things of the same kind, respecting which one who is not a Christian has knowledge derived from most certain reasoning or observation. And it is highly deplorable and mischievous and a thing especially to be guarded against that he should hear a Christian speaking of such matters in accordance with Christian writings and uttering such nonsense that, knowing him to be as wide of the mark as, to use the common expression, east is from west, the unbeliever can scarcely restrain himself from laughing.'[3]

In his allusions to the scientific theories of his age Augustine shows caution. He confesses that he has not been able to spare the time to grasp the subtle and difficult questions of cosmology.[4] But he expresses admiration of the work of the astronomers, contrasting their mathematical calculations of the solstices, equinoxes, and eclipses with the fables of the Manichees.[5] He adheres to the doctrine of the four elements, in which earth as the heaviest element is always seeking the lowest place, while water, air, and fire are ranged above in ascending order.[6] He devotes much attention to the theory of primary matter. The problem arises in connexion with the interpretation of the phrases of Genesis, such as the phrase 'the earth was without form'. Augustine conceives a formless substance endowed with a lowly life, which underlies the definite forms of things. It is the substratum of change.[7]

[1] Op. cit. IX. xxii; C.S.E.L. xl. i. 439.

[2] Cf. De an. IV. x. 14; P.L. xliv. 532, and Encheiridion, ix.

[3] De Gen. ad litt. I. xix; C.S.E.L. xxviii. i. 28.

[4] Ib. II. x; C.S.E.L. xxviii. i. 48.   [5] Confess. v. iii. 6.

[6] De civ. Dei. XXII. xi; C.S.E.L. xl. ii. 616.   [7] Confess. XII. vi 6

It has been pointed out that all Augustine's discussions of physics refer to Platonic theories, not to Aristotelian.[1] This preference was felt till the twelfth century. The principal pagan authors studied on points of cosmology were Chalcidius, Martianus Capella, and Macrobius; and their Platonic theories accorded with the teaching of Augustine, whose writings were the chief Christian authority for physical beliefs. Thus, through him, the *Timaeus* determined the scientific framework of the succeeding centuries.

One side of Augustine's teaching on nature has stirred peculiar interest in modern times. This is his discussion of the creation of biological species. Many commentators have detected a theory of evolution in the account of 'seminal reasons' given in *De Genesi ad litteram*. The question arises for him not from any direct interest in the biological relation of species to one another, but from difficulties in the story of creation given in the early chapters of Genesis. The text clearly signifies that God created all things at one instant; for, argues Augustine, the six days of creation cannot be taken in their literal sense. But in the second chapter of Genesis the appearance of creatures, including man, plainly takes place in a temporal succession. Further, countless new individual creatures have appeared since the first creation of species. The problem is to reconcile these two principles found in Scripture, the total creation of the world and its inhabitants at one moment, and the successive appearance of species and of individuals. The problem has nothing to do with the modification of species by descent.

Augustine meets the apparent contradiction by supposing that the act of creation took place in two stages. In the first stage plants, animals, and men are created potentially and simultaneously, in the second they actually and successively appear. In the first stage creatures are said to be made in their 'seminal reasons'. *Rationes seminales* are interpreted in a variety of ways. They are said to be the germs of seeds of living beings. In other passages they are described as existing in an indeterminate fluid state which precedes the emergence of the seed, and which is invisible to the human eye. This state, in some passages, is still more abstractly defined as a generative power, and even as a law of growth. On the whole it is manifest that the seminal reasons are intended to be activities which determine the fact and order of growth. These forces imply no doctrine of preformism—the germ does not contain the subsequent individual in a contracted form. 'Let us consider the beauty

---

[1] Cf. P. Duhem, *Système du Monde*, Paris, 1913–17, ii, 410.

of some tree, with its trunk, branches, leaves, and fruit. We not only know that this appearance and size have not suddenly come about, but we know also in what order. For the tree began with the root which the germ first fixed in the ground, and from thence all this developed form has grown. Moreover, that germ came from a seed; therefore all these features were in the seed originally, not in a mass of corporeal magnitude, but in a force and causal potency.'[1] But this potential state signifies a predestined development. 'If the causes of all future things were placed in the world when God created all things together, . . . those causes contained not only that man could be made thus, but truly also that he had to be made thus.'[2] But God may modify their effects. Augustine draws a significant conclusion, that it is vain to seek causes for all phenomena.[3] The essential point is that the seminal reasons are conceived within the framework of fixed species. Nowhere does Augustine envisage a development from one species to a different species. It is true that the parent of trees and of animals is said to be the earth.[4] But the active causality which is contained in the earth is specified to produce its kind. God created, at the beginning, seminal reasons appropriate to all species. 'But as in that grain of seed there are together invisibly all those things which develop into a tree in the course of time, so we must think of the world as having together, when God created all things at once, all those things which were in it and with it when the day was made' . . . including 'all those things which the waters and the earth produced potentially and causally before they were to arise in the course of time as they are now known to us.'[5]

The doctrine that all creatures which will appear to the end of time were created *potentialiter et causaliter* has an important corollary. The voluntary activity of created beings cannot produce any genuinely new being. All it can do in this direction is to provide the external conditions for such production. The creation of substantial existence is only possible to God, working through the seminal reasons.

In his book on St. Augustine,[6] Mr. Hugh Pope has collected a large number of examples of his 'devouring curiosity' over natural

[1] De Gen. ad litt. v. 23; C.S.E.L. xxviii. i. 167. The translations given here are those of Dr. E. C. Messenger, to whose discussion of the seminal reasons in *Evolution and Theology*, London, 1931, I am greatly indebted.
[2] Op. cit. vi. 18; C.S.E.L. xxviii. i. 192.   [3] Ib. vi. 16; C.S.E.L. xxviii. i. 191.
[4] Ib. v. 23; C.S.E.L. xxviii. i. 168.   [5] Ib.
[6] *Saint Augustine of Hippo*, London, 1937, chapter vi.

phenomena, especially in the provinces of physiology and of animal behaviour. Augustine even conducted some experiments; he tested, for instance, the belief that the flesh of the peacock does not putrefy. But when all is said, his scientific knowledge, even for the age, is meagre. And it is manifest that the investigation of natural processes for their own sake is fundamentally opposed to his general attitude to knowledge. He frequently warns Christians against vain curiosity which turns the mind away from the contemplation of eternal things.[1] Science must be strictly subordinated to philosophy, that is to say, to the pursuit of wisdom.[2]

This conception of the value of science was prevalent in the age of decadence. The Roman moralists no less than the Neoplatonic philosophers regarded independent inquiry into natural causes as an inferior and elementary activity of mind.[3] The religious mind of the age contributed to this attitude. It accepted the phenomena of nature as the manifestations of God. For precise scrutiny it substituted allegorical interpretation. And for Augustine this method of approach to Nature is supported by his theory of knowledge. He was deeply interested, throughout his life, in the nature of learning. He discusses its psychology at length in *De magistro*.[4] He shows that words, written or uttered, and indeed any significant symbol, are merely the stimuli for capacities which exist already in the mind. The arguments of the teacher are invitations to the learner to 'return to himself', and to discover within the truths that dwell there. Not that these truths are innate, in the sense that men are endowed with them at birth. Still less are they the memories of previous existence, as in the Platonic doctrine of reminiscence. They exist, as we have seen, in the ideal realm which the mind is formed to enter if it will. Now if we try to explain the way in which the human mind acquires its knowledge we find a close parallel between the apprehension of ideas and the apprehension of sensations. We have seen that the mind uses the body 'as a kind of messenger in order to reproduce from within itself what is announced outside'. The messages which the forms and movements of the world bring are spiritual truths.[5] They are patterns or symbols of the moral reality which sustains phenomena. The causal connexions of nature do not embody a structure

---

[1] Cf. De mus. VI. xiii. 39; P.L. xxxii. 1184.
[2] Cf. De Ord. I. viii. 24; C.S.E.L. lxiii. 137.
[3] Cf. for example Seneca, Ep. 88.
[4] Op. cit. Cap. ii ff.; P.L. xxxii. 1196.
[5] Cf. Gilson, *Introduction à l'étude de S. Augustin*, p. 93.

independent of, and indifferent to, man's desires. They are to be viewed teleologically, as means for the instruction of the soul.

This conception hastened the eclipse of scientific investigation. St. Augustine's writings are filled with fanciful analogies between natural phenomena and theological truths. The moon is a symbol of the Church which reflects the divine light; the wind is an image of the spirit; numbers are significant of moral or theological ideas; the number eleven, for instance, stands for sin, for eleven 'transgresses' ten, and ten signifies the law, because of its association with the commandments. The psychological analogies in *De Trinitate* are on a different plane.

In a word, little importance attached to nature in itself. The earth and the stars, trees and animals, convey obscure messages of God's purpose to the human mind.

VI

The mind possesses the power through its bodily senses of perceiving physical objects; it has also the power of discerning the self, and things which though resembling bodies are not corporeal; and lastly it can contemplate objects which are neither bodies nor like bodies; things which have neither colour nor passion, nor any such quality. And it is on such things we ought most intently to dwell.[1] Again 'the intellectual cognition of eternal things is one thing, the rational cognition of temporal things is another; and no one doubts that the former is to be preferred to the latter'.[2] The entire trend of Augustine's analysis of knowledge is towards the establishment of a region of immutable certainty. The relativity of sensory perception requires the regulative power of thought or judgement. It is the fact that the mind appreciates a rule or principle which is important. The mind corrects the impressions of the senses, such as the bent appearance of an oar in water,[3] by reference to a reality, the physical object, which is known by thought. But the mind is compelled to advance beyond this stage. For the judgement of truth and reality is here fallible. In so far as it bears upon the changing scene of events, it is infected with the relativity of their being. Constantly the mind in judging of the truth of appearances, appeals to principles which are untouched by the shifting tide of visible things. The exploration of these principles

---

[1] De an. IV. xx. 31; P.L. xliv. 542.
[2] De Trin. XII. xv. 25; P.L. xlii. 1012.   [3] Cf. p. 15 above.

discovers an intelligible structure in the world. And this structure is timeless.

The approach, then, to these realities lies through the recognition by the judgement of necessary criteria. Now what principles are there of this nature? There are according to Augustine many types of such principles. An important class is the class of mathematical ideas, or more generally, principles of order, rhythm, and symmetry. Mathematical ideas are types of being which are not subject to change; they are certain; and they are not dependent upon the nature of the mind which approaches them.

'The reason and truth of number is present to all who reflect, so that everyone who calculates tries to apprehend it with his reason and understanding. It offers itself equally to all who can grasp it; nor when perceived by anyone is it changed and altered for the nutriment, as it were, of its perceiver; nor does it cease when someone is deceived in it, but he is so much the more in error the less he sees it, while it remains true and whole.'[1]

Seven and three, Augustine adds, are ten, not only now but always.

The vital question for Augustine's theory of knowledge concerns the relation of such Ideas to sensible objects. It is indeed the vital question for medieval philosophy. In treating of mathematical Ideas the question is candidly faced. 'Supposing', he asks, 'someone were to say to you that these numbers are not apprehended by our mind through some property peculiar to them, but that we receive impressions of them in the same way as certain images of things seen which are derived from corporeal objects, how would you answer?' Evodius is made to reply that even if numbers are derived from the senses, the judgements of arithmetic, by which we can detect errors in addition or subtraction, are not so derived. We perceive the truth that seven and three are ten 'by the light of the mind'. And this is a truth which has a permanence that no physical object possesses. It does not, therefore, depend on sensible objects. Further, any sensible object is capable of infinite division. No body, however small, is a simple unity. But to know that no body is one is to know what one is. And this knowledge is not drawn from acquaintance with bodies, that is to say from sense-perception. Lastly, it is pointed out that in mathematical calculations it is possible to transcend the bounds of space and time and predict results throughout infinity. Take any simple arithmetical process, such as the multiplication of a number by two,

[1] De lib. arb. ii. viii. 20; P.L. xxxii. 1251.

and a rule becomes evident to the mind, which applies to all possible numbers. How can this truth be contemplated so surely through countless numbers save by an inner light which the bodily senses do not know?[1]

From these considerations it is concluded that mathematical ideas are one class of realities—and 'there are many such things'[2] —which are in no way inventions of the mind, which are free of the flux of space and time, and which evince a logical system of relations which are necessary and do not, in consequence, depend upon any accumulation of instances. And being themselves non-sensory they are discovered by a process of mind which is independent of sense-perception.

These arguments point to a realm of reality which appears to be completely sundered from the world as it is perceived to exist. Not only do the two regions, the region of Ideas and the region of perception, have no connexion with one another, but the manner by which each is apprehended, the way of sensory-perception and the way of thought tend also to fall apart. Augustine's arguments forcibly suggest the presence in experience of a fundamental structure which is non-sensory, which *intellectus* apprehends. But so far as these arguments go, the operations adduced do not warrant the conclusion that there are two worlds and two ways of knowing them. The truths of arithmetic are not independent of empirical experience. In adding or multiplying we direct attention solely to the quantitative aspect of things. But an aspect is not an independent order. Mathematical propositions concern, not a radically distinct region of experience, but certain formal characteristics of the perceived world. And taken apart from that world they give but abstract knowledge. The knowledge what one is is not knowledge of reality until we know what things are one.

But such criticisms are only applicable at this stage of Augustine's description of Ideas. The abrupt severance of the worlds of sense and of thought must be considered from another angle. The Ideas are not merely intelligible systems standing contrasted with the irrational flux of corporeal objects. Knowledge of Ideas is fundamental for the knowledge of corporeal things. Number lies at the basis of reality. Mathematical Ideas are generalized, and appear under the forms of order, rhythm, symmetry, harmony. From these

---

[1] Ib. II. viii. 23; P.L. xxxii. 1253.
[2] Ib. II. viii. 20; P.L. xxxii. 1251. In *De Trin.* IX. vi. 9–11 norms of truth, beauty, and goodness are named.

principles the objects of perception derive their existence. 'They do not come into being nor perish, but it is through them that all things which can or do come into being or perish are made.'[1] 'Look upon the sky and the earth and the sea and all the things which shine in them or above them, or creep or fly or swim beneath them. They have forms because they have numbers; take that from them and they will cease to be.'[2] Thus the object of our perception as well as those of our scientific understanding derive their substantial being from mathematical forms. In so far as our intellect discerns the rhythmic order in corporeal things, it discerns reality. These forms are the prototypes of the objects presented to our senses. Things exist primarily in their eternal Ideas, but they exist also for us in their material mode.[3] And they exist in the Ideas not only as species or genera but also as individuals.[4] For the doctrine is put forward in close connexion with the interpretation of the work of creation described in Genesis.

We are now in a better position to appreciate the grounds upon which Augustine believes in the external order of objects perceived. The mind, we have seen, has no direct awareness of bodies through the sense; it forms images of them from within itself. Nevertheless 'objects exist without being perceived, and sound exists when there are no ears to hear'.[5] The existence of material bodies in the physical guise in which they appear to us, or, more strictly, in the manner in which the mind reproduces them, remains a point not of knowledge but of belief. This belief is a necessary postulate of practical life. But through 'the mist of corporeal images' the intellect descries the immutable Forms which constitute the stable reality of things. The sensible image is for our feeble minds a necessary aid to the intellectual apprehension of the unchanging Form. For man's thought does not dwell, for example, on the incorporeal and immutable form of a square body in the same way as that form itself remains in it; if indeed the mind could have arrived at the form apart from the image of enclosed space.[6] The mind is helped to intellectual understanding of the eternal structure of the world by 'the transient glance' of sensory perception. But 'if you have looked upon anything mutable, you cannot grasp

---

[1] De div. quaest. qu. 46; P.L. xl. 30.
[2] De lib. arb. II. 42; P.L. xxxii. 1263.
[3] De vera rel. xxii. 42. P.L. xxxiv. 40.
[4] Epist. xiv. 4; P.L. xxxiii. 80.
[5] De mus. VI. ii. 3; P.L. xxxii. 1164.
[6] De Trin. XII. xiv. 23; P.L. xlii. 1011; cf. ib. XI. l. 1; P.L. xlii. 984.

it by the sense of the body or by the consideration of the mind, unless it is held firmly by some form of numbers; and if they are removed it falls back again into nothing'.[1] The mind is led to a knowledge of numbers through the sensible quality of objects, but apart from numbers there would be no object to perceive.

This fundamental order is at the opposite pole of being to mechanism. Augustine frequently associates with quantitative terms such as number or magnitude, terms expressing aesthetic natures. In a remarkable passage in the section of *De libero arbitrio* from which we have been quoting it is asserted that art is number. 'Human artists too have numbers of all bodily forms in art, and it is to them they shape their works. In fashioning they move their hands and instruments until that which is formed outside is referred back to that light of numbers which is within.' The motion of the artist's arms is number; and if we ask what it is that pleases in a dance 'number will answer you, Behold it is I'.[2] *Numeri* reveal at once the rhythmic beauty and the intelligible necessity of the natural world.

But mathematical Ideas are types of reality to which our judgement in every province ultimately refer. The moral principles of practical life rest on immutable standards in which we descry a supreme good, wherein our hearts are fulfilled. 'The rules and certain lights of virtue are true and immutable and are each or all present in common to be contemplated by those who are able to conceive them.'[3] Insight into these principles is *sapientia*, Wisdom.

Finally the question is pressed whether the several classes of universal realities discerned by *sapientia* are aspects of the same fundamental reality. Augustine has no doubt that, in the end, moral wisdom and number are single and identical. 'The learned and the scholarly, the more remote they are from earthly blemish, the more they look upon both number and wisdom in truth itself and hold both dear.'[4] And he seeks to explain the connexion between them by an analogy. As in fire brightness and heat exist together, heat affecting objects which are near it, brightness diffusing its influence more remotely; so rational minds are warm with the fire of wisdom, while bodies are infused with the radiance of numbers. But it is admitted that the question is difficult. Although it cannot be clear to our humble minds whether number is in wisdom

---

[1] De lib. arb. ii. xvi. 44; P.L. xxxii. 1264.
[2] Ib. ii. xvi. 42; P.L. xxxii. 1263.
[3] Ib. ii. x. 29; P.L. xxxii. 1257. [4] Ib. 31.

or derived from wisdom or whether both can be shown to be the names of one thing, this is certainly clear, that both are immutably real.[1]

In the natural sphere, however, the Forms point to a Supreme Form.

'Doubt not that, in order that these mutable things may not be checked in their course, but by measured motions and by distinctive variety of forms bring time to a close like a poem's ending, there must be some eternal and immutable Form, which is neither extended nor varied in time, and through which all mutable things can receive a form and according to their kind fulfil and accomplish their ordered rhythms in space and time.'[2]

Thus Augustine reaches the goal to which all his exploration of the degrees of knowledge tends. The norms of truth by which the mind judges, whether in the realm of nature or of goodness or of beauty, point to an absolute region of the spirit. So the intimations of the religious consciousness are confirmed. The argument is one which has been echoed throughout Christian thought, wherever the influence of Augustine has penetrated. It is the argument of Cudworth in the seventeenth century, no less than that of St. Bonaventure in the thirteenth.

But the process by which the mind approaches the system of absolute Form is complicated in St. Augustine by the doctrine of illumination. His writings are filled with metaphors drawn from light. And in this he follows his masters in philosophy. He tells in the *Confessions*[3] how he came to perceive, through reading the Platonists, that the soul of man is lit by the sun of truth. And in *De civitate Dei* he recalls the explanation given by Plotinus of the great passage in the *Republic* where the Form of the Good is compared with the Sun, 'that not even the spirit which these philosophers hold to be the soul of the Universe draws its joy from any other source than we ourselves, namely, that light which is not itself, but by which it was erected; and its understanding reflects the glory of that Intelligence'.[4]

But Augustine employs the simile in varied ways, and there are widely diverse interpretations of his meaning. Broadly speaking there are two groups of texts. In one the light by which the mind is illuminated refers to the standards of truth, beauty, and goodness which it contemplates above itself. 'That light by which the mind is enlightened is distinct from it, in order that it may behold

[1] De lib. arb. II. x. [2] Ib. xvi. 44. [3] VII. xi. 13.
[4] De civ. Dei. x. 2; C.S.E.L. xl. i. 448.

clearly all truths whether in itself or in it.'[1] The doctrine resembles Descartes's intuition of the 'simple natures'. Here illumination expresses the goal of intellectual endeavour. Other passages, however, teach that illumination is an active intervention by the divine power on the mind. The intellect is irradiated by God; it cannot attain to understanding by its own resources. Here the mind is given a passive role. The notions of goodness and truth are impressed on our mind as a seal imprints its shape on wax.[2] There appears to be no fundamental opposition between these two conceptions, and taken together they qualify theological difficulties inherent in each. When Augustine says that the light of truth is God Himself, it must not be supposed that he tells us that in apprehending the *rationes* of things we are directly aware of the divine mind. Malebranche claimed the authority of St. Augustine for holding that in apprehending the Ideas we are apprehending the mind of God. And from this position he proceeded to assert that we perceive corporeal objects 'in God'.[3] This is certainly not Augustine's view. 'Nor is our mind itself competent to see them (corporeal things) in God, in the actual relations in which they were created, so as to know their number and magnitude and degree, even if we do not see them through the bodily senses.'[4] But bodies are perceived by the senses, and it is only through 'the cloud of corporeal images' that we can contemplate the Ideas. The mind though rational and intellectual is a created being, and when it endeavours to behold the light, it trembles in its weakness, and is unable to attain to it.[5] Our categories, for example the category of substance, cannot be applied to God.[6] The numbers or principles to which reason points reflect a light which is beyond them. The metaphors drawn from light seem to teach, on the one hand, that the principles which guide experience are realities which the mind is led to accept; on the other, that the meaning of these realities is not finally to be appreciated by purely intellectual approach. A theological and religious standpoint bring a more comprehensive enlightenment; and the Forms are found to be revelations of God.

VII

St. Augustine dedicated his thought, from his nineteenth year, to the pursuit of *sapientia*, the contemplation of the divine order

---

[1] De Gen. ad litt. xii. 31; C.S.E.L. xxviii. i. 425. Cf. Confess. VII. xvii. 23.
[2] De Trin. XIV. xv. 21; P.L. xlii. 1052.   [3] *Recherche de la Vérité*, iii. 6.
[4] De Gen. ad litt. v. xvi; C.S.E.L. xxviii. i. 159.
[5] Ib. xii. 31; C.S.E.L. xxviii. i. 425.   [6] De Trin. VII. v. 10; P.L. xlii. 942.

implicit in the changing conditions of human experience. His theory of knowledge is a prolonged vindication of the Neoplatonic idealism through which, as we have seen, he found deliverance from the material philosophy of his early years. All his analyses of the modes of knowing have, indeed, a religious end in view. His treatises often open in a scholarly form, on a point of grammar or the definition of a term. Soon logical and metaphysical implications are debated. The philosophic discussion takes on a religious tone; and theology passes into mysticism and prayer.[1]

His philosophy is presented in a series of detached passages, which are often lacking in precision and coherence.[2] The allusiveness of his discussions and the fluidity of his terms permitted schools of varied complexion to claim his authority. But he is the principal channel through which the tradition of Greek thought passed into the reflection of Christian Europe. He taught the ages that followed the logical priority in all human experience, theoretical, moral, aesthetic, religious, of an ideal order which supplements the fragmentariness and impermanence of our temporal understanding. The universe is permeated with the divine ideas. And to them are due the order and measure upon which not only corporeal things, but also the activities of life are based.

In relation to the discussions which follow, the chief point of interest is the sanction thus given to Realism. The general features of experience and thought, the common elements in virtue of which we recognize particular men as men, or dwell in thought upon shape, or justice or knowledge, are entities subsisting beyond the sensible world, though the objects of sense provide information of them. These universal forms constitute the nature of things. They are the true objects of scientific understanding, and the further they are explored the more is revealed of the unchanging origin of the changing world of experience. This is Realism, and we have seen how profoundly it consorts with Christian beliefs. Yet we shall find it, or extreme forms of it, boldly challenged by medieval

---

[1] See, for example, De mus., bk. vi.

[2] The form of the early dialogues, with their long superficial preludes, irrelevant digressions, and verbal disputes, is deliberate. Augustine intended them to be educational exercises for his disciples. As he says, 'the subject could, of course, be concluded in a few words, but I wished to exercise you, and to prove your powers and zeal; for this is my chief concern'. Contra Acad. i. ix. 25. This point is excellently brought out by Marrou, *Saint Augustin et la fin de la culture antique* (Paris, 1938), pp. 298 ff. He shows that the logical disorder of the mature works, such as De Trinitate, is also due to a desire to lead the mind, by digressions in many analogous fields, to the contemplation of the objects of pure intelligence.

critics. But the great controversy over universals did not become acute till the appearance of the most formidable of these critics in the eleventh century. The attack of Abaelard upon Realism will be followed in some detail in the next chapter.

The distinctive circle of principles that were first asserted by Augustine persists throughout the course of Western thought; the concentration on the eternal reasons, the doctrine of illumination, the dualism of mind and body, the theory of seminal natures. It is true that from the earliest centuries Aristotelian formulae mingle with this scheme of ideas; they were taught in the Carolingian schools from the text-books of Boethius. But the more fundamental tradition, and that which formed the philosophical structure of Christian belief, was Augustinian. In the eleventh century this implicit tradition became fully articulated in the philosophy of Anselm, who rigorously developed the theological consequences of Realism. Nor did the Augustinian way of thought succumb to the advance of Aristotelianism in the thirteenth century. In fact the metaphysical principles of Aristotle were at first interpreted through the glass of preconceptions that were largely drawn from St. Augustine. When the great Aristotelian-Thomist synthesis of thought appeared, a powerful group of scholars, which included such diverse men as Roger Bacon and St. Bonaventura, asserted the claims of the older view of knowledge in opposition to the new doctrine. And in the following century many distinguished thinkers continued to maintain Augustinian positions in the face of vigorous antagonism. Wyclif, for example, proclaimed an extreme Realism, founded upon the teaching of the Bishop of Hippo. In the period of the Renaissance the philosophy of St. Augustine blended with Platonism, but characteristic features of it appeared in the metaphysics of Descartes. In England, not only arguments from Ideas but also the theory of seminal natures were employed by the Cambridge Platonists in refutation of the new materialism. And the Cambridge Platonists were studied by Coleridge.

These slight references indicate the continuity of the tradition of thought that descended from St. Augustine. But at an early stage of the development of this tradition, in the time of Augustine's greatest disciple, Anselm, there appeared a formidable critic of the orthodox view of knowledge. Abaelard's attack on Realism marks the beginning of a new outlook in philosophy. It prepared the way for the grand reconstructions of the thirteenth century.

II

ABAELARD

REFERENCES

The chief texts used in the following account are the *Logica ingredientibus* and the *Logica nostrorum petitioni sociorum* which are printed in *Beiträge zur Geschichte der Philosophie des Mittelalters*, Band xxi (1919), edited by Dr. Bernhard Geyer, pp. 1–32, and 505–83. A portion of the former work has been translated by R. McKeon in *Selections from Medieval Philosophers*, London, 1930, pp. 208–58.

I

AT the opening of the sixth century there appeared at the Court of Theodoric the Goth a scholar whose works exercised a dominant influence upon the thought of the Middle Ages. Boethius was not an original philosopher, but he was a man of eclectic culture, and in an age when few had command even of Latin he was accomplished also in the literature of Greece. His most celebrated work is *The Consolation of Philosophy*, but his philosophical importance depends upon his translations and commentaries. He had studied at Athens and in later years devoted himself to the task of translating and explaining the works of Plato and Aristotle. He succeeded in translating the logical works of Aristotle comprised in the *Organon* before he was put to death on a charge of treason in the year 525. These translations and expositions provided the foundation, until the twelfth century, for the structure of medieval logic.

Among the works of Boethius is a commentary on a treatise composed by Porphyry, a contemporary disciple of Plotinus. Porphyry's treatise is itself an introduction to the *Categories* of Aristotle. In one book of his commentary Boethius, following closely in the steps of his authority, raises a series of questions concerning general ideas or universals. This passage became at a later period the spring from which flowed the copious river of debate concerning Realism and its alternatives. The dispute forms the main theme of our sketch of medieval thought; and it is appropriate at this point to consider broadly the meaning of the issue, and to outline the influences which combined to state it in terms characteristic of medieval philosophy.

In all our perceiving and thinking we find a twofold content. We find throughout our experience singular and general elements in intimate union. The objects we perceive—furniture, people, voices, and guns—are at the same time unique and common to other objects. We perceive *this* book, *that* person; but the book is also *a* book, the person *a* person. Every item to which we direct our attention is an instance of a class or kind. To use medieval terms it is an instance of a species. But the common features in particular objects can be attended to in detachment from the features perceived by the eyes and ears and other senses. To attend to the common elements in abstraction from sensibly perceived objects is to think. We think and speak of books or flowers or bombs in general without referring to any individual book or flower or bomb. And we discuss, and in some cases devote our service to more general entities, shape, colour, learning, beauty, energy, money, the State, Democracy, mysticism. Such entities are universals. The mark of a universal is the presence of elements which appear in a number of things or events numerically distinct. It is an identity in difference. The different elements are the various aspects or instances of an enduring identity which is the subject of our thought and which is fixed in language. And since there is identity in difference throughout the scale of experience, from the perception of a single note of music to the understanding of a philosophical system, universals comprehend the whole range of apprehension and reflection. An inquiry into the nature of universals will embrace the problem of substance, the unity of attributes in things, at one end of the scale; and the validity of the science of physics, or of the Hegelian system, at the other end. It is an inquiry into the veracity of human thinking.

The problem assumed a peculiar importance in the speculation of the Middle Ages for two reasons. It had been transmitted from Greek thought in a manner which distinguished it as the crucial problem for the scientific investigation of the world. And its discussion was profoundly influenced by association with the doctrines of the Christian Faith.

The method of inquiry which is the mark of Scholasticism descends from Socrates and is portrayed in the dialogues of Plato. These conversations discuss the meaning of general notions. They are concerned with asking what some principle really is. Thus the *Charmides* seeks to define the real nature of Temperance, the *Lysis* investigates Friendship, the *Laches*, Courage; and other dialogues examine Love, Virtue, and Justice. In these discussions Socrates criticizes and rejects inadequate definitions with the aim of discovering what essentially characterizes the subject under discussion.

The implications of this method were given far wider significance by Plato. The search for essential characters became the clue to knowledge of reality. The criteria by which we judge what is real in distinction from what is unreal are objectivity, permanence, and coherence. When we reflect on the common-sense world of perception and practical life, we find on all hands variation, indefiniteness, and confusion. The scene which our naïve opinion takes as real is inextricably bound up with our eyes and ears and sense of touch, and varies with changes in them. The hill opposite looks almost perpendicular, the stone feels hot to one hand, lukewarm to the other. Our impressions are corrected by considerations which refer beyond any collection or system of impressions. The further we push the search for consistency and objectivity the more we discover universal relations underlying and connecting the mass of facts with which experience is confronted. The ideal of reason is a system of universals interconnecting all the divisions of reality.

The unities which underlie the changes and the singular aspects of things, beds, or men, or acts of bravery, are not constructions of our minds. They have a being which is independent of our knowledge of them. This principle was applied by Plato to a field which in other ways strikingly fulfilled the characteristics of reality. This is the realm of pure mathematics. Mathematical assertions and the chains of inference which are derived from them supremely display the marks of permanence, coherence, and definiteness. They are independent of the contingent circumstances of time and space; they are absolute and necessary. Plato insists that they are not inventions of our minds but fundamental constituents of reality. Nor are they abstracted from the objects of sense-perception, for they are not found in them.[1] And in very different types of experience Plato pointed to similar orders. Besides mathematical ideas there are norms of beauty and of goodness; and these too are timeless, beyond change. Thus the Ideas are not only logical principles of explanation. They are also standards of perfection.

We have seen how St. Augustine embraced these principles, deriving them in a form transmuted by religious emphasis from the writings of the Neoplatonists. And behind all the controversies of

---

[1] An affirmation of Realism in this field has been recently published in *A Mathematician's Apology*, by Prof. G. H. Hardy. 'I believe', he says, 'that mathematical reality lies outside us, that our function is to discover and *observe it*, and that the theorems which we prove, and which we describe grandiloquently as our 'creations' are simply our notes of our observations.'

the Middle Ages stood the belief that the principles of the world of
common perception were ultimately ideal types constituted by the
divine will. The controversies turned on the question whether it is
possible directly to know these forms. But to the Platonic influences we must now add some features which were inherited from
the fragments of Aristotle and from his Neoplatonic commentators.
The chief source for the knowledge of Aristotle throughout the
early Middle Ages was Boethius, and from his translations of the
elementary logical treatises further distinctions were introduced
into the tradition of Platonic Realism. In his logical writings
Aristotle had sought to make formally explicit the principle upon
which the Socratic method proceeded, and to apply it to the investigation not only of moral but of any subject of inquiry. He
discussed the manner in which the essential character of things
or concepts may be distinguished from inessential features. He
distinguished the accidental features and the properties of a thing
from its essential nature. Accidents are features which are not
necessary to the being of a thing. It is not a necessary part of
man that he should wear boots or be a soldier. But some features
are necessary to a thing which are yet not essential to it. Such
features are properties of a thing. Thus being alive is a property
of man. What further can be said of an essence of a thing? It is
found in those characters which uniquely distinguish the thing
from other things in the same class. Thus the essence of man was
found to be rationality, for it is the possession of reason which
uniquely distinguishes man from other members of the class of
living creatures. This point of distinction was termed a difference.
The search for the universal which constituted the essence of a
species was the search for a definition which expressed the difference of the species within its class or genus. We shall find these
conceptions frequently recurring in the discussions which follow.
The implications for medieval thought of this method of investigation were momentous.

For it was implied that the universal essence of anything, a stone
or a man or piety, can only be defined in one way. It is assumed
that everything possesses a fixed and definite essence. Reality is
composed of a system of unalterable and ultimate entities to which
are attached numerous qualities of varying degrees of relevance.
Philosophical definitions are not relative. An entity, flower or heat
or humanity, cannot be defined in one way at one time and in
another way at another time; for this would be to deny it any

essential qualities. An entity cannot be one thing at one time and another thing at the next moment; if things were in a state of continual flux knowledge would be impossible. If we are to hold to the distinction between reality and appearance, and between truth and error, we are driven to assume that everything has a determinate essence, and that there is one and only one final definition of it. And the method is ruled by the theory. The emphasis is on formal classification into species and genera. In alliance with Biblical conceptions this point of view arrested the development of natural knowledge. By supposing a vast hierarchy of qualitatively different entities it regressed from the insight of the Platonic claim for mathematics in the field of physical science. And in the realm of organisms it precluded any notion of development. But the Aristotelian logic was the mistress of exact thinking in the Middle Ages.

For the few isolated groups of scholars who were in touch by slender threads with the fragments of Greek thought, Realism was philosophy. They learnt it too from the greatest Christian philosopher, St. Augustine. Singular entities, this fever, that person, are what they are only in virtue of the common nature apprehended by thought. In reflecting on the nature of the general essences and the singular cases which reveal them, later philosophers were led to adopt positions which became the target for the shafts of Abaelard. The peculiar form of being which is enjoyed by universals was termed *subsistence* in order to distinguish it from the *existence* of physical entities. Subsistences became fundamental kinds of things side by side with individual objects. Augustinian Realism developed into an extreme Realism in which universals subsist apart from the world of particular colours and shapes and sounds. And yet they are identical essences appearing in different particular things and events. The result is that the singular features which distinguish this man or this book from others of the same species are conceived of as external and adventitious to the essences man and book. Such were some of the dangerous tendencies to which Augustinian Realism was exposed. But this extreme Realism is criticized so thoroughly by Abaelard in the passages which we are shortly to report that it is unnecessary to describe its lineaments further at this point. In modern terms what he attacked was the hypostatization of abstract ideas. Nominalism was a natural reaction to this uncompromising Realism.

But in addition to the traditional and logical sanctions which

have been touched upon there was a second influence which profoundly encouraged a Realistic interpretation of experience. The
belief that universal notions refer to independent realities found
support in the writings of the Fathers and in the rational justifica-
tion of the Faith. The study of Plato was recommended by
Clement and Origen, and the Realism of Augustine dominated the
schools until the eleventh century. We have seen how well
Platonism accorded with the Christian outlook. It envisaged a
realm of absolute, eternal and super-individual realities, arche-
types of all particular and perishing things. Christian thought
interpreted the Forms as divine Ideas, and conceived creation
after the manner of an artist and his works. The realm of Ideas was
also the realm of absolute values, a region infinitely more abiding
than anything revealed to man's senses. The approximate virtues
of the world participate in the eternal heaven of goodness. Reason
and Christian Faith met in this doctrine of the objectivity and
unity of moral judgements. And when we pass from the dogmas of
creation and of the attributes of God to other points of the Creed
we find Realistic arguments employed in their defence. They were
used in discourses on the dogma of the Trinity. If individuals and
not universals are the primary reality the doctrine of the unity of
the Godhead is endangered. If it is denied that persons are one in
virtue of their humanity, it follows that the Persons of the Trinity
do not constitute a substantial unity in virtue of their Divinity.
We shall find Anselm pressing this contention against the Nominalists. Again, Realism was applied to the most sacred practice of
religion. In the ninth century the belief had been formulated that
the consecrated elements of the Mass were transformed literally
into the body and blood of Christ. Its crudity was challenged,
notably by Berengar of Tours, and theologians, led by Lanfranc,
sought to defend the popular faith by drawing a distinction between
the real substance or universal and the accidents of bread and wine.
The real substance of the elements was transformed by the act of
the priest into the substance of the body and blood of Christ, while
the accidents or sensible appearances of the bread and wine
remained unaltered. This is the dogma of Transubstantiation.
And its theoretical basis is realistic, dependent on the distinction between universals apprehended by the understanding, and
sensible expressions of them which are inessential accidents of
real natures.

Finally, medieval social ideas were coloured with Realism.

Corporations were prior to individuals, as the universal was prior to its particulars. Dominating all activities there was the pervasive and unifying reality of the Church. And numerous institutions, the Papacy, the great monastic orders, the ecclesiastical schools, the universities, the towns, the guilds, the manors, and many other corporate personalities expressed the medieval confidence in Realist principles. In our own day there has been a portentous revival of extreme Realism in European politics.

II

Let us now return to Boethius. In the prevailing Realism of the early Middle Ages the questions which he propounded in his commentary on Porphyry provoked no serious controversy for four centuries. Yet the questions raise fundamental considerations for the traditional view of knowledge, and Boethius' own discussion of them offers suggestions which should have startled a more cultured age into discussion. The famous passage is found in the second edition of the commentary on Porphyry's Introduction.[1]

The first problem is: Do we think of species and genera as existing in the same way as objects which we perceive? Are we mistaken when we suppose that general terms, or universals, refer to real entities? Are they no more than the products of our mental processes, having no counterpart in the real world? But secondly, even if it were established that general classes exist in reality, a further and more difficult question arises. What is the nature of these entities? Everything is either material or immaterial. To which order do genus and species belong? Even though we were to succeed in answering these questions, a third problem remains. For if we were to conclude that genus and species were immaterial substances we should be driven to consider their relation to physical objects. Do they subsist with material things (*circa corpora*), or are they immaterial forms of being subsisting apart from material things (*praeter corpora*)? Boethius gives examples of each class. There are immaterial spiritual substances such as God, mind, and the soul, which can exist apart from material things. There are others, such as line, surface, and number, which cannot be separated from bodies without ceasing to be.

The first question is whether universals have being indepen-

---

[1] C.S.E.L. xlviii. 160.

dently of our minds. The characteristic of the general notion or universal is that it is common to many things at once. Boethius points out that this characteristic cannot apply to any simple single entity. The genus, such as animal, is present in each species of men, and present as a whole in each. But if so the genus cannot be one, from which it follows that it is nothing existing at all. For everything which exists is a single entity. The same difficulty can be applied to species. On the other hand, if genus is one it cannot be common to many, for when a single thing is common to many things it is not common to each as a whole. Each of the many share a part of the single thing, or use it at different times. But universals such as genera are said to be not only entirely in each individual at the same time, but to constitute the substance of the individuals to which they are common. Since, therefore, the universal is neither one nor many it does not exist at all.

This is a challenging conclusion. It is directed against a crude literalism which conceived the universal as a kind of thing similar to other existing things. Boethius now proceeds to a description of universals in a passage wherein Aristotelian views are introduced to his age. By the process of abstraction the mind attains ideas which though they do not refer to real objects are not therefore false. The mind receives from the senses a confused mass of impressions. It has the power of uniting what is given in perception as distinct and of separating what it finds united. Thus it apprehends the notion of a line in separation from the notion of a body. Similarly it contemplates genera and other universals apart from the sensible objects in which they actually inhere. The activity of thought consists in noting the common characteristics in a number of different individuals and in comprehending these similar features in themselves. To Porphyry's questions, therefore, Boethius answers firstly that universals are real features of sensible objects. They are implicitly perceived in objects, they become explicit and intelligible through the work of the understanding. Secondly they are immaterial, though they have no substantial existence apart from sensible things. The third question, whether universals exist independently of bodies, is thus also answered.[1]

Boethius has turned from the interpretation of universals in a metaphysical sense as Platonic Ideas, to a psychological account of the formation of abstract concepts. The presupposition of this

[1] C.S.E.L. xlviii. 84–5.

description is that substantial existence is found not in Forms but in sensible objects. It foreshadows the Moderate Realism of the twelfth century. But it must be added that Boethius is here acting as a faithful expositor of Aristotle. He says emphatically that he himself does not hold this interpretation. In other writings he adheres to a Platonic position.

These suggestions were not pursued far in the Dark Ages. And in the centuries which succeeded the work of Boethius the theory of knowledge proposed by St. Augustine prevailed. In the eighth century Alcuin of York recommended him above all philosophers. And in the following century a great system of Neoplatonic thought was propounded by John Scotus Erigena. For him the universal is the essential reality from which the particular is derived; and it is the more real in proportion to its universality. The logical hierarchy of concepts is the scheme of reality, and the most comprehensive abstraction is the fullest Being. The eternal Forms or Ideas are in God and are expressions of the divine will. But genera and species are not true Forms. In spite of his Platonic sympathies it is doubtful whether Erigena can be termed a Realist. For the proper objects of dialectic for him are not the eternal Forms but genera and species, which are found in material things. Yet these secondary forms proceed ultimately from the true Forms.

John Scotus Erigena translated the work of 'Dionysius the Areopagite', a Christian forgery based upon the writings of the Neoplatonist, Proclus. This work continued to exercise an influence throughout the Middle Ages.

But it was not until the generation preceding that of Abaelard that the problem of the status of universals was acutely revived. Controversy was suddenly excited throughout the schools of Europe by the appearance of the unorthodox thesis of extreme Nominalism. The most prominent advocate of this heretical doctrine was Roscelin of Compiègne (1050—circa 1125). Unfortunately little of the writings of this original thinker have so far been discovered and we are left to infer his views from the remarks of his critics, such as St. Anselm and Abaelard.

Concepts and propositions do not express reality. What they express are various forms of assertion determined by the rules of grammar and by arbitrary meanings. Language does not express things as they are, for it names wholes of things, whereas in reality there are only indivisible sensible entities, which do not compose the wholes named by terms. And just as it regards the distinction of parts within an individual as purely subjective, so this theory considers the totality of several individuals as an arbitrary collection. Accordingly, general ideas, universals, are merely names, *nomina*, and even noises, *flatus vocis*. The common nature which they assert is wholly subjective.

The theory had been advanced in Greece by many thinkers; by Democritus, by the Sophist Gorgias, and by the Epicureans. But for the Middle Ages it was heresy. At the basis of this Nominalism lies an empiricist theory of knowledge. As Anslem says: 'In the minds of these philosophers reason, which ought to be the guide and judge of all that exists in men, is so wrapped up in material imaginations, that it cannot extricate itself from them, nor distinguish from them those things which ought to be contemplated in their intrinsic purity.'[1]

The lively antagonism excited by this theory was, however, less due to its logical novelty than to the fact that it conflicted with theological orthodoxy. It appeared, for example, to involve a denial of the doctrine of the Trinity. Anselm warmly pointed out that anyone who could not grasp the way in which many individual men are one in the species man, could not admit that several Persons are united in one God. And the man who found it difficult to distinguish between his horse and its colour could hardly distinguish between God and His attributes.[2] Roscelin was indicted for Tritheism. But for our purposes the important step taken by Roscelin was that it rejected any reference to reality in general conceptions. *Universale est vox.* The contrast with Realism is complete. For Realism the universal resides in the nature governing the individual. For Nominalism this unity resides only in the common term.[3]

We shall find that in spite of the scornful language which Abaelard uses concerning Roscelin, describing him as a *pseudo-dialecticus* and even as a *pseudo-christianus*, his own doctrine of universals bears the impress of the teaching he received from the revolutionary philosopher of Compiègne. And when he passed from the school of Roscelin to the lectures of the leading champion of Realism, William of Champeaux, he was able to criticize his master's position by arguments which he had learnt from Roscelin. His attacks on Roscelin are on the ground rather of theology than of

[1] Anselm, *De Fide Trinitatis*, 2; P.L. clviii. 265.   [2] Ib.
[3] Nominalism is treated more fully in Chapter IV.

logic; though we shall find that Abaelard departed in a significant way from the Nominalism of his first master. Before proceeding to unfold the manner in which he met the situation let us glance at his character and history.

III

Peter Abaelard was born in 1079 at Pallot, near Nantes, in Brittany. As a youth he had the singular good fortune to receive instruction from two masters who taught opposing principles of philosophy, Roscelin and William of Champeaux. This education sharpened his native facility in dialectical controversy and he displayed early the qualities of a brilliant teacher and philosopher. His fame as a logician brought throngs of young students to his lectures. They followed him from place to place, delighting not only in his extraordinary skill in disputation but also in his trenchant way with opponents. His ruthless methods earned him the formidable nickname of *rhinocerus indomitus*. At Paris he engaged his former teacher, William of Champeaux, in sharp debate on the dominant issue of the day, the problem of the status of universals; and his resounding success excited the jealousy and suspicion of the established schools. For many years he drew eager bands of scholars to the slopes of St. Geneviève. Abaelard had so far directed his impetuous but clear intellect to logical questions, but at the age of thirty-four he suddenly deserted dialectics for theology, and put himself to school with the most famous masters of theology in France. But once more he soon changed the rôle of pupil for that of rival instructor; nor did he scruple to declare his contempt for the learning of his masters. He resumed his lectures at Paris, discoursing now on theology as well as on philosophy. Here he met Heloïse. The tragic story of their relations, the most famous and the most affecting romance of the Middle Ages, has often been told. It was succeeded by a period of profound bitterness, during which the philosopher secluded himself in the monastery of St. Denys. He emerged with powers enhanced. The renown of his teaching spread through Europe. In after years a friend in writing to him thus describes this period of his career:

'The fearful seas of the Channel were no terror to the throng of English youths; at the sound of your name they scorned every danger, and flocked to hear you. The distant regions of Brittany sent its savages to be taught by you. The inhabitants of Anjou curbing their natural brutality, came humbly to sit at your feet. Natives of Scotland, of the

Pyrenees, of Ireland; Teutons and Swabians from Normandy and Flanders were roused to fervour by your genius.'

Allowing for some amicable flattery in this description, it is manifest that Abaelard was at this time the supreme teacher of the age. From the vast concourse of students who crowded to hear him lecture at Paris or Nôgent-sur-Seine sprang the first and greatest of the medieval universities.

Meanwhile his enemies were watching. The publication of his book *On the Trinity* gave them their opportunity. A special council was called at Soissons and the book was solemnly condemned. Abaelard found himself an outcast. But the devotion of the wandering scholars would not leave him to the solitude to which he had retired. They gathered round him at Nôgent-sur-Seine, rebuilt his hut, erected a lecture hall, and established the brotherhood of the Paraclete. A few years later, on the departure of Abaelard and his pupils, the buildings were transferred to the sisterhood of which Heloïse was now a member.

After many turns of fortune, during which he narrowly escaped destruction at the hands of his enemies, Abaelard returned to Paris. Now at length he was confronted with an opponent more formidable than any whom he had faced before. Certain of his utterances had been brought to the notice of Bernard, Abbot of Clairvaux. The great religious leader was gravely disturbed by the unorthodoxy which he detected in them. A debate between Bernard and Abaelard was arranged to take place at Sens, though Bernard shrank from the prospect of meeting the great controversialist. It was Abaelard, however, who declined the contest. He appealed to Rome. The Pope, acting under the guidance of Bernard, condemned Abaelard to silence, and his disciples to excommunication. He set out to Rome to plead his cause. On the way he stayed at the Abbey of Cluny and was persuaded to remain there. For two years he was suffered to live in peace, 'allowing no moment to escape unoccupied by prayer, reading, writing, or dictation'. At the end of this period, in 1142, he died at the age of sixty-three.

There are few more impressive figures in the Middle Ages than Peter Abaelard. If he had lived four centuries later he would have been regarded as a signal example of the versatile individuality of the Renaissance. He was the pre-eminent poet of his time in secular as well as in religious verse. The self-revelation of the letters to Heloïse rivals the intimacy of the age of Cellini or

Montaigne. And the varied interests which they show, delight in the beauty of this world, in the literature of paganism, in the pleasures of life, express the very spirit of Humanism. But the main concern of Abaelard's stormy and tragic life was philosophy, and philosophy in the service of religion. 'I have no wish to be a philosopher,' he wrote to Heloïse, 'if I must abandon my allegiance to Paul; I do not desire to become Aristotle if I must separate myself from Christ.'

In addition to the *Dialectica* and other logical works he wrote an ethical dialogue, *Scito te ipsum*, in which the inward rule of conscience is vindicated, even though God should appear to enjoin otherwise. An early theological work, the celebrated *Sic et Non*, is a collection of contradictory statements to be found in the Bible and the Fathers. It was composed in order to stimulate students to exercise their wits upon the problems of theology.

Abaelard composed a number of treatises on logic in the course of which the problem of universals is discussed at length. These treatises consist, for the most part, of commentaries on the works of Porphyry and of Boethius. From these writings we may select for consideration portions of two commentaries known from their opening words as the *Logica ingredientibus*, 'Logic for Beginners', and the *Logica nostrorum petitioni sociorum*, 'Written in response to the request of our friends'.[1] We are to follow somewhat closely his discussion in these treatises. They are valuable sources for the philosophical interests of the beginning of the twelfth century, for Abaelard is at pains to describe carefully the theories which he is attacking. In the vigorous and often sardonic criticism to which he subjects the orthodox views we hear an echo of the challenging methods of the *rhinocerus indomitus* and catch a glimpse of the eager crowded debates at Nôtre Dame or Nôgent.

IV

Abaelard introduces the discussion by recalling Porphyry's questions. He had inquired, in the first place, whether universals, such as man, animal, rose, exist apart from the mind that conceives them. Are they no more than mental operations? Secondly, if it is found that universal entities actually exist, that rose in general is a form of being not dependent on the mental process that apprehends

---

[1] The texts are to be found in *Beiträge zur Geschichte der Philosophie des Mittelalters*, Band xxi (1919), edited by Dr. Bernhard Geyer, pp. 1–32 and 505–83. The references which follow give the pages of the text in the *Beiträge*.

it, what is the nature of these forms of being? Are they material or immaterial substances? Thirdly, the problem of their relation to the objects perceived by the senses arises. Do they exist apart from sensible objects or are they united with them? To these questions of Porphyry, Abaelard adds a further inquiry concerning the relation between the individual instances and the universal term. If the objects to which the general name refers were abolished, could the universal retain a meaning for thought? For example, could the generic term rose continue to have significance if no particular roses were to exist?[1]

These problems are approached by means of a survey of current doctrines. The main division is between those philosophers who hold that universals are only words (*voces*) and those who maintain that they refer also to things (*res*). And since genera and species are acknowledged to be universals, we are invited to inquire into the nature of universals by an examination of these types. At the outset it is necessary to be agreed upon the general meaning of the terms universal and particular. Here Abaelard cites the accepted Aristotelian definition. A universal is that which refers to many items at once, *quod de pluribus natum est aptum praedicari*. It embraces a number of different particulars; flower refers to all types and colour and shapes of flowers. A particular or an individual, according to Porphyry, is asserted only of one item. We shall find that these traditional definitions are strictly adhered to during the discussion. Abaelard next cites the main authorities. Aristotle and Porphyry state that universals are things, but Aristotle in another passage, and Boethius, assert that they are names or terms, *nomina*. They are said to be signs of the way in which things are determined. If this latter version were accepted we should be obliged to deny that universals are species in the realist sense, for a term is not a substantial thing but an accident. Yet terms can be accepted as universals, for they can be asserted of many things. This interpretation, for which he here claims high authority, is, in fact, close to Abaelard's own position; and he anticipates his conclusion in the phrase that words which are universal terms perform the function of predicates of propositions.[2]

The first school of contemporary thought to be considered is the teaching of emphatic Realism. It is the doctrine that universals are kinds of object, existing independently of the mind. What is the meaning of this account? How can any thing, or even a

[1] p. 8.   [2] pp. 9–10.

collection of things, be asserted of many things? This house, and
Socrates, are instances of things. How can they be asserted of
many things? How can universals be things? Let us consider by
what arguments this theory is defended.[1]

The view that universals are *res* holds that they are the substantial essences manifested in a number of particular instances, the
particular instances differing from one another only in their forms,
that is to say, in their special natures. The universal essence of a
class of things, such as men, is one; it assumes variety by becoming
embodied in forms of differing degrees of particularity. Now,
consider the logic of this position. If these particular modifications of the identical substance were removed there would be no
difference whatsoever between particular things. All things would
be the same. 'Man', for example, is the single material essence of
both Plato and Socrates. The modifications of the identical substance in virtue of which Plato and Socrates are individuals with
different characteristics are accidents. These individual characteristics may be present or absent without affecting the essence of
man. So, too, creatures which differ in kind are presumed to
be expressions of the essential and identical substance, animal.
The different kinds of animals are derived by assuming that a
number of accidental differences have been introduced into the
identical substance. This substance is like a piece of wax that can
be moulded into many shapes; though the analogy is not precise,
since the material of the universal substance remains the same in
all the models which are made from it. The universal, then, becomes individual by means of external, adventitious forms. In the
language of this school, it is said to *subsist* in itself naturally or in
reality, apart from its forms, but to *exist* actually, through the
forms or physical expressions of it. The real subsistence of the
universal can be apprehended only by pure thought or understanding, *intellectus*, untouched by sense-perception. And thought
apprehends it as immaterial and absolute.[2]

Such is Abaelard's summary of extreme Realism. The doctrine
was endowed, as we have seen, with high sanction. And, as he
here observes, it was the dominant theory of the time. He makes
no mention of the arguments from which it drew its strength. He
describes only the conclusion which it reaches, that genuine substances are principles apprehended in general ideas. And these
realities that underlie the changing and manifold objects of percep-

[1] p. 10.   [2] pp. 10–11.

tion retain their identity unaffected by change and difference. In this Platonic and Augustinian citadel of thought Abaelard, for the first time, makes a formidable breach.

His first criticism of the doctrine is that it destroys all distinctions between things. The doctrine implies that one thing is in essence the same as another thing, however different its special forms may be. Consequently a rational animal will be the same in essence as an irrational animal. Two individuals, in fact, possessing contrary or incompatible qualities will be fundamentally the same. And this contravenes the rule that contrary qualities cannot exist at the same time in the same thing. It is true that some qualities that appear to be incompatible may occur in the same substance without being really incompatible. Thus 'great' and 'small' can both be present in the same thing at the same time. The thing is great in one respect and small in another. But this explanation does not apply to qualities such as rationality and irrationality. These are genuinely incompatible.[1]

It may be said that, in spite of this contradiction, these qualities are actually found existing together in the same individual, for example, in Socrates. But if they are both in Socrates at the same time, they must be not only in Socrates but also in an ass at the same time. For, in this philosophy, Socrates and the ass are fundamentally the same being; both are, in essence, animal. Whatever is present in Socrates apart from the peculiar and accidental characteristics of Socrates is identical with what is present in the ass apart from the accidental characteristics of the ass. The features that make the ass Socrates and Socrates the ass are essential features. The individual differences between them are external and accidental.[2] The force of the argument rests, in part, upon the sharp division assumed in medieval thought between man and other animals. An ass could not be rational. Yet on this theory it inevitably follows that it is. But the main point is that by making individual differences adjectival or superficial, everything becomes everything else and clear thinking becomes impossible.

Some realists, he proceeds, seek to escape these conclusions by affirming that the difficulties are verbal. No real contradiction is involved in saying that a rational animal is also an irrational animal. Certainly the words refer to the same thing, namely, animal. But they signify that it is rational in one respect and irrational in another. They refer in fact, not to the thing's essence,

[1] p. 11.   [2] pp. 11–12, 515.

but to its forms or specific features. And forms, since they are relative and accidental, may occur together without conflicting. There is no contradiction in such propositions as 'a rational animal is a mortal animal' and 'a white animal is an animal which walks'. Rationality and mortality, whiteness and walking, are not mutually exclusive terms; each pair of terms may qualify a subject at the same time without contradiction. Otherwise one might as well say that no animal is man because nothing, in so far as it is animal, is man.[1] In this way the identity of substances may be defended in spite of the presence in them of contrary forms.

But Abaelard rejects this argument, not by insisting further on the incompatibility of some forms in a substance which is presumed to be identical, but by denying that forms can serve to distinguish particular expressions of substance. For they too dissolve into identity. His reasoning here is based on the Aristotelian doctrine of categories. There are ten modes into which things may be fundamentally classified. Substance, quantity, quality, relation are examples of these fundamental classifications. Now substance is presupposed by all the other categories. Variety is due to the forms by which the substantial and general characters are made particular. But since each of the categories expresses essence or substance all instances of them are fundamentally identical. Two individuals, Socrates and Plato, contain in themselves characteristics belonging to each of the categories. Since each of these features are fundamentally the same all the forms of one are also forms of the other. Forms, therefore, do not serve to distinguish individuals any more than substances distinguish them. For they too dissolve into substance.[1]

Abaelard does not scruple to bring a charge of heresy against the doctrine. For if it be admitted, it would follow that the divine substance which excludes all forms is identical with physical substance, that is to say, primary matter, which also excludes them.[2] This ingenious accusation of pantheism must have sorely tried William of Champeaux. And further difficulties are pressed with inexhaustible persistence. We need not describe them all here. He concludes this part of his examination by reiterating the point that the differences between individuals cannot rest upon accidents. The qualities that constitute the nature of a thing must be intrinsic to its nature, not external features of it. And if these qualities constitute the nature of a thing they must be universals.

[1] p. 12.   [2] p. 515.

The suggestion here is that there is a manifold variety of independent substances.[1]

The doctrine that universality lies in a metaphysical identity
which is the essential nature of things has been rejected. Abaelard
now turns to examine the teaching of a more recent variety of
Realism, a version which in his view comes nearer to the truth than
the theory which he has so far been discussing. This type of
Realism is known as the doctrine of *indifference*. We have notices
that it was the doctrine which William of Champeaux was driven
to uphold in the face of Abaelard's criticisms of orthodox Realism.
This theory departs so far from Realism as to accept a pluralist
basis of knowledge. Individual things not only differ from one
another in their forms, the features which distinguish them in
their species, but are substantially distinct existences. What exists
in one thing does not in any way exist in another thing, whether
it be a point of matter (the uniform underlying substance of
things) or of form (the determinate expression). If these differences
were not ultimate we should be led into an infinite regress; we
should be obliged to refer the different forms or essences to more
fundamental forms or essences, and so *ad infinitum*. But this
school of thought while holding that all things are fundamentally
distinct from one another, contrive at the same time to believe in
universals. How do they reconcile this belief with their pluralist
principles? They teach that things which are distinct are yet the
same not essentially but *indifferently*, that is to say in so far as they
are not different. The upshot of this view is that the same thing
may be described as universal or particular according to the way in
which it is taken. Things have universal characteristics in so far
as they share the same characteristics. Individual men are man in
so far as they resemble one another. They are individual and
particular in so far as they differ from one another.

Abaelard's examination of this position relies upon a literal
adherence to the preliminary definitions. These philosophers say
that individuals are themselves universals in virtue of their similarity to other individuals. Similar individuals, let us say trees, are
referred to as classes or universals, not because they are in essence
universals, but because numbers of individuals are like them. But
this conflicts with the definition of individual, namely, that it is one,
not many. One thing taken by itself cannot resemble anything
else. And how is it possible on this theory to distinguish between

[1] p. 13.

a universal and a particular by reference to predication? For in the same way in which 'man' expresses the common features of numbers of particular men, an individual such as Socrates also resembles many men. Certainly man in so far as he is man, and Socrates in so far as he is man, resembles others. But neither man in so far as he is Socrates, nor Socrates in so far as he is Socrates, resembles others. On this view 'man' and 'Socrates' are defined in the same way. Universals and particulars are not therefore distinguished.[1]

The general entity man which is in Socrates and the individual Socrates himself refer to the same being; just as Socrates is at the same time white and a grammarian. But though these characteristics are in him, they are not different from him. The fact that he is white or a grammarian cannot be distinguished from himself. It is said that Socrates resembles Plato in the fact of being man. But men differ from one another both in matter and form. As himself Socrates is different from Plato. The phrase 'resemblance in the fact of man' is taken by some authorities in a negative sense, to imply that Socrates does not differ from Plato in being man. Here Abaelard is recording the reply made by William of Champeaux to his own earlier criticisms. It is certainly not a happy contribution to the debate. It is like saying, he caustically observes, that Socrates does not differ from Plato in being stone, since neither is a stone. If the proposition is taken affirmatively, that they do not differ in being man, it is false. For if Socrates does differ from Plato in being man, he does not differ from him in himself. If he differs in himself from him, while he is himself the thing which is man, he must also differ from himself in the same respect.[1]

In the discussion over universals philosophers were fond of using the phrases 'in so far as', or 'to the extent of'. Abaelard finds them ambiguous and confusing. As an aid towards a clearer definition of the universal or of the particular, such limiting phrases are useless. In place of the definition 'the genus is that which refers to many things' is substituted the definition 'the genus, to the extent of being a genus, refers to many'. This phrase throws no further light upon the nature of genus; it merely repeats the subject which is to be defined. And so when it is said that men are identical in so far as they are men, the question remains what nature and status this identity possesses. Moreover, how is it possible on this theory to distinguish between the genus or universal and the individual?

The genus is defined as that which refers to many. But the individual is also said to be universal in this sense. An individual man is said also to be man, and even animal. These philosophers attempt to distinguish between the two on the ground that genus in its capacity of being individual is excluded from this definition. But the description is not applied to the genus nor to the individual absolutely (*simpliciter*) but only 'in respect of being' genus, and 'in respect of being' individual. They are not, therefore, distinguished, since what is asserted concerning genus can be with equal truth asserted of the individual, for both refer, in an absolute sense, to the same thing. It is impossible, in fact, to combine a clearly distinct and a relative sense of the terms universal and particular; and this is what the Indifference theory tries to do.

Again, it is said that the proposition 'a man is walking' is false for the species, but true for the particular. How can this distinction be maintained if the same thing is both species and particular? It is replied that the universal man in so far as it is universal does not walk. This is like saying 'a man, in so far as he is an animal, does not have a head'. It could equally well be said that a particular man in so far as he is a particular man has no head, nor walks; or that, in so far as a being is rational, it is not mortal.[1] But there are conflicts of opinion within this school of thought, and Abaelard proceeds to discuss a further interpretation of the general doctrine which seeks to combine a belief in the uniqueness of things with an acceptance of their universality. One party maintained this position by proclaiming the doctrine of *collectio*. A universal is no more than a collection of things. Individuals such as Socrates or Plato are not species in themselves; all individual men taken together constitute the species man, all individual animals collected into one unit form the genus animal. Another group of philosophers combined this interpretation of the universal with the view discussed above. They asserted that a species is not only the collection of individuals, but is also in an individual in so far as it is also universal. When these philosophers say that the particular object Socrates is asserted of many they intend the description to be taken in a figurative sense as meaning many are the same as he, or he has qualities which correspond with those of other men. Consequently, they postulate as many species and genera as there are individuals, but according to the similarity between different things they assume a smaller number of universals.[2]

[1] Cf. p. 37.　　　[2] p. 14.

Against the view that universals are collections of things Abaelard brings the following objections. How can the mass of men
taken as one, he asks, be asserted of many? If what is meant is
that the whole is asserted part by part of many different things, so
that distinct portions of the whole refer to different things, then
the doctrine has no bearing on the nature of universals, as or-
dinarily understood, that nature which the doctrine professes to
explain. For universals are understood to be pervasive, that is to
say, they exist wholly in each individual. The relation of the
universal to individuals does not consist in the relation of parts
to a whole, as parts of a field are shared between different persons.
On this interpretation any individual, such as Socrates, would be
a universal since it includes many parts. And any group of men
would constitute a universal or a species. Any type of material
or mental collection of entities would be a universal substance.
A combination of collections of substances would constitute a
supreme genus or class. If one group were taken away, the
remaining groups, since they formed a total, would form a supreme
class. Consequently groups could be classified in different ways
to form a supreme class. But (Abaelard appeals to an accepted
principle of logic) there cannot be any number of supreme genera.
It may be replied that no collection of things which is included
under the supreme genus is itself a supreme genus. But it is still
true that when one collection or substance is taken away from the
total collection of substances, if the remaining collection is not
the supreme genus, it must be a species. For it is a universal. And
if it is a species it must possess a correlative species under its genus.
What could this be? For there would be no other collection to form
a species.

Further, every universal is said to be prior in nature to its
individuals of which it is composed. Again a collective whole and a
universal are traditionally distinguished thus; in a collection the
part is different from the whole, in a universal the species is the same
as the genus, in the sense that the genus is implicit in the species.
But how can the total number of men constitute the aggregate of
animals?[1] For these reasons the doctrine that the universal is a
collection of things must be put aside.

Abaelard has now concluded the first part of his discussion.
What is the significance of the series of criticisms which we have
been following? Contemporary philosophic thought was preoccu-

[1] p. 15.

pied with the problem of the meaning of general terms, for reasons which we here outlined above. The identity of characteristics in things was considered to be a fundamental kind of thing. General terms referred to types of real being. These types of reality are immanent in all the particular instances which are comprehended in the universal term, in all reds and men. But the cardinal point of this theory was that the particular instances are inessential features of these realities. The particular reds, the individual men, are accidents. They are appearances, expressions of realities whose nature is utterly different from them. For these realities are general; and they are the only genuine realities. It is these assertions of Realism, that individuals are radically distinct from universals and that individuals are unreal, which Abaelard mercilessly assails. He exposes the monistic consequences of the doctrine; everything would, in the end, be everything else. He unmasks its contradictions; the multiplicity of things is traced to the presence of accidents, yet there are said to be many immaterial substances. And he exhibits the confusions into which defenders of the doctrine were led by such resorts as the Indifference theory, and the interpretation of universals as an assemblage of particulars. The positive outcome of his assault on these types of Realism is that the manifold variety of things is not an illusion. The negative result is the destruction of extreme Realism. By the former conclusion a more careful restatement of Realism was made necessary in closer sympathy with Aristotelian conceptions, in which the empirical aspects of experience should be recognized. The intimate association of Realism with the principles of Faith is a measure of Abaelard's achievement in criticism. It is not to be wondered at that the rumours of his onslaught stirred Europe and drew throngs of earnest scholars to the lectures on the slopes of St. Geneviève. Far-reaching changes in philosophy were due; Abaelard's attacks on the incautious Realism prevalent in his day opened men's minds for the renaissance of Aristotelian thought in the thirteenth century.

V

Abaelard now turns to the second part of the inquiry into contemporary theories of universals. The theories that remain to be considered assert that universals are not things but words. But Nominalism is not treated in the critical vein in which Realism has been approached. The extreme form advocated by Roscelin, that universals are *voces*, mere words, is repudiated. It is simply pointed out that words express meaning, and the discussion passes on to analyse the meaning of terms. This leads to an account of Abaelard's own theory in which the problems of universals find solution.

He turns, as is usual with him, to consider language. In what way can words function as universals? The grammarians name certain terms *appellative* and others *proper*. The former refer to a general class, the latter to individuals. In a parallel way, philosophers name certain elementary forms of discourse (*sermones*) universals, and others particulars. A universal word is one which is designed to be predicated as a single word of many items at once. The term 'man' can be united to the particular names of many men. A particular word can be referred to one subject only, such as the word 'Socrates', so long as it indicates one particular person. But, Abaelard points out, grammatical parallels will not take us far. The construction of sentences in which the philosopher is concerned are different operations. The grammarian is occupied with the formal conjunction of any nominative term with another term by means of the copula 'is'. The philosopher is interested in the meaning of sentences. He is concerned with the status of the objects to which terms refer. No error of grammar is contained in the proposition 'man is a stone'; in philosophy the statement is inadmissible.[1]

He now attacks the problem directly. Let us, he says, carefully investigate the property of universal words. It is a matter of some difficulty. They do not appear to refer to anything, nor to give a clear conception of anything. The universal 'man' does not apply to any definite person, nor, as we have seen, to the whole body of men. We have noticed that certain philosophers suppose that universal terms refer to the individual in so far as he is man. If in fact Socrates alone is sitting in this house, then the proposition 'a man is sitting in this house' is true. But the universal term 'man' does not necessarily designate Socrates. Otherwise we could infer from the proposition that the man sitting in this house was Socrates. To what, then, do universal terms refer?[2]

General terms, it is insisted, are not, as the Nominalists averred, merely words, but refer to general notions. The word 'man' is a name given to individuals in virtue of an element which is common to many individuals. If we are to avoid a return to Realism we

[1] pp. 16–17.   [2] p. 18.

must examine this common principle more closely. Is the term called common because of a common nature in which different things share? Or is the common character imputed to things by the mind? Or is it due to both principles?[1]

The common or general nature to which universal terms refer calls first for consideration. Individual men are distinct from one another both in form and essence. But they are united in the fact that they are men. Now this does not mean that different men are united in the entity man. No such entity exists. In saying that individuals are united in being man the words do not refer to any essence. The nature of man or of any universal (he is never tired of insisting) is not a thing. What, then, is it? He terms it a *status*, which we may translate 'a thing's nature in the order of things'. The common principle in virtue of which the universal term is attached to things is to be found in the fact that individual things can be grouped together in thought on the basis of identical features; but the groups are not also real objects, still less essences. Identity is a relation between things. The common features which are discerned in different men belong indeed to the real nature of men. The mind apprehends these common qualities through the process of forming conceptions.

This position, in admitting a common nature in things, is so far realist, though Abaelard is anxious not to identify this nature with the transcendent object of the extreme realists. But let us follow his further explanations. The key to the problem he finds in a psychological analysis of the processes of knowledge. He turns from metaphysical inquiries concerning the common nature to which concepts refer to discuss the operation of conceiving itself. He sketches the components of knowledge in the following terms.

Sense-perception and pure thought (*intellectus*) are sharply distinguished from one another. Both perception and thought are activities of the mind. But perception is exercised through bodily instruments, and senses perceive only bodies and what are in them. Thought does not require a bodily instrument and in consequence does not need a physical object. It is satisfied with the image of a thing. The mind forms this representation for itself, directing the activity of its intelligence upon it. I perceive a tower standing in the plain. If the tower is removed sense-perception vanishes with it but thought remains, since the tower's likeness is retained by

[1] p. 19.

the mind. So far this account conforms with Augustine's theory. The mind forms its material from within itself receiving no aid from the body. Abaelard now points out that the act of thought must be distinguished from its object, just as the process of perceiving is not identical with the object perceived. Thought is an activity of the mind, in virtue of which it is said to understand. But before the act of understanding can take place the process of imagination must intervene. The understanding is directed on an imaginary and fictitious object which the mind constructs for itself whenever it wishes to do so and in any way it desires. Such representations resemble the imaginary countries seen in a dream or the form of a building which a craftsman is in course of designing. He conceives in his mind an ideal image of the work to be achieved.[1] In a word thought is free to construct its own objects.

Abaelard emphasizes these distinctions because he found that some philosophers tended to identify thinking and its objects. They called the image of the tower the same as the thought of the tower. He rejects this subjective idealism. The image is a likeness of the thing. And this is the proper object of thought. But if we stop at this point we have not reached true knowledge. Real qualities, the squareness and height of the tower, exist only in bodies. Conceptual thinking cannot be formed from fictitious qualities. We may say that the image in a mirror to which sight seems to refer is in reality nothing, since it is clear that in the white surface of the mirror a contrary quality often appears.[2] Conceiving is not like this. It refers to reality. Something more than an image which may turn out to be fictitious is required. The understanding operates on the image so as to apprehend the nature of objects.[3] Here we have a dim foreshadowing of St. Thomas's account.

Thinking, then, is an activity directed upon an image, and the mind can form images at will. We have now to distinguish between thoughts which are directed to universals and those which are applied to particulars. Now the universal term refers to a generalized and confused image of a number of things, while the particular term calls up one only. When I hear the word 'man' an image arises in my mind which is so related to individual men that it is common to all of them, specific to none. When, however, I hear the word 'Socrates', the likeness of a definite person arises in my mind. The common form to which a universal term refers is the

[1] p. 20.   [2] p. 21.   [3] Cf. p. 317.

generalized image of many individuals, like a painting of a lion, which does not portray the characteristics of any particular lion, but a typical lion.[1]

The conclusion which Abaelard has now reached, that universals consist of generalized images, is an unfortunate one. The position is exposed to the criticism which Berkeley afterwards levelled against Locke. It is an inadequate description of the manner in which the mind comes to form general conceptions. In coming to understand what is meant by 'lion' we do not put together all pictures of lions which we have seen and produce in our minds a composite picture. Still less do we mean by the universal 'lion' any form of image. Our philosopher is struggling to produce a theory of abstraction upon the basis of particular images.

In a later passage he proceeds farther into the psychology of the matter. Now matter and form are always found in combination, but reason has the power of contemplating now matter by itself, now form. And it may conceive of them in combination. In the two former activities the mind is abstracting. It abstracts an element from a complex object for the purpose of considering its nature. The third instance is one of synthesis. But it also supposes abstraction. For example, the substance of this man is body and animal and man, and it is clothed with infinite forms. So long as I restrict myself to the material essence of the substance ignoring all other forms, I have a concept of abstraction. Again when I attend only to its physical quality, combining it with the substance, this concept is also formed by abstraction, although it involves some process of synthesis compared with the former abstractions, for it considers the physical quality as well as the substance. But other forms, such as life, sensation, reason, whiteness, I ignore.[2]

Conceptions of this kind are considered by some philosophers to be misleading and vain for the reason that they apprehend an object in a way which does not relate to its real nature. We can think of matter and of form separately; but neither in reality exist separately. The process of abstraction, however, does not misconceive the object. When I consider this man from the point of view only of substance, ignoring the fact that he is also animal and man and a grammarian, I am not thinking of anything which is not really in the man: though I am not apprehending all that is in him. And when I say that I am considering only one quality of the real object,

[1] p. 22. [2] p. 25.

the emphasis is on the way in which the object is looked at, not to the way in which it really exists. The abstract quality is not in reality the only character of the thing. The act of thought takes it as the only character. The quality is conceived separately from other qualities, not as though it existed in reality separated from them. Sense-perception, indeed, often operates in the same manner in relation to composite objects. If an image consists partly of gold, partly of silver, I can turn my attention now to the gold aspect, now to the silver.[1]

The act of conceiving universals, therefore, always presumes a process of abstraction. It is a partial view of many individuals. When I hear the word 'men' or 'whiteness' or 'white', the import of the word is not the whole of any object. The term 'man' provides me with the ideas of animal and rational mortals, not with the idea of particular individuals. The content of the general idea (he persists in holding) is a general composite image. A very important point is now mentioned. Universals are involved in the conception even of an individual. In the consciousness of 'this man' the abstract character is perceived in the particular instance. This is the basis of Abaelard's view, and requires more explanation than it receives here. It implies a rejection of the theory of *universalia post rem*, the theory of the Nominalists. But the implications which point to a distinction between substantive universals and abstract universals are not developed. The former unify our impressions in the object as perceived and recognized; the latter unify qualities of many objects. The text, however, goes on to justify Porphyry's description of universals as *sola, nuda,* and *pura.* They are separate from sense-perception, empty of specific characters and free from reference to any thing.[2]

VI

Abaelard is now in a position to answer Porphyry's questions. The first question was whether universals are real entities existing independently of the mind which conceives them. The question raises the postulate of Realism. Abaelard's reply is that universal terms refer indeed to reality. They do not refer to nothing at all as the extreme Nominalists maintain. Yet in a certain sense universals exist only for thought. For they embrace abstract not concrete views of things. Confusion has arisen over this question only because a false dilemma has been presented. The question has

[1] p. 25.   [2] p. 28.

been taken to imply that universals are either real or not real, or that they either exist wholly in the mind or do not so exist. But the truth does not lie with these alternatives.

The second question was whether universals are material or immaterial entities. Abaelard demurs to the terms of the question. He observes acutely that the alternatives are better expressed in terms of what is discrete or locally distinct and what is not discrete. Every existent thing is discrete. In this sense universals are material in the fact that they refer to real discrete objects, immaterial in respect to the way in which they conceive these objects. Thought takes objects, or rather features of objects, together though they are perceived as distinct entities.

The answer to the third and critical problem whether or not universals are found in sensible objects or apart from them follows from the answers given to the previous questions. There are three ways in which immaterial entities may be related to sensible objects. They may exist only in sensible objects; mind is given as an instance of this type. They may be found in connexion with sensible objects, without being distinct existences. In this case, of which whiteness is an example, they are said to subsist in the sensible things. Finally there are some immaterial entities which exist entirely apart from sensible objects, such as the divine spirit and the soul.

Now Realist philosophers maintain that universals subsist in the sensible objects in the sense that they are substances inherent in objects which are sensible in virtue of external forms attached to substances. These substances can subsist in reality apart from the sensible object. Accordingly genera and species are traditionally described as being apprehensible by thought apart from them. Here the real nature of genera and species are considered by reason as continuing to subsist by themselves even when the external forms through which the senses become aware of them have been removed. Universals, according to this view, are both in sensible objects and at the same time continue to have being outside them. It is from this standpoint that the third question was raised. But Abaelard does not accept this position, except in so far as universals may have real being in the divine mind. A universal term does not point to any kind of sensible object, for this is the function of perception. And the objects of perception are the only kind of objects which possess genuine reality for human thought. Yet because universals are elicited from perceived objects they may be described as being in them; while they can equally well be termed non-sensible in so far as they are due to the activity of the mind.

And to the further question whether universals could continue to exist if there were no particulars, Abaelard returns an emphatic negative. For if their particulars were to vanish universals could not refer to many things. Yet the universal would still have meaning for thought, in spite of being deprived of particular reference. Otherwise the negative proposition 'there is no rose' could not be expressed.[1]

He concludes by pointing to the principal source of confusion in the discussions, the confusion between words and the things to which they refer. When the significance of terms is under discussion the argument is apt to move from words to objects and from objects to words. This ambiguity in logic as well as in grammar leads many into error. They fail to grasp that it is the function of terms to be applied to things in various ways, and they suppose that they are treating of things when they are treating of logical terms.[2]

Universals, then, are neither *voces* nor *res*, neither words nor things. Here Abaelard introduces his own modification of the Nominalism of Roscelin. Universals are *sermones*, concepts. The *vox* of Roscelin is a mere physical occurrence, a displacement of air. But the word means something. The word 'flower' is not merely a physical event; it refers to a general nature. But this general nature is arbitrarily selected. The human mind imposes itself upon the natural order as a sculptor fashions the stone to form a statue. Universal terms, *sermones*, imply a judgement about things, the judgement, namely that many different things have common qualities.[3]

The entities to which universal words refer are genuine through abstract properties of things. General conceptions are derived from the nature of things as they exist. Thought cannot grasp the concrete and total being of classes of objects. The *modus intelligendi* falls short of the *modus subsistendi*.[4] But by its conceptions the mind is enabled to grasp cross-sections of the manifold data of experience. These aspects are similarities discerned in a number of different individuals and contemplated in detachment from them. The universal man does not present to the mind a metaphysical reality to which individual men owe their being. It registers the observation that men are alike in being men.

[1] p. 30.   [2] pp. 30–2.   [3] p. 522; cf. p. 323.   [4] p. 25.

The position is now clear. The activity of thought isolates features which are common to a number of particular objects or events and attends to them as separate entities. These entities, whiteness, substance, rose, are genuine aspects of the discrete objects perceived by the senses. But they are not forms of being distinct from objects. In thinking the mind breaks up the complex detail of the concrete world and refashions it into objects of thought. The doubtful doctrine of the generalized image is improved by the notion of *sermo*, logical construction. And this process of analysis and synthesis is implicit in knowledge of particulars. Sense and thought co-operate fundamentally in all experience. When the mind perceives, general ideas are already implicitly present.[1]

The doctrine takes discrete individual things as real and as the point from which knowledge starts. Concepts are formed from an acquaintance with objects. Knowledge begins with particulars and progresses to the general. But this is not to move away from particulars to a separate realm of being. Theological thought was too deeply based upon Augustine for Abaelard to offer no acknowledgements to the Platonic Ideas. Ideas exist as patterns of things in the divine mind. But his theory of human knowledge is Aristotelian. The understanding knows ideas by abstracting them from things; and abstract knowledge must refer to the details of perception. 'Intellectus per abstractionem divisim attendit, non divisa, alioquin cassus esset.' Thought in virtue of its power of abstraction apprehends separate aspects of objects. It does not suppose these features to be distinct entities; for since there are no such entities it would be void of content.

VII

Abaelard's position has often been described as Conceptualism. This term indicates a qualified form of Nominalism. Those philosophers in medieval and modern times who have adopted Conceptualism are at one with the Nominalists in denying that there are any universal realities. But they admit that general notions of concepts provide the content of thinking. Concepts, however, are constructions of our minds. They are arbitrarily framed according to our purposes by a process of abstraction from particular impressions, such impressions being our sole genuine contact with the external world. Partial aspects of separate perceived items are selected and

[1] p. 95.

grouped into unities, man, green, goodness; the other features in the complex perceived individual being ignored. The abstract entities are fixed by language and exist for our minds as independent objects of thought. We argue about them as though they corresponded to real facts. On this view universals are derived entirely from the mind.

This position certainly corresponds with much that Abaelard asserts in the latter part of the passage we have been following. His interest in the process of abstraction instead of in the metaphysical problem has a decided conceptualist note. It presumes that things are known in perception prior to universalizing them. Relations as well as general ideas appear to be arbitrary. He speaks of conceiving a common likeness and of imposing general terms on things in virtue of this conception. If these and similar phrases comprised his view he would assuredly be exposed to the charge of Conceptualism which is brought against him by historians of medieval philosophy. For Conceptualism (at any rate of this order) is a plainly inadequate account of the nature of universals. It begs the question. Before the mind can abstract a common element from its experience of different individuals it must judge that they possess it. In order to construct the ideas of man, blue or shape, we have to notice similar elements in a variety of men, blue objects, and things with form. We may arbitrarily select this or that common quality, but the common quality must be already there distributed among numerous different entities; it cannot be a pure invention of our minds. There are indeed many difficulties here. But such a minimum of Realism seems to be necessary to account not merely for the relevance of thinking, but even of perceiving. For an individual object, a dog or a pen, is an implicit universal. As has been shown often in the history of thought the mind could never be aware of a train of mere particulars. But these considerations will be developed further when we come to examine the Nominalism and Conceptualism of William of Ockham.

Now, Abaelard clearly admits the minimum of Realism to which we have referred. He insists against Roscelin that the process of abstraction does not necessarily falsify our knowledge of the object. Universals are grounded in the nature of things. Man or green or Divinity are not mere sounds nor mental figments. 'Universal terms are both corporeal in respect to the nature of things'—that is to say greenness or humanity are actual features of things—'and incorporeal in respect to their meaning'—for they refer to general qualities artificially isolated from individual things. Universals are faithful representations of reality, but they are partial aspects, never reaching the concreteness of perception. This is not Conceptualism. It is an early expression of Moderate Realism.

In seeking for a middle way between a Realism that severed the universal from the particular, and a Nominalism which abolished meaning, Abaelard is led to find reality in the field of individual objects. Universals are derivative. Not that he was any friend to empirical methods in the modern sense. 'The discerning man', he says, 'is he who has the ability to grasp and ponder the hidden causes of things. And by hidden causes I mean those which concern the origin of things. These must be investigated more by reason than by practical experiments.'[1] This is an utterance typical of the medieval view of knowledge.

Yet it must be admitted that Abaelard is happier in exposing the difficulties of contemporary Realism, in ridiculing verbalism and the hypostatization of general terms, than in working out a satisfactory theory of abstraction and of the universal. This task was left to St. Thomas, who was aided by a wider acquaintance with the works of Aristotle. But already before Abaelard's death the logical treatises were being circulated and studied. We obtain a comprehensive picture of philosophical opinion on the problem of universals shortly after the time of Abaelard from a passage in the *Metalogicon* of the Englishman, John of Salisbury. John is one of the most agreeable figures in medieval literature. But scholarship was not his main concern. He was adviser to kings and archbishops and played a conspicuous part in the ecclesiastical politics of twelfth-century England. In his student days he attended for a brief period the lectures of Abaelard at Paris. His principal works were dedicated to his friend and master, Thomas Becket. The main purpose of the *Metalogicon* is to recommend the study of Aristotle's logic, but it throws a most interesting light on the intellectual life of the time. In the second book John describes the various schools of thought on the question of universals.[2] (The work was finished in the year 1159.) A few philosophers still maintain the theory of Roscellinus that universals consist of words (*voces*), though this extreme Nominalism almost disappeared with its author. The view of Abaelard, that universals are judgements (*sermones*), finds adherents, and John hails those who adopt this

[1] p. 506.　　[2] *Metalogicon*, ii. 17, ed. C. C. J. Webb, Oxford, 1929

position as his friends. But he thinks they have sadly distorted the teaching. They think it incredible that a thing can be predicated of another thing, in spite of the fact that Aristotle is the author of this incredible doctrine. Another school holds that genera and species are intellectual principles in the mind, an opinion which springs from Cicero and Boethius. These innate principles they call 'notions'. Turning to the Realists John finds that those who think that universals are realities comprise many divisions of belief. Some say that because everything that exists must be a single entity, universals must be single entities. But they allow that distinct substantial universals can be united in essence, putting forward the doctrine of *status*. John says, however, that this view is not now held. A further party follows Bernard of Chartres in asserting the Platonic theory of Ideas, in the sense that universals are counterparts of eternal realities. This view, that universals are supersensible realities, is not wholly alien to the teaching of Aristotle, and recent philosophers have laboured to reconcile Plato with Aristotle; but John deems the attempt futile. It is clear that they differed. Another group of Realists holds that universals are natural forms, images of the divine Ideas dwelling in created things. Others assert that universality consists in the combination of particulars; while others propound the doctrine of *maneries*, the meaning of which John is unable to interpret.[1]

Thus, soon after the death of Abaelard, all the opinions discussed by him were still being warmly debated. It must be added that John himself in a careful discussion of the question, closely faithful to Aristotle, arrives at conclusions similar to those of his master. The mind has the power of abstracting and recombining common aspects of particulars. Anyone who seeks to grasp these abstractions apart from the particulars is searching for dreams. A man would not thank you for the gift of a horse-in-general. Universals are ways of apprehending and of thinking of particulars, ways which are necessary to our minds; they are not objects in their own right.[2]

Abaelard's place in the history of Scholasticism lies in his analytical method. The distinctive characteristic of his manner of philosophizing is his persistent criticisms of the meaning of words.

---

[1] The word appears to be derived from *mannaria*, meaning 'way of handling' or 'manner'. C. C. J. Webb, *Metalogicon*, p. 95, note.
[2] Cf. op. cit. ii. 20.

Later sections of the treatises we have been describing contain
many examples of this method. There are acute examinations of
the meaning of the words 'and', 'all', 'anyone', and 'someone'.
And there is an elaborate treatment of the import of propositions.
Logical conceptions, he is always insisting, must not be taken as
referring naïvely to things. Words and sentences express various
arbitrary senses given to things. Philosophy is the science of the
meanings which words express. The theory of knowledge must be
preceded by a critical discussion of language. This method founded
a school of logicians who based their science upon an investigation
into the meaning of grammatical forms. 'Grammar is the cradle of
all philosophy', wrote John of Salisbury. The names of representa-
tives of this school, Lambert of Auxerre, Peter of Spain, William of
Shyreswood, indicate the range of this movement. Through these
philosophers the method passed to William of Ockham whose
Nominalism developed the conceptual elements in Abaelard, with
disturbing results for Scholastic thought.

III

ST. THOMAS AQUINAS

REFERENCES

All references to the *Summa Theologica* are to the Questions and Articles of the First Part. Other references are to the *Summa contra Gentiles, De Ente et Essentia, De Potentiis Animae, Quaestiones Disputatae de Veritate, IV libri Sententiarum,* and *De Anima.*

I

DURING the thirteenth century the philosophical thought of Europe was transformed. The chief factor in this new development was the rediscovery of some of the cardinal works of ancient reflection. From the middle of the twelfth century in Sicily and in the Spanish peninsula numerous translators were engaged in producing Latin versions from the Arabic records of Greek science and philosophy. A generation earlier Abaelard, as we have seen, was acquainted with but a few of the minor logical works of Aristotle. Now not only the major logical treatises but the *Physics* and the *Metaphysics* were for the first time made available for study. The impact was disturbing, for it was revealed that on many vital points of Christian thought Aristotle's views were at variance with the teaching of the Church. The disparity was exaggerated by the way in which the philosopher's thought was interpreted by Avicenna and Averroës, the great Arab scholars through whom Aristotle's writings were first transmitted to Christian students. Aristotle was presented as maintaining views on providence, on the eternity of the world, on the reality of individuals, on freedom, and on immortality, which were in direct contradiction with Christian beliefs. Repeatedly throughout the thirteenth century masters were forbidden to instruct their students in the doctrines of the philosopher who was soon to become the standard authority of medieval reflection. Conservative theologians recoiled from these dangerous innovations and reasserted the claims of Augustinianism and of Neoplatonism. Others interpreted Aristotle in Augustinian terms.

In order to appreciate the work achieved by Thomas Aquinas it is essential to realize that his independent analysis of thought and reality led him into conflict with both the influential schools of philosophy which were actively disputing at his side. He was compelled to criticize the Neoplatonism of Bonaventura on the one hand, the Arabian conception of Aristotle on the other. The latter position was being powerfully advocated by Siger of Brabant and other contemporary philosophers. It is true that a comprehensive exploration into the implications of Aristotle had been made by Thomas's master, Albert the Great (1206–80). It was he who attempted for the first time the task of reconciling Aristotle with Christian doctrine. He addressed himself to the formidable labour of paraphrasing and commenting upon the entire range of treatises of the Stagirite. In carrying through this colossal work Albert performed an inestimable service to medieval thought. Unfortunately he was content to describe many theories which in default of more precise interpretation appeared to be inconsistent with one another; and to this eclecticism is added a diffuseness which constantly leads the reader from the point at issue.

But the immense labour by which the mass of new material was examined and incorporated into Christian thought was accomplished by Thomas of Aquino. Early in his career he encouraged the distinguished scholar, William of Moerbeke, to undertake a series of translations from the authentic text of Aristotle. And his own numerous commentaries on the treatises of the philosopher sought to expound the genuine meaning of the conceptions found in them. What Thomas perceived in this philosophy, freed from Arabic and from Augustinian interpretation, was a systematic doctrine of knowledge and reality that fulfilled the demands of experience and of human nature. The constant endeavour of his doctrine of knowledge is directed to bringing together into one pattern of experience both the universal, immaterial elements, and the particular, material features of thought. Such a programme means, in the sphere of mental processes, the work of harmonizing the claims of sensation and conception; in relation to objects it means the due recognition of both contingent material entities and necessary universal 'ideas'. In the Aristotelian theory he found justice done to both sides of experience.

Thomas's father was the Count of Aquino and he was born at the castle of Roccasicca near Naples in 1225. He received his early education at the local Benedictine Abbey of Monte Cassino, leaving there at the age of fourteen to continue his studies at the University of Naples which had lately been founded by the Emperor Frederick II. At the age of twenty Thomas decided to enter the teaching order of the Dominicans, and was sent by his superiors to Paris in order to pursue higher studies in theology.

His decision to become a friar annoyed his family, and he was seized on his journey by his two brothers and held captive in the castle of St. Giovanni. Here he was detained for a year. All efforts to persuade him to abandon the religious life for one more appropriate to his noble station proved unavailing, and he was at length allowed to continue his journey to Paris. There he came under the immediate influence of Albert of Cologne. Much has been written on the relation of Thomas's thought to the work of Albert the Great. The debt of the disciple has been exaggerated; but Thomas's reflections certainly owed much to the vast scholarship of Albert. Thomas accompanied his master to Cologne in 1248, where Albert had been charged with the task of establishing a school of higher studies. On his return to Paris four years later he entered on his course for the degree of Master of Theology. He attained his licence for teaching in 1256. A letter from the Pope Alexander IV has been preserved in which he expresses his pleasure to the Chancellor of the University 'in having granted the licence for teaching in the faculty of theology to our beloved son friar Thomas of Aquino of the Order of Preachers, a man of noble birth and renowned for the regularity of his life and by the grace of God learned in the whole range of letters'. Thomas had already published several works which gave promise of the strength of his mind.

A short period of teaching at the University was followed by a recall to Italy where he composed his *Summa Contra Gentiles*. During nine years he taught theology in his native country, chiefly at the papal court. Already he had attained a position of high distinction as a philosopher, and he was also called upon to perform many tasks in educational administration. In 1268 he was appointed to lecture on Theology at the University of Paris, where he found himself plunged in controversy with the leaders of the secular clergy on the one hand and with the followers of the traditional method of Aristotelianism, whose spokesman was Siger of Brabant. The Averroistic interpretation of Aristotle was finally condemned by the Bishop of Paris in 1270, principally owing to Thomas's incisive exposure of its fallacies. But at the height of his fame he was in 1272 once more recalled to Italy, where he was entrusted with the direction of the theological curriculum for the Dominican Order in that country. He worked for two years in Naples. In 1274 he was invited by Pope Gregory X to take part in the Council of Lyons which had been summoned to discuss the unity of the Church. On the journey he fell ill, and at the Cistercian monastery of Fossanuova near Terracina he died on 7 March 1274 at the early age of forty-eight.

Thomas produced an astonishing amount of works ranging throughout the compass of philosophy and theology. He wrote twelve books of commentaries on Aristotle, twenty philosophical treatises, and a large number of works on theology, on the religious life, and on exegesis. His two most celebrated works are the *Summa Contra Gentiles*, which he composed for the benefit of Catholic missionaries among the heathen, and the vast *Summa Theologica*. In this work, which comprises three parts, thirty-eight treatises, 631 questions, and about 3,000 articles, the entire range of theology and philosophy is surveyed, the nature of God, the life of the angels, and that world of mingled intelligence and matter, the human mind.

The rigorous style of the philosopher affords few glimpses of the man. From his biographers we receive a picture of a saintly scholar with extraordinary powers of application. His day was so filled with prayer, composition, and teaching that he had little time for food and sleep. He was always engrossed in reflection and it was found necessary to appoint a companion to guide him in the practical necessities of life. His intellectual concentration was so remarkable that he was able to dictate to several secretaries at the same time. Thomas's writings display an almost Euclidean clarity and rigour. The question at issue is first stated. This is followed by a series of difficulties or objections to the position stated. Next, arguments or pronouncements expressing a contrary view are given. Now follows the main body of the article, in which the position advocated by the author is set forth. Finally the objections proposed at the beginning are criticized or explained in the light of the principles expounded in the main section of the article. An example of this method, the finest development of Scholastic procedure, is given on a later page.

II

St. Thomas's language concerning the relation of mind to the world it apprehends seems at first sight to embrace contrary positions. On the one hand we are told that the mind grasps immediately, without representative interference, the objects which confront it. The objects of knowledge differ radically from mental processes. That which is primarily known is not composed of states of consciousness, whether impressions or ideas or the self.

For human understanding the first object of knowledge is 'aliquid extrinsecum, scilicet natura materialis rei', something external, the nature of a material thing. The operations by which the subject is known is a secondary and indirect type of knowledge, *secundario cognoscitur ipse actus*.[1]

On the other hand, Thomas's assertions frequently appear to deny this position. We find him saying that the first thing understood by the intellect is its own act of understanding. The world of which the mind is aware is described in terms that seem to mean that it is infected with subjective elements. Material things so far as they are known must exist in the knower, not indeed materially, but immaterially. The intellect in act is the object understood in act. The realm of objects is a mode of the same reality which is found in consciousness; there is an essential kinship, a correspondence, between mind and things. In its relation to mind being must first correspond to the intellect. Things are ideas.[2]

The business of knowing is therefore both a direct approach to objects external to the mind, and also the expression of what is in some way already in the mind. 'All knowledge is through some form which is the principle of knowledge in the knower.' But, 'it is the stone which is understood not the likeness of the stone'.[3]

The resolution of these apparent contradictions naturally follows upon an interpretation of Thomas's terms; and the attempt to explain them must take us to the heart not merely of his doctrine of knowledge but also of his conception of reality. His accounts of perception and of thought will be totally misconceived if they are detached from his philosophy of being. A summary description of the cardinal principles of his metaphysics must, however inadequately, be attempted.

These principles are Aristotelian. Fundamentally, Reality is absolute and unchanging. But the Real is conceived of as an End, and every aspect of the Universe is teleological. All that exists and all that happens exists and happens for the sake of some outcome, near or remote. The ultimate explanation of individual things and events lies in the end which they subserve. For our experience things are pervaded by change.[4] And no change is meaningless; it is, on the one hand, relative to some stage or culmination,

---

[1] Q. lxxxv. 2, lxxxvii. 3.
[2] Q. lxxxvii. 3, lxxxiv. 2, lxxxvii. 1.   [3] Q. lxxvi. 2 and 4.
[4] As we shall notice later forms are not subject to change. They are always actual.

on the other hand, it implies preparation. It is a becoming. But becoming presupposes something which does not become, an attainment and state of rest. Accordingly there is implicated in every type of existence and event a twofold condition. These two aspects of being are expressed by the terms *actus* and *potentia* which represent Aristotle's ἐνέργεια and δύναμις. The conception of act and potency animates every department of Thomas's thought. All modes of being, a stone, an oak-tree, a man, are conceived of as realizations. Every form of activity and change, all growth and decay, are to be understood in relation to ends or fulfilments. They are tendencies. At any stage of its existence a thing whether animate or inanimate, whether a rock or a dog, is in respect to another stage in potency. For any entity that is undergoing change is not complete. It is approaching a determination of its nature, or it is receding from it. And this determination *is* its real nature. In so far as a thing has achieved stability or perfection it is *in actu*. In so far as it shows aptitude for a more enduring and determinate state of existence it is *in potentia*. A thing is indeterminate the more it expresses its nature independently of other things. In a word, the more immanent the process which sustains the thing the more it possesses of reality. The further it is self-determined the higher it is in the scale of being.

It is important to notice that neither act nor potency can occur independently of one another. Potency presupposes act. It is only through the actual that what is potential can exist. All learning, to adopt an example of St. Thomas's, comes from knowledge that exists already, not only in the teacher but also in the learner. On the other hand if potency disappeared there would be no movement, process, activity. But the process is not independent of the outcome. Entities are not produced by it. There *is* something, an identity, which changes. Modern principles such as an *élan vital* or a space-time which creates orders different from themselves would be, on this view, abstractions. For all processes are actuated by ends which are already implicit in them.[1] Change of any kind is the invasion of a potency by an act. Acts are in fact ideals to which any activity approximates, and the ideal governs and pervades each stage of the activity. Thomas thus avoids on the one hand a naturalism which tries to account for the higher levels of experience in terms of the lower; while he escapes on the other side an all-engulfing absolute for which every process is an appearance,

---

[1] Q. lxxxiii. 3 ad 2.

a pseudo-reality. For if the whole is ultimately in act, nothing can become. But potency is not an illusion. It is a constant aspect of the real finite world. Beyond this world, indeed, Faith points to an infinite Reality, a Being to whom no change can be attributed; for what is absolutely real cannot cease to be itself.

The numerous further distinctions which Thomas elaborates within Being, substance and accident, being and essence, essence and existence, effect and end, analogy and causality, the doctrine of degrees of perfection, must all be understood in the light of this fundamental rhythm. Its applications are indeed infinite. All the categories evince this twofold character. But for the theory of knowledge the dominating application is that of Matter and Form.[1] Matter is the underlying amorphous element of which things are made. It is pure passive potency and requires form for its actual expression. Form is the realization of matter in definite structures or patterns. Matter is constantly being transformed by an inherent activity into determinate shapes. The nebulous substratum, ὕλη, becomes substances in virtue of form. We have notices that the process and direction of potency is governed by act. So the movement immanent in matter is due to form. *Omnis actio est per formam.* Form is the principle of completion and accordingly it is the essential principle of everything's existence. 'The substantial form makes a thing to exist absolutely.'[2] Health is determined by a form of health; heat by a form of heat. Above all, as we shall see, mind is the form of the body. But the form of anything is not to be conceived as an entity or nucleus alongside the material element. It is the organizing principle of the material element, that which makes it a unity, or a thing.

Form, in fact, gives existence to matter, for matter cannot exist without some structure. But form is not dependent on matter. Thomas believed that intellectual beings can, in principle, exist without material embodiment. But such beings would be simple substances. Human beings are composite substances and their essences embrace form and matter.[3]

In all this what is potency and matter, what is act and form, are points of relative emphasis. In different references what is potency may become act and what is act may be seen to be potency. The

---

[1] Some authorities regard Potency and Act as themselves derived from Matter and Form. See Sertillanges, *Saint Thomas d'Aquin*, Paris, 1910, ii, p. 8.

[2] Q. lxxvii. 6. Thomas distinguishes substances of various kinds from accidental forms. The former are natural, the latter are artificial and man-made.

[3] *De Ente et Essentia*, 4.

stones of a house are potency in relation to the house, but the stones may be viewed as themselves acts for they are the consummation of processes which have gone to make them. In bare matter these correlative principles are expressed in the distinction between the elements into which anything can be analysed and the thing itself as a unity. It is one in virtue of a Form, it is many in virtue of its matter. In the field of living creatures it is due to their materiality that they are many individuals.[1]

It is in the organic realm that the application of these principles is most clear. The growth of a blade of grass or a horse or a man is intelligible only in relation to the maturity of these types of being. Growth in organisms points throughout to a culminating stage in which the structural plan found in detail throughout the organism discovers its completion. The principle still further illuminates ethical and aesthetic experience. It throws light on the teleological character of goodness. The nature of a person, and indeed the nature of any activity judged good, is directed to a certain fulfilment. Goodness is the domination of an activity by an immanent form which is also its end. Not that a person makes his own goodness. For St. Thomas goodness is ultimately communicated.[2]

This central principle is further developed in another celebrated and difficult Thomistic doctrine, that of essence and existence. In the content of my awareness of anything, this inkpot or this dog, I can distinguish in theory two elements. I am aware that it is an inkpot and I am aware that it exists. In the former aspect I apprehend the object as possessing a characteristic shape and a particular purpose, and by these I am able to define it and to distinguish it from other objects. The essence is what an object is. It is the source of all its properties. Essences are universals. The essence or nature of an object includes only those elements which fall under the definition of species, just as humanity or man in general includes those features which fall under the definition of man. In virtue of these features man *is* man; humanity means that by which man is man.[3] But we can conceive such essences without assuming that they actually exist. Actual existence implies a further principle. To the unity of the inkpot, dog, or man is added

[1] It must be admitted that there seems to be incompatibility between the conception of matter as the unconditioned manifold and the principle, equally cardinal in Thomas, that matter is the foundation of individuality.

[2] On the application of *actus* and *potentia* to goodness see A. E. Taylor, *Aristotelian Society*, Supplementary Vol., xi, p. 158.

[3] Q. iii. 3.

the contingent multiple shapes by which these natures are actually expressed. It does not follow that essences have any form of being, or subsist, apart from existence. What the principle does assert is that existence is not necessary to essence. Thomas believed in and describes at length an order of beings, the angels, whose natures approach a unity of essence and existence.[1] The essence of an angel is fully expressed in himself. Yet even here the two principles fall apart. An angel does not derive his existence from his essence. He does not create himself. The existence of a thing cannot be caused by the essence of the thing. If this were so the thing would bring itself into existence. Everything which exists derives its existence from something else. If we press this derivation back far enough we arrive at an ultimate cause of all things, a being which essentially exists.[2]

We have here another facet of the idea of act and potency. Essences are potencies to the act of existence. But no creatures attain fully to their potency; all contingent existences fall short of their capabilities.

III

St. Thomas's theory of knowledge must be understood according to the general conceptions of which we have given an outline. The passage from ignorance to knowledge is an aspect of the universal rhythm of potency and act. And it is a specialized expression of the determination of matter by form. It displays a mode of the growth of an organism to maturity. Knowing is a manner of being, a maturing of the immanent life of mind. In the process of understanding from simple apprehension to philosophical reflection the mind seeks the perfection of its own nature. Cognition is the peculiar achievement of life at the level of mind. A new synthesis of being is here reached. Mind or intentional being transcends life and physical existence, natural being. The activities of the vegetable and animal world are concerned with their immediate environment. The life of mind is aware of wider reaches of time and space; and it is conscious of its own awareness. But the distinctive mark of mental activity is that it does not effect any alteration in the objects with which it unites. Inferior orders of life, plants and lowly animal organisms, 'know' their environment by assimilating it or by other action upon it. Mind feeds on the world without altering it. Objects do not enter in any bodily form into mind, nor does mind contribute anything to the nature of objects. An object is

[1] Q. lii ff.   [2] De Ente et Essentia, 4.

external and yet it is known as a mode of mental being. In the object the form has a natural being, *esse naturale*, in the mind it has a mental being, *esse spirituale* or *intentionale*.

On a rationalist metaphysic Thomas thus imposes an empiricist theory of knowledge, in the modern senses of these terms. In a celebrated passage he states the position thus. The ancient naturalists, of whom Democritus was typical, saw that object and subject must have something in common, but they concluded that this common principle was identical in nature with either mind or matter. These naturalists resolved the dualism by materializing mind. Plato, on the other hand, resolved it by idealizing objects. He observed that mind is immaterial and believed that the things which it knows subsist as immaterial forms. Thomas replies to the materialists, firstly, that the process of knowing is not the production of physical objects; secondly, that if the material objects exist in their material form in the knower, one might as well say that anything knows. 'If by fire the mind knows fire, fire itself would be conscious of itself. But things which only receive forms materially are determined to a particular thing; the form does not extend to other things. Now the characteristic of knowing is that it refers to a number of things outside the particular knower.'[1] On the one hand, then, the primary object of knowledge is in no way a psychic entity; it is material. Yet, on the other, there is an identity of subject and object which is fundamental to experience. The mind in exploring the external world expresses itself. 'Cognoscens in actu est cognitum in actu.' The problem of knowledge is to explain this transference; to show how mind without ceasing to be itself becomes something strangely different. And on the other hand, the external object of which mind is aware must be shown to unite with mind without modification of its own nature.

There are two modes by which things can influence or act upon one another. All transformations, as we have seen, take place under the influence of a form. We have now to notice that the form may be transferred in two ways. It may be physically transferred from one body to another. When, for example, a piece of bread is heated the heat in the fire passes into the bread. This type of action is termed natural change, *immutatio naturalis*. 'Natural alteration takes place when the form of that which alters is received into that which is altered in its actual state as heat passes into what is heated.'[2]

---

[1] Q. lxxxiv. 2.   [2] Q. lxxviii. 3, cf. 2.

Now in sense-perception some natural change occurs. The physical change may occur in the object. In order to produce sound the object must be struck; in order to produce smell 'a body must to·some degree be affected by heat'. But the change occurs also in the physical organ. 'The hand that touches something hot becomes hot, while the tongue is moistened by the humidity of the flavoured morsel.'[1] But there is another mode of the alteration of one object by another. This is mental change, *immutatio spiritualis*. Here the form of the object is received into the thing which is changed by it 'according to a spiritual mode of existence'. What receives the form does not do so in any physical manner. Materially it is unaffected by the change. The operation of knowledge is of this kind. The form of colour received into the pupil of the eye does not change the colour of the eye. In Thomas's language an *intentio* of the sensible form is affected in the sensory organ. By *intentio* is meant an apprehension of something.

The forms of objects are incarnate; they are expressed in matter. The mind cannot attain the materialized forms of objects. It reaches out to and assimilates the forms only in so far as they are communicable. And what renders them communicable are *similitudines*, likenesses of objects. But consciousness of objects does not lie in the mere possession of a likeness by the mind. It consists in the degree according to which the likeness represents the object. But we must defer for the moment further discussion of the status of *similitudo*.

Knowledge, then, takes place in virtue of an assimilation of the knower to the object known.[2] 'The more anything is known, the more intimate is the understanding of it, the more is it one with the knower.' Mind and its objects are thus linked by an essential kinship. Knowledge is due to the presence and effects of the object; object is different from the subject; but it is also a phase of the self-actualization of the subject. The mind in the course of perfecting itself seeks to know objects.

We are perhaps now in a position to grasp the paradoxical phrases quoted earlier. Knowledge is concerned immediately with objects, but also with what is already in the mind. For reality is expressed not only in matter but also under certain conditions in a conscious subject. The chief of these conditions is the immateriality of the subject. For the object, as we have seen, penetrates the subject by means of an ideal form of which it is the material

---

[1] Q. lxxviii. 3.   [2] De Ver. i. 1.

embodiment. Its material configuration is controlled by a form so as to be what it is, a stone, a fire, or a work of art. On the other hand, the mind in knowing passes beyond itself without ceasing to be itself. The ideal form in the subject unites with the forms of the external world. This is the meaning of Thomas's oft-repeated assertions that the form of that which is known is in the knower, and that understanding in act is the object understood in act.

But in order to study more precisely the bearing of these principles upon perception and thought we must turn to St. Thomas's view of the relation between body and mind.

IV

We have noticed that for St. Augustine and for the dominant tradition of medieval thought which followed him the mind is a nature wholly different from the body. The body belongs to the physical realm. It is, in the main, passive to external influences of a material type, and has no influence on the mind. The mind is active and produces sensations from its own substance.

St. Thomas begins by asserting no less the incorporeal nature of mind. Mind is *intellectus* or understanding and understanding is immaterial and subsistent. Mind is not composed of matter and form. In principle *intellectus* knows a thing absolutely. It knows the form of a stone, that is to say it knows it as substance in general. If it apprehended the stone as matter it would apprehend it through a bodily organ and therefore as an individual object. Further St. Thomas maintains that the understanding as such is immune from decay. It is not liable to change because it is not an existent; it is a subsistent form. The senses do not know existence save under conditions of *here* and *now*, whereas the understanding knows things absolutely and eternally. So far, Thomas adheres completely to St. Augustine's way of thought.[1]

But the great difference between that philosophy and his own is that he does not think that the mind as such, pure understanding, functions in our experience. The mind of man is not a pure intelligence (such as an angel) nor is it a spirit in a corpse. It is an organic composite of mind and body. For human beings mind is the form of the body. The cause of activity is a form of the thing which is active. For example, the fundamental cause of healing is the form of health, and the fundamental cause of the mind's

[1] Q. lxxv. 5, 6.

knowledge is the form of knowledge. Now mind is manifested at all levels of nature, and at the lower levels it appears as life. Life shows itself according to different operations in different degrees of living things; but the principle of all vital functions, whether nourishment or sensation or movement, is the mind. Mind is the organic principle; it cannot be severed from the organism without ceasing to be itself. Thus when St. Thomas says that the mind is the form of the body he means that it determines the character of the body. A human body could not be a body apart from mind; and a mind divided from its body ceases to be a mind.[1]

Mind, in fact, virtually contains the sensitive and nutritive functions and all inferior forms.[2] Looked at as functions these inferior forms *are* mind. We must not suppose, however, that the human mind is composed of several distinct forms. The doctrine of the plurality of forms, warmly defended in the thirteenth century, is rejected. The organic mind, the perceptive mind, and the understanding constitute one mind. And this mind pervades the whole body.[3] Mind cannot function at the level of sensation without material expression; for the process of sensing is accompanied by changes in the body. The act of seeing is accompanied by changes in the eye, and so with the other senses. Every operation of the sensory mind is an operation of the joint activity of body-mind.[4] And man's knowledge is rooted in sensation. Without this reference to particulars man's knowledge would be imperfect, of a general nature and confused. It is therefore with a view to having perfect and proper knowledge of things that human minds are constituted by nature to be united to bodies, and thus to receive the proper and adequate knowledge of sensible things from the actual things; they are like uneducated persons who cannot be instructed without concrete examples. It is clear, then, that the greater good of the mind requires its union with the body and that it understands by relying on sensible images.[5] But the understanding knows corporeal objects by a knowledge which is immaterial. In so far, then, as human knowledge can attain understanding it transcends the body.

The position is approached in one passage in the following way. Anyone who examines his consciousness is aware that it is one and the same self who experiences both thinking and sensation. But sensation requires a body; therefore the body must be a part of self.[6]

[1] Q. lxxxix. 1.   [2] Q. lxxvi. 4.   [3] Q. iii. 8.
[4] Q. lxxvi. 3.   [5] Q. lxxxix. 1.   [6] Q. lxxvi. 1.

Body and mind form one complex being, man. His mind is not disembodied; it is not a soul in a machine. The unity which Thomas seeks to explain is an intimate one. The mind is not related to the body as an agent to his instrument nor as a pilot to his ship, as Plato maintained. The assumption here is that the essential nature of man lies in his mind; his body is as external to him as his clothes. But the body and its organs form part of the essence of man, for the mind is expressed in sensation as well as in thought.[1]

One consequence of this union is that minds are individualized; for the bodies of which they are parts are, as matter, necessarily particular. All men do not constitute one mind, as certain types of extreme Realism had held. St. Thomas points out, in the manner of Abaelard, that if this position were true it would follow that two men would be essentially one, differing only in accidents. Socrates and Plato would differ in no other respect than one man with a shirt differs from another with a cloak. And this, Thomas observes, is quite absurd.[2]

Since, then, the human mind is intimately allied with matter its thinking is throughout infected with sensible experience. This interpretation of the roots of human knowledge is a striking departure from the traditional position, which, as we have noticed, was still being asserted and developed by St. Bonaventura and the Franciscans. The central thesis that the mind knows material objects in the 'eternal reasons' is directly examined. Thomas begins by quoting a text from St. Augustine's *Confessions* in which the objectivity of truth is maintained. 'If we both see that what you say is true and if we both see that what I say is true, where do we see this, pray? I do not see it in you, nor do you see it in me; but we both see it in the unchangeable truth which is above our minds.'[3] The unchangeable truth lies in the eternal Ideas, and in them all reality, including the reality of material objects, is known. In his reply to this position Thomas first points out the difference between the formulation of the Platonic doctrine by Augustine and Plato's own expression of it. Plato had held that the Forms of things subsist apart from matter. These Forms are conceived of as creative substances, the source of a thing's existence. Such a view is inadmissible in the Christian Faith for which God alone is the source of all being. For this reason Augustine set the Ideas in the divine mind.

Thomas now directly considers the Realist position by inquiring

[1] *De Anima* Q. i. i.   [2] Q. lxxvi. 2.   [3] Confess. XII. xxv. 35.

what is meant by a thing being known in something. There are two senses in which this statement can be taken. Firstly it can be taken literally. An object can be known, or apprehended, in another object which is itself already known, as for example in a mirror. Now under the conditions of human life the mind cannot see things in the eternal reasons in this sense, that is to say, as reflections of the divine mind. This is only possible to spiritual beings, who see God. But secondly, a thing can be apprehended in something in the sense of being known by means of something. Thus we might say that we see in the sun what we see by means of the sun. In this sense we can say that the human mind knows all things in the eternal reasons since all intelligent experience is ultimately derived from God; our light of reason bears some likeness to the uncreated Light. But the vital consideration is that the intelligible content of experience is for us derived from things, not from eternal reasons. Thomas happily quotes a passage from Augustine himself in which the importance of perceptual experience is pointed out.[1] 'Although the philosophers prove by convincing arguments that all things occur in time according to the eternal reasons, were they able to see in the eternal reasons or to find out from them how many kinds of animals there are and the origin of each? Did not they seek this information from the story of times and places?' Our knowledge is dependent upon sensory experience.[2]

Again he rejects the Platonic belief that the mind contains innate ideas through which it has knowledge independently of experience. The argument of the *Meno* is recalled, where Plato seeks to prove that we have *a priori* knowledge. In the course of that dialogue a person of no education gives true answers to a series of questions in geometry. In considering this point Thomas relies on the principles of potency and act. Mind apart from experience is in potency; its thought is only in act when instruction or experience is brought to bear on the potential state. Plato had maintained that the mind has the capacity of attaining knowledge of universals but is hindered by its connexion with the body and with sensation. But if the mind possesses by nature this universal knowledge it is difficult to understand why it should forget it. The root of the Platonic belief is a denial of the natural unity of body and mind. If mind is by nature united with the body it is unreasonable to maintain that it is hindered by the body. Knowledge of the type insisted on by the Platonists, knowledge of universals divorced

---

[1] De Trin. iv. 16.   [2] Q. lxxxiv. a 5.

from sensory reference, could not include apprehension of material objects. For this apprehension requires sensory experience. A man born blind has no knowledge of colour. As for the argument of the *Meno*, universal self-evident principles are not known previously to being elicitated. Then they are known for the first time. Once seen their consequence can be also seen under systematic questioning.[1]

Human knowledge is dependent upon perceptual experience. Our minds cannot free themselves of sensory references even in reflection upon 'the eternal truths'. Even in these regions we do not attain a mode of knowledge which shares in an order of perfectly intelligible and certain ideas, devoid of all the contingency of sense. Incorporeal principles are known to us only through sensible bodies. The human mind holds a middle place between organic beings whose information extends no further than the environment with which they are in immediate contact, and the angels who are able to know material objects not through the senses, but in the immaterial principles. In our present state we cannot understand separate immaterial substances in themselves. If our intellectual power were capable of acting apart from sense it could not be obstructed by damage to a sensory organ. But we find that such damage, as in epilepsy, makes a man unable to use his mind.[2]

V

The human mind exhibits a number of capacities or potencies because it lies in the order of being between the spiritual and physical realms and the activities proper to each meet together in it. But it is not therefore resoluble into a number of separated functions. For the various activities which enter into knowing are potencies; they are tendencies which seek fulfilment. Mind is in essence act; and this means that it is a unity in which activities are completed, and to which they are subordinate.[3]

The broad division of powers is between the sensitive and intellectual. The former is effected by the particular. Its seat is the composite body-mind, where various activities consequent upon the stimulus of a sense-organ combine to form the elementary perception of the external world. The seat of the intellectual power, the processes of thought and reason, is that part of the mind which surpasses matter. Its object is the essence of particular things.

[1] Q. lxxxiv. 3.　　　[2] Q. lxxxiv. 7.　　　[3] Q. lxxvii. 2.

In describing the psychological elements which enter into perception Thomas, following Aristotle, adopts a biological approach. These processes are the outcome of activities which are manifested at humbler levels of life. The activities of living bodies are distinguished in general from the movements of wholly material bodies by the fact that they are directed from without. The various levels of life and mind are accordingly marked off from one another by the scope of the field of reality to which they are capable of referring. At a lowly level the creature is concerned with no more than the fundamental functions of its body, the rhythms of generation, growth, and nutrition. This is the vegetative level of existence, characteristic of plants. What knowledge they possess extends no further than what is immediately present to them. It is expressed in movements which respond to actual stimulus. Knowledge proper begins at a further stage. For the sensitive or perceptual order of life there is awareness of a world existing independently of the creature. But this experience is intrinsically united with appetite and instinct, and it becomes more explicit with increasing range of movement.[1]

The psychology of this perceptual and animal level of mind, in which the mind of man is rooted, is elaborated, with some modifications, upon the Aristotelian model of which Thomas is able to make better use than his predecessors. Perception requires not only the five outer senses, but also a number of inner senses. Among these Thomas distinguishes firstly a *sensus communis* or general sensibility. All experience presupposes the unity of organic life, an enduring and pervasive centre of awareness from which the special senses are derived and to which they refer. To this organic sensibility are assigned several types of experience. Not only does it co-ordinate the deliverances of the separate senses; by it the mind is enabled to be aware that it is conscious.[2] Self-consciousness grows from this root. Further, *sensus communis* distinguishes between the experiences of the different senses.[3] The simultaneous perception of two qualities such as hard and sweet implies a common sensibility. Lastly an important function must be mentioned. This sense perceives the common sensibles, such qualities in things, that is to say, as movement, rest, size, shape, number. These properties are not apprehended by any particular sense, as are the sense qualities, odour, sound, colour, yet they are sensory qualities.[4]

[1] Q. lxxviii. 1, 2.   [2] Q. lxxviii. 4.   [3] Q. i. 3 ad 2.   [4] De Pot. An. iv.

In the animal mind Thomas finds a capacity which he names *vis aestimativa*. It corresponds closely to the modern conception of instinct. In placing it at the basis of primitive apprehension Thomas rejects hedonist theories of action. An animal is not moved to avoid or to desire the objects before it only because they are felt to be pleasing or not pleasing, but also on account of other benefits and uses, or disadvantages. Thus a sheep runs away when it sees a wolf, not on account of the ugliness of the creature's colour or shape, but because it is a natural enemy. And in the same way a bird gathers together straw, not because it gives pleasure to its senses, but because the straw is useful for building its nest. An animal, therefore, must recognize ideas (*intentiones*) of this kind, though its external senses do not apprehend their significance.[1] Animals, in fact, are predisposed to attend to certain sensory patterns; their behaviour cannot be accounted for on the basis of associations derived from experience, still less on the score of unrelated presentations. In man the ideas which are implicit in instinct become explicit by the exercise of a kind of comparison (*per quandam collationem*). In *De Potentiis Animae*[2] Thomas makes a suggestive comparison between this instinctive capacity in animals and man's intellectual life. Just as the animal through its *vis aestimativa* is aware of more than what is given to it in sensation, so man knows more than what his senses reveal, even though his knowledge arises from sense.

The awareness of sensory images, *phantasmata*, is placed among the interior senses. But *phantasia* or *imaginatio* includes also, somewhat confusingly, the power of retaining impressions, and this form of retention is distinguished from memory, *vis memorativa*, which is devoted to the preservation of ideas. In man this power develops into recall, *reminiscentia*, the active effort to form associations.

Now that the psychological processes which may be discerned at the perceptual level of life have been sketched, we may appropriately raise the philosophical issue concerning the validity of these activities. Knowledge, we have seen, begins with mental sensations which are the counterpart of physical impressions. We must bear in mind the immanent character of the activity implied in this description. Sensible knowledge unfolds in response to a physical alteration of the sense-organ, but the process is fundamentally a movement of the form which exists in different modes in mind and

[1] Q. lxxviii. 4.   [2] Op. cit. iv.

in thing. Sensation is to the sense-organ what mind is to body. Sensation is the realization, the act, of the sense-organ.

The mental sensory elements are *phantasmata*, and our thought is dependent upon them. But they do not comprise the only content of perception. For their objects are particular and private, while the objects we perceive are universal and public. When I perceive a stone I receive a multitude of different images, and another man has a series of images which differ from mine. Yet I perceive one stone and I and my friend perceive the same stone. What is apprehended is not a pattern of evanescent images but an object. And this must be, at least, a unity having diverse aspects.[1] In a word it must be a universal, and this, we shall see, is the only element which mind can directly apprehend.

Images are not objects, but they are necessary to the experience of objects. Their function is to provoke consciousness and to orientate thought. Sensorial impressions free the intelligible. They are signs. Mind responds to the stimulus of the *phantasmata* in the sense of using them in the production of the generalized form which is the object of consciousness. The form implicated in matter is unknowable. Only in so far as it is extracted, that is to say becomes universal, can it be apprehended.[2]

It follows that *phantasmata* are not directly known. Our minds know only the universal directly. But the particular element in experience can be known indirectly, by a kind of reflection. We can attend to images as elements in our experience by isolating them artificially. The sensible images as such can only enter into consciousness when they are stripped of sensibility. If we try to take them as representations we must be careful to say that they represent no more than subjective contacts with objects, not the objects as they are. These references show the remarkable advance made by Thomas on the psychology of his predecessors. There is a nice recognition of both the universal and particular ingredients of experience.

Augustine's observation that *phantasmata* taken by themselves (so far as they can be so taken) are only able to report the pictures they present, and that these are subjectively true, is quoted with approval.[3] It is only when they are referred to objects that the question of their truth or falsity arises. For instance when we see a white object through green glass we question the validity of the appearance. 'The understanding judges of the pretensions offered

[1] Q. lxxvi. 2.   [2] Contra Gent. 1. 44; cf. ib. iii. 84.   [3] Q. Disp. i, De Ver. 11.

by the senses.' If sensations were the only components of knowledge every sensation would be true, even contradictory ones.
There would be no means of distinguishing reality from illusion.[1]

The cardinal error is the separation of two modes of knowledge,
perception and thought. Two extreme positions have been held,
each determined by exclusive interest in one aspect of experience.
For two orders are discovered in reflection, one the order of
unchanging and necessary entities such as logical and mathematical principles, the other the realm of changing and contingent
things, material objects and the bodies of creatures. These are
perceived by the senses, the former are known by the understanding. Augustine, we have seen, had denied that bodies could be
known by the understanding. Intellect and sense are distinct and
have different spheres. Understanding cannot know bodies, nor
sense essences or forms.

Thomas points out that if sense is divided from thought knowledge becomes impossible. If we suppose, with Heraclitus, that
there is nothing in experience but what is apprehended by the
senses, experience becomes a perpetual flux. And what is in a state
of continual flux cannot be an object of knowledge; for *this* state
ceases to be and is replaced by another before the mind can say
what it is. If on the other hand we hold, with Plato, that over
and above material things there is a realm of eternal Ideas, from
which particular existences draw their being, other difficulties arise.
In the first place, if genuine knowledge were confined to immaterial
entities we should possess no understanding of bodies in motion.
There would be no science of matter in change. In the second
place in order to understand objects we are asked to refer to
entities which have no connexion with them.

It is error to believe that the understanding is constituted so as
not to know bodies. Universality is indeed the characteristic of
thought, but the objects of thought need not exist also as universals. The form of the thing known need not be in the knower in the
same way. The sensible form exists in the real world outside the
mind in one way; it appears in another way in the mental apprehension of it. And the understanding grasps in its own way the
species of bodies. They are material and in motion; in the understanding they become immaterial amd motionless. Yet it is knowledge of them and not of another order of being. For what is
received is in the receiver according to the nature of the receiver.[2]

[1] Q. lxxxv. 2.   [2] Q. lxxxiv. 1; cf. ib. 6.

But let us now proceed to elucidate more closely the manner in which understanding co-operates with sense in the act of awareness.

VI

For human beings the forms of objects are embodied in particular material things. The forms, the essences of things, have accordingly to be grasped indirectly, by activities which supervene upon sensation. The contents presented by the outer and inner senses are particular, and so they cannot provide of themselves the objects of knowledge. For the mind, or in Thomas's language the possible intellect, receives only universal species. A purely particular entity is an abstraction; it could not be an object of consciousness. It is necessary, then, that the contents of sensory apprehension should be extracted from their material setting, stripped of their unique determinations, in order to become items of thought. In a word, the sensory particulars have to be made general. This process is performed by the active understanding or intellect, *intellectus agens.*

Thomas is fond of comparing its function to that of light. As the colours of objects are made visible for the eye by light, so material entities are rendered intelligible by the active intellect. It reveals objects by illuminating the phantasms.[1] It is an active not a passive power. It is not provoked by the action of bodies on the mind; it exhibits the action of the mind on bodies. The mind produces itself the force by which it is enlightened. Knowledge is not wholly derived from sensory factors, though they play their part.

The activity of the *intellectus agens* is manifested in the constant movement of thought from the concrete to the abstract, from the ideas implicit in the bare apprehensions of external objects to general notions of science and philosophy. The more abstract the object of thought the nobler and higher it is in itself.[2]

The active intellect is not a power outside the mind, an Intelligence in which the mind can share. For it is imperfect and attains truth, not by direct intuition, but by a process of inquiry and partial approaches, in fact by reasoning. The Augustinian view that the active intellect is the divine Mind must be rejected.[3] The limitations of our minds, the ideals to which knowledge points, and the teaching of Faith, lead us to believe in a substantially separate and supreme Intelligence. But the active intellect is human. It is

[1] Q. lxxix. [2] Q. lxxxii. [3] Q. lxxix. 4.

a power not of Mind, but of minds. Many minds are not in reality one mind as Realism had maintained. There are as many active intellects as there are men.[1]

The primary work of the active intellect is to make general and so apprehensible the disappearing and disconnected *phantasmata* of sensory experience. It performs this in Thomas's terms by abstracting the intelligible species from the *phantasmata*. The significance of *species intelligibilis* in Thomas's scheme is complex and difficult. It is a form, that is to say it is an immanent activity which expresses the nature of the knowing subject. But it also expresses the nature of the object. It is an emanation or likeness of the object which is fitted by its physical character to combine with mind and produce the act of awareness. For objects cannot enter our minds in concrete form. In order that apprehension should occur the object must meet our mind without ceasing to be itself and at the same time without physical invasion of the mind. The species is the ideal intermediary which unites object and subject in the act of consciousness.

Accordingly it is not an object of thought; it is that by which we think. What we apprehend is the object, this house, or justice, not the way in which we apprehend. Theories of representative thinking are ruled out by this interpretation of the species. Our knowledge is directly concerned with external realities, not with representations of them. But it can grasp external objects only by freeing the intelligible form which is implicit in them.[2] In the realm of spirit mind corresponds to pure matter in the world of physical being. It is potency, indetermination, unintelligent. It can only become intelligent when it is informed by the intelligible species of a body.

The intelligible species is a principle of unity. The mind can only perform at one time a single act of understanding. It embraces many objects or elements in one perspective. The presence of several intelligible species necessarily means several acts of consciousness.[3] Our knowledge of relations rests on this principle. Take, for example, the relation of whole and part. If we attend to the parts by themselves the whole recedes from view; each part constitutes a whole in its turn. If, on the contrary, we consider the whole the parts are apprehended only in a vague manner as existing in the whole.[4] Or take the perception of the difference between objects, or the process of comparing them. It is true that

---

[1] Q. lxxix. 4, 5; lxxvi. 2.　　[2] Q. lxxxv. 2.　　[3] Q. lxxxv. 4.　　[4] Ib. ad 3.

the mind must know both the objects at the same time in order to distinguish and compare them. But the terms of these judgements are not known separately in themselves, but in relation to the judgement of comparing or distinguishing.[1] In any judgement, in fact, the parts of the proposition, the subject and the predicate, are not understood as distinct items. It is the proposition as a whole which is understood. All the parts are known according to a single species of the whole.[2]

Besides introducing unity into the *phantasmata* the active intellect in bringing to light the intelligible species generalizes the sensible images. Thomas describes abstraction in language closely resembling that of Abaelard, for here as at every stage of his philosophical reflections he was obliged to guard his doctrine from the current teachings of extreme Realism. In thinking of the qualities of objects we do not refer to items which have distinct existence. In abstraction we attend to aspects of things in isolation from other aspects. This separation occurs on the perceptual level of experience.

'For if we mean or assert that colour is not in the coloured object or that it exists separately from it, there would be error in thought or expression. But if we consider colour and its properties without at all referring in our minds to the coloured apple, or if we express what we think, there will be no error either of thought or expression. For the apple is not essential to the colour. There is no difficulty in thinking of the colour without thinking of the apple. In the same way I maintain that the features which essentially belong to the species of any material object, such as a stone or a man or a horse, can be thought of apart from the individual characteristics which do not belong essentially to the species. And this is what is meant by abstracting the universal from the particular or the intelligible species from the phantasms. The species is thought of apart from the individual principles which the phantasms represent.'[3]

There are two points here. In thought we attend to features cut loose as it were from the objects in which they inhere. And these features are general; we do not mean by colour the image of any particular colour we may have in our minds when we think of colour.

Thomas gives a brief survey of various levels of abstraction. Abstraction may be of the general or of the particular. We may think of flesh and bones in general or of some particular flesh and

---

[1] Q. lxxxv. 4 ad 4.   [2] Cont. Gent. i. 55.   [3] Q. lxxxv. 1 ad 1.

bones. Now the active intellect abstracts the species of an object from particular sensible matter, not from sensible matter in general. The notion of a man is formed from some particular flesh and bones. But it is possible to abstract species from matter in general. General features of matter are qualities such as cold and hot, hard and soft. This is we may presume the province of physics. But the mind can proceed further in the realm of the abstract. It can descry an order beyond the general sensibles. Now this is substance as subject to quantity, and Thomas names it intelligible matter. Quantity is prior to other sensible forms. Quantities, for example number, dimension, and figure, can be treated apart from other sensible qualities. Finally we may take a further step, beyond intelligible or mathematical matter. All that now remains for our thought are elements such as being, unity, potency, and act. These can be studies apart from all matter. Here we reach the province of metaphysics.[1]

The *species intelligibilis* is thus made explicit and becomes the *species intellecta*, the general object or concept of which the mind is conscious. Thomas is accustomed to refer to it as *verbum* or expression, thus emphasizing the intimate connexion between thinking and language. The language, however, may be interior, *verbum cordis*. The concept is directed to being expressed either to oneself or to others; and Thomas accordingly excludes 'simple intuition' or 'implicit apprehension' from conception.[2] A general term is a similitude of an actual thing, not, of course, the likeness which holds between the intelligible species and the object, but a resemblance existing between an ideational representation and concrete individual thing. The likeness has only intentional being. It is not a thing, nor is it in things. It is a way of comprehending things to which we are compelled by the deficiencies of our understandings.

The immediate foundation of the general ideas which form the main texture of our thought is not in things but in the mind. What the mind knows are abstractions. The particularity of things can never be seized. Conceptual thought is indistinct. 'It is evident that to apprehend an object that comprises many things, without proper knowledge of each thing contained in it, is to apprehend that object in a confused way.[3] The senses have intuitions; thought strives after intuitions but must be content with partial views of reality. This human knowledge is midway between the

[1] Ib. ad 2.
[2] In IV libri Sententiarum, i, d. 27, q. 2, a 1.   [3] Q. lxxxv. 3.

potentiality of conceptual thought and perfect act, the intellectual intuition of objects, which is the prerogative of the angels.

Thomas frequently asserts that the natural object of the human mind is the 'quiddity' or essence of a material thing.[1] Yet to these affirmations must be joined statements which seem directly to contradict this position. Thus he often says that the essences of things are unknown to us. The contradiction appears sometimes in the same article. The solution of the antinomy must be sought in an analysis of the structure of the intelligible form. What is first known by mind is being, to which it refers all its conceptions. All other conceptions of the understanding must be arrived at by an addition to that which is.[2] We understand being in ways which variously qualify it. Thus we break the unity of being, piecing it into genera and species, into classes and things. On the other hand, we preserve the indeterminate unity of being, but only by expressing general modes which are no being in particular, such as unity, real, good. But all being possesses both special and general modes. We attain then the essence immediately, in so far as we apprehend the general features before the particular.[3] And the mind in apprehending the quiddity in this sense is always apprehending the truth.[4] It is in conformity with reality.

But the truth is not consciously seen to be truth until the mind distinguishes between itself and the objects of its thought. It asks how far its conceptions, arbitrarily abstracted from experience, conform to experience.

'But the understanding forming quiddities has only the likeness of the thing existing outside the mind, as sense has in so far as it receives the species of the sensible thing. When, however, it begins to judge concerning the thing apprehended, then the very judgement of the understanding is something proper to it which is not found outside the thing. But when it is adequated to that which is outside the thing, the judgement is said to be true.'

The concept which is produced by the operation of the active intellect has, as we have seen, a counterpart immanent in particular things. Truth is the conformity of the mind with this pervading form.

VII

There is a passage in the *Summa Theologica*[5] in which Thomas defines his position on the nature of knowledge in relation to

---

[1] Cf. Q. lxxxv. 5.   [2] De Ver. Q. i. 1.   [3] Q. lxxxv. 3.
[4] De Ver. i. 3.   [5] Q. lxxxiv. 6.

sensationalism on the one hand and Augustinian idealism on the other. We cannot conclude our brief survey of his philosophy of knowledge more appropriately than by presenting the argument of this passage. It clearly epitomizes the Thomistic account of knowledge.

He begins, as usual, by stating several of the texts which reject the position for which he proposes to argue. The traditional texts are naturally drawn from St. Augustine. In the work named *Eighty-three Problems* he had asserted that genuine truth cannot be sought for in the bodily senses. For, in the first place, whatever the bodily senses reach is in process of continual change. And what has no permanence cannot be perceived. In the second place everything which we perceive through the body, even when it is not present to the senses, may be apprehended by us in the form of images. This occurs when we are asleep or in a state of excitement. But we cannot distinguish, so long as we rely on the senses, whether what we are perceiving are sensible objects or illusory images of them. Augustine concludes that we cannot seek the truth in the senses. Yet we do, in thought (*cognitio intellectualis*), apprehend the truth. Therefore it cannot rely upon sense-experience.

These are typical Platonic arguments against sensationalism. The objects of sensation are evanescent, and it is impossible to distinguish percepts from images. But Augustine assumes that perception is composed of sensations, and he therefore severs it from thought. Thomas now quotes the passage from Augustine in which he asserts that the mind produces the counterpart of impressions from its own substance.[1] 'It is inconceivable', he had said, 'that the body can make any impression on the mind, as though the mind were a substitute for matter in the activities of the body. For that which acts is in every way superior to that which is subject to action.' Hence he inferred that the bodily image is not produced in the mind by the body, but the mind itself causes it to arise within itself. Intellectual knowledge is not therefore derived from sensible objects.

He adds a further objection drawn from a prevailing precept of medieval thought. No effect surpasses its cause in power. But intellectual knowledge extends further than knowledge of sensible objects, for we have understanding of things which cannot be perceived by the senses, and so it cannot be a consequent sensation.

[1] Gen. ad. lit. xii. 16. Cf. p. 13 above.

He concludes his preliminary citation of opinions by a contrary statement from Aristotle that the foundation of our knowledge is in the senses.

Thomas now proceeds to discuss the question as follows. Three views have been held by philosophers on this problem. Democritus maintained that the only cause of our knowledge are images which flow from the bodies of which we are aware and pass into our minds, as Augustine records in his letter to Dioscorus.[1] Aristotle also says in his work *On Prophecy in Sleep* that Democritus held that knowledge takes place by means of images and fluxions emanating from objects. And the reason for this theory was that both Democritus and the other ancient natural philosophers did not consider that thought can be distinguished from sensation, as Aristotle points out in his treatise *On Mind*. In consequence, since sensation is a response to sensible entities, these philosophers thought that all our knowledge can be reduced to the impression of sensible entities on the mind. And this impression Democritus maintained was brought about by discharges of images from objects.

Plato, on the other hand, held that thought is distinct from sensation. He considered it to be an immaterial power which makes no use of a bodily organ. And since what is without body cannot be affected by body, he held that intellectual knowledge does not take place through the operation of sensible objects on the intellect, but in virtue of the intellect's participation in separate intelligible forms. He held further that sensation is a self-active power. It follows that sensation, since it is a spiritual power, is not a response to sensible objects; it is only the organs of sensation which are affected by sensible objects. In virtue of this distinction we can say that the mind is moved to form within itself the species of sensible entities. Thomas here recalls Augustine's doctrine which we have discussed above,[2] that it is not the body which experiences sensation but the mind through the body. The mind uses the body in the manner of a messenger in order to produce in itself what is announced from outside. He concludes his summary of the Platonic position thus. On the one hand, thought does not spring from sensation; on the other hand, sensation does not wholly arise from the impressions of sensible objects. Sensible objects excite the sensitive level of the mind to experience sensation, and in the same way sensations produce intellectual activity in the intellectual part of the mind.

---

[1] Ep. cxviii; P.L. xxxiii. 446.   [2] p. 14 above.

But there is a middle course open to us between sensationalism and Platonism and it is this middle course which, Thomas points out, was adopted by Aristotle. He agreed with Plato in distinguishing between thought and sensation. But he held that sensation cannot actually take place apart from the co-operation of the body. Sensation is not the activity of the mind alone, but the activity of the complex being, the body-mind. And this is true of all the activities of the sensory part of the mind. It is to be expected that the sensible objects outside the mind should produce some effect on the composite entity. Accordingly Aristotle so far agreed with Democritus that he considered the activities of the sensory part of the mind are caused by the impression of the sensible object; though he held that this took place not by an influx of atoms, but by a peculiar type of activity appropriate to the body-mind. But intellectual activity he thought was independent of the body's activity. Now nothing material can make any impression on an entity which is immaterial, and therefore, according to Aristotle, in order to bring about intellectual activity the mere impression of material sensible objects is not sufficient, but a higher form of process is necessary. For that which is active is nobler than that which is passive. But in subscribing to this principle Thomas adds that it does not follow that the intellectual activity is caused only by the impression on our minds of a higher order of reality. This was the view of Plato. The meaning is that the higher and nobler activity of which Aristotle speaks, and which is in fact the active intellect which has been discussed above, causes the images received from the senses to be expressed by a process of abstraction.

Thought, or intellectual activity, depends on sensation. But images cannot of themselves affect the mind.[1] They become intelligible through the work of the active intellect. Consequently it is impossible to maintain that sensory knowledge is the whole cause of thought; it is rather the material cause or occasion.

Such is Thomas's doctrine. The sensory and generalizing factors in perception are aspects of a process which includes them both. This complex activity is in part dependent upon physical stimulus, in part upon a preliminary grasp of the physical particulars by the mind. This process is one of generalization and from it spring reflection on abstract qualities and beings. When I perceive a pen the particular physical forces which impinge on the eye are

---

[1] *intellectus possibilis.*

apprehended in the form of a particular image, and this is necessary in order that the perception to take place. But it is not this changing image which I perceive, but the object. And this has general features. The pen possesses permanence and continuity, and the qualities which are perceived in it, its brown colour, shape, and hardness are implicitly abstract notions capable of being further abstracted from their particular embodiment in the pen. But before we proceed to describe Thomas's account of the non-sensory components of experience let us complete our description of the present section. What remains are the replies to the objections quoted at the beginning of the article.

To the first, that sensation gives no permanence, and that if there were nothing but sensation it would be impossible to distinguish between perceptions and illusions, Thomas briefly replies, that all Augustine means is that truth or real knowledge is not to be sought in sensory experience. The light of the active intellect is also required. And by it we apprehend the unchanging truth amid changing entities; and are enabled to distinguish real objects from illusory images.

To the second objection Thomas replies thus. When Augustine asserts that the mind produces images from within itself and is not affected by physical forces, he is referring not to thought but to imagination. But according to Plato imagination is a process which takes place only in the mind. Augustine follows this view in order to point out that bodies do not impress their images on the imagination, but that it is only the mind which does this. Here he employs the same argument as does Aristotle when he seeks to show that the active intellect is a separate process, the argument namely that what is active is superior in nature to what is passive. It is clear that, according to this position, we must assign to the imagination not only a passive but also an active role. But if we hold with Aristotle that the activity of imagination is an activity of the composite being, the body-mind, there is no difficulty. For the sensible body is superior to the animal organ, in that the former is related to the latter as what is in act to what is in potency, just as what is actually coloured is related to the pupil of the eye, which is only potentially coloured. It may be said, however, that although the primary effect of the imagination occurs by means of motions on the part of the sensible objects, since, as Aristotle says, the awareness of images is motion in accordance with sense, yet there is in man a mental activity which forms various images of things by analysis and synthesis, even of things which are not perceived by the senses. It is possible, Thomas concludes, to interpret Augustine's works in this sense.

These replies to the objections cited from Augustine illustrate Thomas's custom of adapting the Platonism of the great Church Father so as to avoid conflict with his own position. But it is doubtful whether Augustine can be interpreted in this way. For him sensation is a mental parallel of physical stimulus and apprehends the stimulus directly.

In reply to the third point Thomas observes that sensory awareness is not the whole basis of thought. Hence it is not strange that thought should surpass sensation in range.

VIII

Thomas founds knowledge upon sensible experience. But he gives no encouragement to the development of scientific investigation. He is respectful towards natural knowledge and echoing Augustine[1] he warns Christians against displaying their ignorance in discussing scientific questions. He lays down the principle that Holy Scripture can be explained in a number of ways and no one should abide by any particular interpretation so rigidly as to be unwilling to abandon it if it should clearly be shown to be false. Otherwise Scripture is exposed to the ridicule of unbelievers and obstacles placed in the way of their assent to the Faith.[2] The Angelic doctor is credited with a work of irrigation and mechanical engineering. But it is plain that his interest in empirical inquiry was meagre. He adopts without question the cosmology of Aristotle, the concentric spheres of the four elements, earth, water, air, and fire, the unchanging celestial spheres beyond the terrestrial order. He believed in demons, witchcraft, and divination, though he distinguished magic from legitimate science. But in two ways he prepared opinion, by criticizing prevailing error, to attend to the phenomena of nature. The errors which he strove to defeat were the refusal to recognize the independent working of secondary causes, and the belief that Nature was evil.

God is the ultimate cause of all the processes of nature. But Thomas does not agree with those theologians who, in the light of this premiss, tended to exclude and belittle the action of natural causation. He refuses to attribute the cause of heat to God and not to the fire. He traces this denial of natural efficiency to the

---

[1] Cf. p. 19 above.   [2] Q. lxviii. 1.

influence of Platonism, for in conformity with the theological view of nature Platonism had ascribed causal sequences to immaterial forms separated from the sensible realm. A similar opinion was held by Moslem theologians. Thus from many quarters direct interest in the operations of nature was disparaged.

Thomas attacks the orthodox view on the following grounds. If the action of all bodies on one another is due to nothing but the work of God, no effects appropriate to the special nature of things would necessarily follow. For God suffers no change through working by means of different creatures, and He could cause any effect to follow any cause. Actually, however, we see a uniform sequence of causes and effects; a hot body invariably produces heat and not cold, a human being always generates another human being. The necessary sequence of nature would be incomprehensible and otiose if God were the direct cause of all phenomena. Indeed such a view, in disparaging nature, disparages God; for if nothing effects anything, the world, which is the creation of God, becomes valueless. If the genuine interaction of things is not recognized we deny any order in the world, for the only way in which things radically different from one another form an order is through being connected by cause and effect. To attribute all effects not to things but to the immediate action of God makes it impossible to detect a cause from an examination of its effects, and thus all natural science is denied us.

A further point is that an effect in the realm of nature is a composite of matter and form; it is not simply form. But on the rule that like is produced by like the cause also must be not a form but a composite being. It must be a particular thing composed of matter and form. The distinct species of the Platonists and the active intellect as conceived by Avicenna must both be rejected as accounts of natural cause, since both are purely formal principles.[1]

But no medieval philosopher would deny that, however strongly the operation of secondary causes is insisted on, God is also present in the activities of nature. No difficulty, Thomas points out, arises from admitting both types of causation if certain distinctions are borne in mind. We must distinguish in every activity the thing which is active and the force in virtue of which it is active. A fire is a thing which is active in virtue of its heat. Now the effective power of a thing which is active is dependent on the power of an

[1] Contra Gent. iii. 69.

activity beyond it. Thus a craftsman directs a tool to its proper use. The lower agent, the instrument, is none the less a genuine and immediate cause of the effect, though it does not act, except under the control of the higher agent. The application to the divine activity in the natural universe is easily seen. Nature is God's instrument. He is the primary cause, the impact of things upon one another is the secondary cause. The most trivial event produces its special effects, but it is only able to do this in virtue of all the superior causes to which it is subject. But the analogy between God's relation to the world and that of a craftsman to his instrument must not be pressed too far. God is not external to the world, as a craftsman is external to his tool. The causal sequences of nature reveal, says St. Thomas, the immensity of God's goodness. He has communicated His Being to the multiplicity of events; and every natural activity exists, not for its own sake, but as a manifestation of the divine Life.[1]

Thomas is never tired of demonstrating the goodness of nature. And here it is important to appreciate the circumstances under which he wrote. In attacking the assumption that nature is evil he is not merely criticizing a perverse theory. He is concerned with the greatest danger that ever assailed the Medieval Church. The thirteenth century saw a widespread revival of Manichaean beliefs, against which, as we have noticed, Augustine had strenuously fought. The most notorious example of this rigid Puritan creed was the Albigensian heresy, on which the Church had exacted such terrible punishment. But the heresy had been almost as general as the Catholic Faith. The doctrines of this movement were based upon a dualism of spirit and matter, and it was believed that all forms of matter were evil. Nature, including the bodies of animals and men, was indiscriminatingly condemned. The Albigenses rejected the fundamental doctrines of orthodox Christianity and advocated social practices which threatened the continuance of the human race.

In his refutation of this pessimistic view of nature, which he traces back to Origen, Thomas rests upon a belief in the organic character of reality. We must think of the universe as an organic whole, in which all the parts contribute to the whole. In the attempt to discern the purpose of any particular unity or its parts, we find that each part exists for the sake of its particular function. Thus the eyes exist for the purpose of seeing. We observe further

[1] Ib. 70.

that the less important parts exist for the sake of the more important. The senses, for example, serve thought, and the lungs the heart. We see, too, that all parts are directed to the perfection of the whole, in the way in which matter serves form. Indeed, parts may be deemed matter in relation to the whole which can be conceived as form. If we now think of man as a whole we must look beyond him to the end which he serves. And this is the enjoyment of God.

Every creature, then, in the universe exists for the performance of its function. The inferior exists for the sake of the superior, and in the end every created thing exists to serve the entire universe. And reaching further Thomas asserts that the universe of nature with all its parts tends towards God. The divine goodness is the goal of all material things.[1]

IX

In sum, then, the progress of thought is the effort to realize the ideal unity which is the common ground of mind and its objects. It is an endeavour, the goal of which is fulfilment of being, and accordingly it is a facet of the all-pervading rhythm of potency and act. The understanding and what is understood are fundamentally of the same order. The movement of the spirit in the process of knowledge, in the process that is to say of identifying itself with its objects, constitutes the activity of the *species intelligibilis*. This approach of mind to its objects is expressed in various modes of unity by which general being is grasped, modes such as existence and essence, substance and accidents, genera and species. St. Thomas extends and deepens the notion of universals to include these primordial forms of being, which are the necessary conditions of awareness of objects. Accordingly he maintains that the mind apprehends universals directly, particulars indirectly. And the oft-repeated assertion that the proper object of the mind is the *nature* of some material thing expresses the same doctrine.

But this apprehension of universals in material things· is an awareness of extremely general features, of thinghood or being or oneness. In the effort to understand things more nearly, whether they be men, or trees, or rocks, we are led to specify and define the implicit universals. And here the human mind is limited by the presence of matter which confronts it at every turn. The universal element is in itself intelligible, and provides insight into the

[1] Q. lxv. 2.

foundation of things. But it is never found in itself. Thomas criticizes Platonism, that is to say the extreme Realism of the Medieval School, from every angle. We can only know Form directly in matter, and this means that it is always for us immersed in particular things. The intellectual element in mind cannot grasp particulars, for they are in themselves unintelligible. They are apprehended by corporeal organs through the senses of our bodies. Sensory awareness or perception is a condition of further understanding of the nature of things; and this further exploration of universal principles, of genera and species and of other relations is obtained by the process of abstraction and comparison. This is the work of the *intellectus agens*, which disengages universals from their sensory expression. The conceptions which we thus construct, ever reaching for more concrete universals, are likenesses of things. They are phenomena. We cannot attain the essences of things, for our dependence on perception compels our thought to be discursive.

Thus Thomas stands midway between extreme Realism and Nominalism. Whiteness and colour are reached by a process of analysis and synthesis, and must fall short of the concrete reality known in perception. In comparison the genera and species of thought and science are appearances, and exist *quoad modum concipiendi*. The modes of thought by which the mind understands the world differ from the mode of being in which nature exists. But the implicit universals which are given in sensible things and the abstract universals of reflection are not collections of sense-impressions nor mental signs by which singular images are conventionally taken to apply to a class. Our concepts refer to a universality in things though not apart from things. The business of discovering what are the essential characteristics of things demands an incessant revision of our abstractions. It requires a perpetual reference to the data of perception and a constant pursuit of logical coherence. St. Thomas is not concerned with working out a logic of empirical investigation. Duns Scotus pursued this problem. But the final lesson of his philosophy of knowledge is that human understanding is based upon sensory experience and that intuition of intelligible realities is impossible. The task of thought is to approach the complex realm of things by many paths, and so draw nearer to the concrete universal where essence and understanding are one. But we can never pass beyond similitudes. The proper object of thought is the knowledge of Form in matter. Such a position is capable of providing a foundation for natural science, while extreme Rea m and Nominalism assuredly cannot do so. Nevertheless the theory of knowledge is an incidental feature in the vast edifice of the *Summa Theologica*. The theme of St. Thomas's tremendous work is Sacred Doctrine, a science which is higher in dignity than other speculative sciences.[1] The impulse to develop scientific methods was not derived from the greatest of the Schoolmen, though beyond all other medieval thinkers his philosophical teaching was destined to endure.

Q i. a 5.

WILLIAM OF OCKHAM

REFERENCES

There are no modern editions of the philosophical works of William of Ockham. *The Commentary on the Sentences* has not been reprinted since 1495; the latest edition of the *Summa Totius Logicae* is the Oxford edition of 1675. The chief sources for the following account are the references in N. Abbagnano, *Guglielmo di Ockham*, Lanciano, 1931; S. C. Tornay, *Ockham, Studies and Selections*, La Salle, 1938; R. McKeon, *Selections from Medieval Philosophers*, London, 1931, vol. ii, pp. 351–421; E. A. Moody, *The Logic of William of Ockham*, London, 1935; E. Gilson, *The Unity of Philosophical Experience*, London, 1938; and the extensive quotations in C. Prantl, *Geschichte der Logik im Abendlande*, 1867, vol. iii, cap. 19. Abbagnano gives a useful bibliography up to 1930. A work of doubtful authenticity, *De Principiis Theologicae*, has been edited by L. Baudry, Paris, 1936.

I

In the fourteenth century medieval philosophy began to disintegrate. The decline in thought was part of the general collapse of the old order of Christendom to which many factors contributed. Among these events were the public scandals in the Church, the Hundred Years War, and the Black Death. A period of moral confusion set in, and mental activity deteriorated. Confidence in reason decreased, and an era of scepticism and theological irrationalism ensued. One mark of the destructive forces of the time was the revival of Nominalism, the chief advocate of which was William of Ockham.

He was born about the year 1300 at the village of Ockham near Guildford in Surrey. At an early age he became a student at Oxford, and soon afterwards entered the Franciscan Order. He completed his course at Oxford as far as the Bachelor stage, and taught there until 1324. But he never attained to the degree of Master in Theology. Students who did not proceed beyond the

The abbreviations refer to the following works:

Cent. Theolog.	Centilogium Theologicum.
Expos. Aur.	Expositio Aurea et admodum utilis super artem veterem.
Quodlib.	Quodlibeta septem.
Sum. tot. log.	Summa totius logicae.
Summulae	Summulae in libros physicorum.
Sent.	Super quatuor libros sententiarum subtilissimae quaestiones earundumque decisiones.

Bachelor stage of the degree were known as *inceptores*, and Ockham became renowned as the *venerabilis inceptor*. It is probable that the originality of his views even at this early period of his life was disapproved of by the Doctors of the University. Certainly the vigour with which he announced them soon brought him into disfavour in the highest quarter. It had long been customary for a teacher in philosophy to enter on his career with a course of lectures on the Four Books of *Sentences* of Peter Lombard. This work, which was composed about 1150, is a collection of the opinions of the Church Fathers, especially those of St. Augustine, upon the principal topics of theology. It had become the chief text-book of the University, and Roger Bacon declared that at Paris the *Sentences* were more studied than the Bible. The lectures of the young *inceptor* proved to be dangerously unorthodox; he propounded a doctrine of empiricism, and did not shrink from objecting to the grounds upon which the tenets of theology were traditionally supported. His doctrines were referred to the Curia; and in 1324 he was summoned by the Pope to Avignon in order to face an investigation of his opinions. Judgement was delayed, and for some years William was confined in the Franciscan house at Avignon.

But meanwhile the provocative young scholar had become prominent in a more formidable controversy. The Pope, the ruthless and avaricious John XXII, had attempted to suppress the teaching of the mendicant party of the Franciscans, a body which believed in and practised the doctrine of the absolute poverty of Christ. The movement was bitterly hostile to the Papacy, nor could the tortures of the Inquisition check its rapid growth in north Italy and France. In a sermon delivered at Bologna, Ockham publicly allied himself with these spirituals, who were led by the general of the Franciscan Order, Michael of Cesena. He was arrested and imprisoned at Avignon. In 1326 a commission of six theologians found that fifty-one articles in his commentary on the *Sentences* were heretical and pestilential. But Ockham refused to retract them, and in 1328 added to the danger of his position by signing the protest drawn up by Cesena against the Papal Bull which had condemned the doctrine of apostolic poverty. On the night of 24 May of that year, in company with Cesena and Bonagratia, the brilliant Franciscan lawyer, he escaped from the prison at Avignon and made a perilous journey to Pisa. Here he placed himself under the protection of the Emperor, Louis of Bavaria. By this action he finally severed himself from the authority of the Pope. In the previous year Louis had descended on Rome, proclaimed the deposition of John XXII, and set up an anti-Pope of his own election. Ockham was solemnly excommunicated upon joining himself with the monarch against whom the Pope had already exhausted his spiritual maledictions.

Soon after this critical event in Ockham's career the Emperor and his court moved to Munich. The youthful philosopher had promised to defend Louis with his pen in return for the protection of the Emperor's sword; and now from the seclusion of the Franciscan monastery at Munich he poured forth a series of pamphlets directed against the Pope. The most important of these are the *Eight Questions concerning the Power and Dignity of the Pope* and the *Dialogue between Master and Disciples upon the Power of Emperors and Popes*. His main purpose in these works is to advocate a loftier discipline for the Church, but he expresses a remarkable defence of the principle of political representation both in Church and State. In conformity with his theory of knowledge he placed the emphasis upon the individual person in opposition to the corporate body; and he asserts that the actions of the State must be judged according to the law of nature. He finds the seat of the law of nature in the moral decisions of individual citizens. In such reflections he lent assistance to the reforming ideas of his great contemporary, Marsilio of Padua, the author of *Defensor Pacis*.

Ockham remained at Munich engaged in polemical writing in every field of discussion. He produced a comprehensive logical treatise entitled *Summa totius logicae*. During these years he was compelled to witness the decline of his protector's resolution. The Emperor entered into negotiations with Pope Benedict XXII. He wrote pitiful excuses for his past action and foreswore all his former partisans. Among these was Cesena with whose cause Ockham had been so deeply identified. Ockham took part in the numerous Diets of prelates, princes, and nobles which met to discuss the reconciliation of the Empire and the Papacy, and it is possible to detect the influence of his ideas in a declaration which asserted that the right of electing the Emperor was independent of the approbation of the Pope. But after numerous vacillations Louis, in 1344, agreed to the most humiliating terms at the hands of Clement VI. He was deserted by his supporters and died in 1347. Amid the tribulations caused by these events Ockham had also to endure the devastation spread by the Black Death, and in 1349 he himself succumbed to the plague.

William of Ockham was a revolutionary figure. His life was spent in polemics. His logical criticisms shook the foundations of Scholasticism, and the dialectics of the following centuries revolved round the problems which he had raised. His three most important philosophical works are the *Commentary on the Sentences*, the *Sum of All Logic*, and the *Golden Exposition of the Ancient Art*. Let us now proceed to indicate the circumstances in which these works were composed.

II

Thomas Aquinas died in 1274. The remaining quarter of the thirteenth century was filled with controversies excited by his challenge to the accepted views, and the current of thought for a time prevailed against the new Aristotelianism. Three years after the death of Thomas, the Bishop of Paris received instructions from the Pope to make an inquiry into the doctrines taught at the University. The Bishop found himself obliged to condemn no less than two hundred and nineteen theses maintained in the schools; and though the bulk of the censored propositions were Averroistic, a number of important doctrines taught by Thomas were also included in the ban. The ascription of the principle of individuation to matter, for instance, and the teaching that the body participated in the intellectual operations of the mind, were forbidden. A few days after the decree of Paris a similar condemnation of Thomist theories was declared at Oxford. This indictment of certain principles of the new school was the signal for renewed confidence in Augustinian ideas, and a number of Franciscan philosophers asserted the traditional theory of knowledge and reality in opposition to the Thomist philosophy.

For Augustine our conceptions are not obtained by recourse to objects perceived by the senses; the mind illumined by the divine Light directly apprehends the immutable truth in the eternal reasons. To the problem of abstraction Augustine, as we have seen, gives no clear answer.[1] Accordingly philosophers who held that he was the teacher *par excellence*, philosophers such as Matthew of Aquasparta[2] and Roger Marston, attempted a compromise between

---

[1] Cf. p. 17 above.

[2] Matthew of Aquasparta was born about 1240 and died in 1302. He was a pupil of Bonaventura and was general of the Franciscan Order in 1287. The references to his views are taken from *Quaestiones de Fide et Cognitione*, Q. 2.

the doctrines of their master and the analysis of knowledge presented in the new system. Matthew agreed that Thomas's account of knowledge as the production of sense, memory, and experience, and that the description of the way in which the active intellect abstracts the intelligible species from the sensory images, furnished an adequate representation of the processes of temporal knowledge or *scientia*. But he refused to admit that *scientia* was the whole of knowledge. Our knowledge has *a priori* as well as an *a posteriori* source; and certain demonstrations, those for example which lead to proofs of God's existence and of the spiritual nature of the self, are open to it apart from sense-experience. But Matthew adds a curiously Kantian interpretation to the 'ideal reasons'. They are not objects of our thought, but motives which lead and direct our understanding. 'The material principle of knowing is from external things from which the species of the things to be known are derived, but the formal principle is partly within, that is from the light of reason, partly from above, but fully and finally from the eternal rules and reasons.' Roger Marston held that the active intellect is nothing but the divine illumination in which we perceive with certitude all the truth implicit in our judgements of reality. Thus in the face of Thomas's arguments the characteristic position of Augustine was reaffirmed.

Many other writers contributed to this reassertion of the older view of knowledge. Even Roger Bacon,[1] despite his eloquent advocacy of experimental methods, insisted that they must be supplemented by inner illumination. He argued at length against the view that the active intellect is part of the mind. It is, he averred, a substance separate from the mind subject to the divine inspiration. And in other respects he adhered to the principles of Neoplatonism.

But the end of the century produced a young philosopher of greater power and ingenuity than any of these authorities; one of the pre-eminent thinkers of the Middle Ages. 'Subtle' is the traditional and appropriate epithet applied to Duns Scotus.[2] The interpretation of his views is difficult; but he appears on some

---

[1] Roger Bacon was born about 1215 and lectured at Paris and at Oxford. His works contain extraordinarily prophetic conclusions on such matters as plant-life, the habits of animals, the nature of tides and rainbows, and the density of the air. He sketched the principles of an embracing science which should bring all natural phenomena under mathematical principles. He died in 1294.

[2] He was born about 1270 in Scotland, studied at Cambridge and at Oxford, frequently visited Paris, and died at Cologne in 1308.

issues to range himself in opposition to the doctrines of St. Thomas. Thus he rejects the distinction between essence and existence, and refuses to admit the Thomist view of matter as pure potency. For our purpose, the modifications which he introduced into the new theory of knowledge are of interest. He agrees with Thomas in recognizing that all knowledge springs from sensory apprehension of particular entities. This perceptual apprehension is, however, complex, corresponding to the complexity of the individual thing. The mind discovers a number of formal elements in the objective world, in the light of which particular things are *formalitates*, perceived and understood. Causal connexion is one of these principles. We shall find that Ockham criticizes this view of knowledge, which resembles that of Kant, as a variety of extreme Realism. Yet Scotus also refuses to accept principles dear to the followers of Augustine, and considers the doctrine of Illumination an invitation to scepticism.

Thus at the close of the century resistance to Thomism was strong. Thomas indeed had many disciples, and his prestige was established by the support of the Dominican Order. But the revival of Augustinian interpretations of knowledge throughout the universities inspired much of the polemics of William of Ockham.

And there is another less negative tradition of which William was the heir. We have seen that Abaelard in the twelfth century founded a school of logicians who directed their attention to the relation between thought and language.[1] A conspicuous writer in this field was Petrus Hispanus (1226–77), who in his *Summulae Logicales* discusses at length the properties of words. He treats of words as signs, the expansion and restriction of signs; the principles of naming and other properties of terms. The connexions of logical thinking are regarded as ways in which words can be arranged. Many philosophers were led to investigate, after Petrus, 'the modes of signification'. These teachers concentrated more upon correct expression than upon truth. For them metaphysical questions concerning the nature of the objects to which terms refer became matters of secondary interest. When the principle consideration is the way in which things are understood and expressed, the path is open for a development of conceptualism and nominalism. Thus a typical utterance of this school is the following: 'It is clear that the notion of man and of animal in so far as it is distinguished from Socrates is a fabrication of the intellect

[1] p. 65 above.

and is nothing but a concept; for nature has not formed distinct principles of this kind as actual existences.'[1] Here are Conceptualism and Nominalism in a sentence. The generality in our thinking is subjective.

But none of these writers developed the implications of these ideas in the persistent manner of Ockham. In points where the theory of knowledge touches theology Peter Aureol followed Augustine.

III

Ockham's popular fame rests upon the celebrated razor. It is continually at hand throughout his works. 'To employ a number of principles when it is possible to use a few is a waste of time.' 'We must never assume a number of elements unless we are forced to do so.' To work with more entities where it is possible to work with fewer is futile. 'Frustra fit per plura quod potest fieri per paucoria.'[2] The rule is invoked against the excessive verbal divisions which filled the writings of contemporary logicians. At the same time Ockham is critical of loose language in philosophy. 'Aristotle and Averroës', he complains, 'frequently use terms in a misleading metaphorical and figurative sense.'[3] But the rule of economy in explanation is chiefly directed against every form of Realism, against the tendency he found among the *moderni* to treat terms as metaphysical substances. It is upon the entities of the new realist schools who confused words with things that the razor constantly descends. 'Sufficiunt singularia et ita tales res universales omnino frustra ponuntur.' The pervading note of Ockham's philosophical discussions is the rejection of all facets of Realism. Universals have no existence in reality. They are convenient mental fictions, signs standing for many particulars at once.

Ockham bears witness to the domination of Realism in contemporary thought. He declares that all whom he meets agree in asserting that the entity which is in some way universal actually exists in the individual object.[4] From the immense number of arguments against Realism which fill his logical works we may select the following. There was the extreme type of Realism which

---

[1] Petrus Aureoli (died 1322), Ueberweg-Geyer, *Geschichte der Philosophie*, p. 257.
[2] The maxim is employed by other Oxford Franciscans, for instance, Richard of Middleton and Duns Scotus.
[3] Summulae i. 13; Tornay, p. 41.
[4] Sent. i, dist. 2, qu. 7; Tornay, p. 126.

asserted that the universal exists as a mode of being distinct from the individual instance which exemplifies it. Echoing a criticism which we have heard levelled by Abaelard against William of Champeaux, Ockham protests that there is no single identical and simple entity which is present in each of a number of particular things at the same moment. On this view the particular thing and the universal are two distinct existences; and a single thing cannot exist in several other things. But some philosophers offered another interpretation of the universal. They maintained that the universal was capable of being *communicated* to many things at the same time. What is the nature of this communication? If it means that the universal is imparted to many things at once without causing any alteration in itself or multiplying itself in the things, it remains a single identity or an individual; and our former difficulty returns.

We have noticed that it was a cardinal doctrine of Scholastic thought that universals were the essences of things. Duns Scotus had recently given a peculiar turn to this principle. He argued that the universal is not the whole of the essence of an individual but part of its essence. If it were the whole essence the individual thing or person would be the universal. Nevertheless, formal distinctions made by reason in the thing have status in the thing. They are *formalitates*. Ockham replies that even to say that the universals or *formalitates* are part of the essence of an individual implies that in any individual there would be as many distinct objects as there are universals which could be predicated of it.[1] If the universal 'humanity' were an entity distinct from a particular individual and at the same time part of its essence, it would be in a number of different places at the same time. And, what is worse, it would be Judas and Christ simultaneously.

Similar objections are pressed against a further theory proposed by the subtle doctor. The universal, according to him, is not actually different from the individual. It is present in particular things in a contracted form. Humanity is present in Socrates in a specific way. Once more Ockham points out that it would follow that there would be as many universals as there are individuals. And this would mean the denial of universals; there would be no common nature.[2]

Most of Ockham's criticisms against universals are variations on the theme that a single distinct entity appearing in a multiplicity

---

[1] Sent. i, dist. 2, qu. 4; Tornay, pp. 126–7.   [2] Ib.; Tornay, pp. 127–8.

of individual things is a contradiction in terms. For the universal is described in language proper to the individual. But if it is an individual it is incomprehensible how it can appear in a multitude of individuals. If it is present in a number of particulars it cannot be a single entity. He roundly concludes that there is no such being as a universal in the sense of an entity present in each of a number of items of experiences and common to them. It is as great an impossibility that anything should exist outside the mind in any universal form as it is that a man should at the same time be an ass. To say that the universal has objective being is like saying that the word 'man' is part of the individual to which it refers.[1] Realism is denied, as we shall notice, even to the divine mind. The acceptance of universal realities, apart from the confusions to which it leads, violates the Law of Economy. Knowledge can be described without introducing such types of existence. Universals are unnecessary.

Ockham uncompromisely rejects all modes of Realism. We turn with interest to his own view of knowledge; for we are at a crisis in the history of European thought. It is here that there occurs most markedly the breach with the magnanimous tradition of *philosophia perennis*.

The basis of experience is provided by *notitia intuitiva*, intuition. It alone gives clearness and conviction. The other main division of knowledge, abstract knowledge, gives in comparison doubtful and confused information. Confusion arises when the mind fails to distinguish accurately between items of experience. Whether an object is part of another object, all distinctions in fact, can ultimately be decided only by direct perception. All knowledge of the elements of which terms or objects are composed is derived from this intuition, and the mind can fail to attain truth only when it cannot reach the objects of intuition or when intuition suffers some obstruction. Now the objects of intuition are in the first place individual things. They are not essences or quiddities, but the objects of sense-perception, each of which may differ as much from another as an individual person differs from another person. But intuition is not only of individual objects in the sensible world. It also perceives immediately the relations between objects. When anyone sees Socrates and white at the same time, he is certain that Socrates is white.[2] But before we refer to further elements

---

[1] Sent. i, dist. 2, qu. 7; Abbagnano, p. 88 n.
[2] Sent. i, dist. 2, qu. 7, and ib. Prol. qu. 1; Cornay, p. 120.

revealed by intuition we must draw attention to the most important evidence which it provides. Intuition gives knowledge of reality. It informs us whether an object exists or does not exist. 'Notitia intuitiva rei est talis notitia virtute cujus potest sciri utrum res sit vel non.'[1] Reality is most securely known in immediate present experience. Intuitive knowledge is then said to be perfect. It is imperfect when it passes judgement on past experience. For even memory images are classified as abstract in this strict empiricism. When I see a wall or touch a flame, I know certainly that the wall or flame exists. But if I recall them or imagine them I am not sure that they exist.[2]

But intuition is not mere sensation. Within it a sensory and an intellectual factor are distinguished. Sensation is associated with appetite, of which it is said to be the cause. But sensation, for example of sight, is not sufficient to produce awareness of an object; an 'intellectual' intuition is further required. The function of this factor is to classify the object of our intuition, to pronounce what it is.[3] The sensory factor tells us *that* the thing exists, the intellectual factor allows us to recognize it; and any perception requires both elements. This doctrine that *intellectus* knows sensible things intuitively is a revolution in medieval ways of thought. That the intellect or understanding could not know particular sensible things was a cardinal point of Scholastic teaching. Even for St. Thomas our minds can grasp no more than the abstract nature of each individual object. We cannot seize its individuality, for this is conditioned by matter. Our knowledge is confined to universals. But for Ockham there are no universal essences immanent in things. Matter is not the limiting factor in individuality; it is the individual itself (so far as it is a sensible object), and it is apprehended as a recognizable object by the combined activities of intellect and sensation in intuition.

The world is directly perceived. All theories of representative knowledge are repudiated. Ideas which are asserted to resemble the reality of which they are copies assume acquaintance with that reality. If anyone saw the statue of Hercules without having any previous knowledge of Hercules, he might take it to represent Achilles. Ideas or species which convey a similitude of the real

---

[1] Sent. Prol. qu. 1; Abbagnano, p. 58 n.
[2] *De Princip. Theolog.*, ed. Baudry, p. 133.
[3] Quodlib. i, qu. 15; McKeon, ii, p. 368.

world are logically impossible, and the introduction of them offends against the principle of economy.[1]

In abolishing any idea or other intermediary between experience and its object Ockham sweeps away at a stroke the *species intelligibilis* of St. Thomas. The account which the Angelic Doctor gives of knowledge requires, as we have seen, an intermediary between object and subject that makes possible the passage of thought. The view rests on the belief that thought is immanent; knowing is a mode of being, a realization of Form, and when the active intellect extracts the intelligible species from the phantoms it is expressing no less the nature of the object than the nature of the subject. Thomas often speaks of the intelligible species as though it were a copy or substitute for the object. But he insists that it is not the species which is known but the object. But if this is the case Ockham argues that the intelligible species is otiose. The object and the mind in direct relation are all that it is necessary to postulate. Moreover, it is impossible to understand how matter which is presumed to be incapable of causal action on the immaterial mind can produce the immaterial species.[2]

Experience is simple and direct. But here two interesting qualifications in Ockham's empiricism must be described. The first widens the range of objects which can be intuitively perceived; the second introduces a reservation into the guarantee given by the act of perception that objects exist. As regards the first point it is not only objects perceived by means of the external senses which can be directly known. Actually it is the region of inner experience, comprising acts of will, pleasure, or sorrow, that are most immediately and convincingly known. Judgements based on these processes carry greater certainty than any other class of contingent propositions. In asserting that the experiences of the self are better known than external objects, Ockham refers to the authority of St. Augustine, quoting his argument that while anyone can doubt the delivery of sense perception no one can be sceptical regarding his own existence.[3]

Some hesitation concerning the existence of objects perceived by our external senses is here indicated. And this leads to the second qualification in Ockham's empiricism. For intuitions may sometimes be clear without giving guarantee of their existence.

[1] Sent. Prol. qu. 9; Tornay, p. 16; Abbagnano, p. 70 n.
[2] Sent. ii, qu. 15; Tornay, p. 4; cf. Sent. i, dist. 3, qu. 2; Abbagnano, p. 72 n.
[3] Sent. Prol. qu. 1; Tornay, p. 121.

In a passage which has a highly modern ring, it is pointed out that we may continue to see a star after it has been destroyed.[1] And God can give an intuition of an object which has no real existence. But in the natural course of things intuitive knowledge is always caused by objects. It is a contradiction that sight should refer to nothing. A chimera cannot be perceived. Puzzles such as those due to after-images are easily solved. If a person looks at the sun and then goes into a dark room he will have an image of the sun before his eyes; but it is not the sun he sees but the 'light impressed on his eyes'.[2]

The final references of truth, then, are the testimonies of the external or internal senses. These alone in Ockham's terms give evident knowledge. But he does not deny that propositions even of the most general character are not immediately apprehended and recognized as true. 'We apprehend not only simple things, but also propositions and demonstrations.'[3] But the 'assent' by which we judge propositions to be true ultimately depends, when analysed, on the evident awareness of individual experiences. This is so, even of propositions which claim to be self-evident, such as the proposition that the whole is greater than the part. They presuppose the apprehension of individual things, though the immediate assent is not to them.[4]

IV

Ockham has categorically rejected all forms of Realism, and grounded knowledge on direct apprehension of individual objects. 'Nihil est in rerum natura extra animam nisi singulare.' What, then, does he conceive to be the nature of universals? The answer will have a profound effect on medieval life and thought. Unfortunately a precise answer to the question is not easy. He expresses views which are not obviously consistent with one another. The position adopted in the *Commentary on the Sentences* differs from the theory which is maintained in the later works. It is reasonable to suppose that when he wrote the *Summa totius logicae*, the *Septem quodlibeta*, and the *Expositio Aurea* he had changed his opinion.[5]

Berkeley, writing from the standpoint of extreme empiricism four

---

[1] Sent. Prol. qu. 1; Tornay, p. 120.
[2] Quod. vi, qu. 6; McKeon, ii, p. 374; Sent. ii, qu. 15; Abbagnano, p. 68 n.
[3] Sent. Prol. qu. 1; Tornay, p. 122.   [4] Quodlib. iv. 17; McKeon, ii, p. 384.
[5] Mr. Tornay attempts to combine the earlier and the later positions into a coherent doctrine, but the texts plainly point to divergent theories. On this point cf. J. R. Weinberg, *The Philosophical Review*, vol. l, no. 5, pp. 523 ff.

hundred years later, recognized that knowledge is concerned with universals. He observed: 'It is I know a point much insisted on that all knowledge and demonstration are about universal notions, to which I fully agree.'[1] Ockham writes that 'properly speaking there is no science of individuals, but of universals.[2] And so far both the fourteenth- and the eighteenth-century empiricists follow Aristotle and the medieval tradition. But Berkeley immediately went on to add that universality does not consist 'in the absolute positive nature or conception of anything, but in the relations it bears to the particulars signified by it; by virtue whereof it is that things, names, or notions being in their own nature particular are rendered universal. . . . The particular triangle . . . doth stand for and represent all rectilinear triangles whatsoever, and is, in that sense universal.' Ockham's interpretation of thought resembles this position but is more satisfactory, both with regard to the empirical basis of experience and to the function of general ideas.

At the outset one fact must be made clear. Ockham rejects extreme Nominalism. The universal concept is not a mere *vox*, an arbitrary and conventional noise. He rejects the position of Roscellinus on the ground that in this case there would be no species or genus at all; and also on the ground that God and any object external to the mind could become universal equally with what is in the mind. In other words, he assumes that some kind of reality attaches to general notions, and insists that they must be distinguished from the particular objects of intuition.

In the *Commentary on the Sentences* he admits as plausible the view which he afterwards adopted, that universals possess actual existence as a quality of the thinking process, as a psychical experience. But he decides against this theory in favour of another principle. This principle is that universals have only logical status. Their function is to enter propositions as predicates, asserting universality of groups of particular subjects. This logical function does not endow universal terms with any real existence. They are 'meanings'. 'There are certain entities which have only logical being. Thus propositions, syllogisms, and similar topics dealt with by logic possess no objective being, but only logical being. Their being consists in being thought, *eorum esse est eorum cognosci.*'[3]

---

[1] *Principles of Human Knowledge* (1710), Introd. 15.
[2] Sent. i, dist. 2, qu. 8; Abbagnano, p. 90 n.
[3] Ib.; Tornay, p. 132.

Universals have a being of this kind. In order to understand the principle it is necessary to touch on some technical terms which occupy important places in Ockham's doctrine. He classifies the contents of thought under the heading of first and second intentions. First intentions or primary experiences are direct intuitions of things, the mental responses to objects. But they also include complex intuitions of truths. There are immediately evident propositions as well as evident perceptions. The main point is that first intentions refer to elements which are not signs of something other than themselves. Second intentions, or secondary concepts, are defined as signs of first intentions. Here the terms do not refer directly to actual things but to features of things abstracted for special investigation. Two important types of such investigation are grammar and logic. At this point another expression of great significance in Ockham's philosophy is introduced, the expression *suppositio*, substitution. Following the current grammatical logic he classifies terms under three types of *suppositio*, namely *simplex, materialis*, and *personalis*; and it is in connexion with the first of these forms of substitution that he makes an important innovation. Terms that are material substitutes refer to grammatical symbols, such as 'nouns', 'adjectives'. Terms that are personal substitutes stand for the particular items referred to in a general term; thus the word 'man' is a personal substitute when it stands for individual men. Now, in the current logic terms that are simple substitutes stand for universals; 'man' stands for 'man-in-general'. For Ockham, terms of this class, *suppositiones simplices*, can only refer to 'intentions' of the mind, to concepts. They cannot refer to any realities. 'A substitution is simple when a term is a substitute for a mental concept. . . . Hence the error of those who believed that there was something in reality besides the singular entity and who held that humanity distinguished from singular instances is something that exists in individuals and is related to their essence.'[1] In all this Ockham is drawing attention to the difference between real meaning and logical meaning, between assertions about forms of discourse and assertions about things. He is distinguishing discussions about what actually exists from discussions about the rational operations which are used in the first type of discourse. Terms of second intention are formal. To confuse them with realities which are individual things

[1] Sum. tot. log. i. 66; Prantl, iii, p. 351, n. 796. Cf. ib. i. 64; Abbagnano, p. 128.

is to abolish the distinction between logic and science. In knowledge about reality, *scientia realis*, the propositions stand for things;
in rational knowledge they stand for mental constructions. The
fatal error is to mix forms of thought with the things thought of,
signs with what they signify. Thus the Aristotelian categories do
not refer to things but to concepts of second intention. There is
nothing actually outside the mind but particular things.

The same point is driven home in a passage in the *Commentary
on the Sentences*. Let us take the proposition *homo est risibilis*.
When this sentence is uttered we hear it, and we hear it with our
bodily ears just as we also perceive colour or light with our
bodily eyes. Accordingly there exist true propositions which are
composed of words or sounds, and concerning which we have some
knowledge. But our knowledge, which is represented by the
spoken propositions, is sometimes a knowledge of reality, sometimes a logical knowledge, although in both cases only words are
given. In the first instance the words stand for certain real things
outside the mind; it is then a question of knowledge of reality. In
the second instance the words represent, not real things, but only
ideas; then it is a question of logical knowledge. But whether their
contents are real or only logical, these propositions always consist of
words. They belong to different branches of knowledge only for this
reason, that some signify objects, while others signify ideas only.[1]

Universals then are second intentions of the simple order. They
refer to terms, not things. 'The secondary process produces the
universals and second intentions and does not presuppose them.'[2]
Universals are signs, standing for a set of qualities or objects; they
are universal by meaning. Thus the historic controversy over the
nature of universals becomes pointless. For to discuss whether a
universal is related to an individual is like discussing whether the
name or sign 'table' is part of the table. Some signs stand for one
thing, others stand for many things, and these are universals; but
everything which actually exists is a single thing. All the difficulties about universals spring from the attempt to make them both
singular and plural at the same time. Species and genus do not
name substances, but signs.

How disturbing these principles were to the traditional beliefs
can be illustrated by Ockham's application of them to theology;
and when we read the passages in the first book of the *Commentary
on the Sentences* in which he criticizes the historic conceptions we

---

[1] Sent. i, dist. 2, qu. 4.   [2] Sent. ii, qu. 25; Tornay, p. 124.

can understand the charges of heresy which kept him prisoner at Avignon. For St. Augustine and the realists formless matter becomes an individual thing, a rock or a tree, in virtue of its participation in an idea, and ideas subsist in the mind of God. Ockham rejects this view completely. An idea is not a thing; it is a logical entity, *habet tantum quid nominis*. Ideas cannot therefore constitute part of the divine being. They are rather ideals according to which God creates individual things, and an ideal can be entertained only by acquaintance with actual instances which suggest it. A builder keeps a house before his eyes in order to make another similar to it. Exemplary ideas, then, arise from acquaintance with singular things. There are no ideas of genera or essences. When it is maintained that God knows by means of ideas, the only acceptable sense is that He knows the infinite number of particular things which are created by Him. This knowledge is particular, not general. If Plato said that ideas referred to the species and not to singular objects he was wrong.[1]

Thus the *universale ante rem* is discarded and the divine Ideas are described as God's creative knowledge of particular things. The interpretation moves away from the ancient assumptions which conceived reality in terms of immutable patterns and eternal reasons. It points to the productive will of God as the ground of the universe, rather than to His unchangeable essence.

In his later works Ockham, as we have noticed, changes his position concerning the nature of universals. He adheres to the main point that they are signs standing for groups of things. But instead of conceiving them as logical contents formed by the mind he maintains that they are qualities or aspects of the mind itself. They inform the mind as white informs a wall.[2] The assumption of logical fictions interposed between mind and the real objects known in intuition offends against the Law of Economy.[3] Second intentions no less than first intentions are acts of the mind; they are real beings or qualities existing in the mind.[4] The process is described as follows. There is first the direct apprehension of single things in intuition; the mind then produces an *intentio* or *passio* which refers to these objects and can stand for them. These concepts are quite general. Just as the word 'man' no

---

[1] Sent. i, dist. 35, qu. 5; Tornay, p. 137 f.
[2] Expos. Aur. Lib. Perierm. Proem. Abbagnano, p. 92 n.
[3] Quòdlib. iv. 19; McKeon, p. 389.
[4] Ib., pp. 390, 391; cf. Summ. tot. log. i. 12; Abbagnano, p. 93 n.

more signifies Socrates than Plato, so the concept is equally general. Accordingly, concepts or affections (*passiones*) of the mind are natural substitutes for the things themselves, just as words are artificial substitutes.[1]

An interesting distinction is here drawn between universals in the sense of natural expressions of the mind and in the sense of conventional expressions. The latter are words. The former are spontaneous expressions of the mind's relationship with things. Animals and men emit sounds in order to express their feelings; a groan signifies the pain of a sick man, a smile indicates inner joy. In the same way the mind utters expressions which are symbols of groups or patterns of things. These spontaneous mental universals have no external reality.[2] They are mental signs, essential features of the mind's activity.

Ockham does not pursue this theory of natural mental language, *representative* response to the world underlying artificial speech. If pressed further I imagine he would say that natural intentions are ultimately forms of behaviour. He complicates and indeed confuses the theory by frequently speaking of *intentiones* as like-nesses of a thing, *similitudines rei*. Such phrases suggest a uniformity of nature between mental concepts and the objects which they represent. What is plain is that the similarity which is predicated of things and in virtue of which the mind is able to express mental concepts and verbal signs standing for groups of objects does not imply any reality beyond distinct similar things. There is no whiteness, only different white things.[3] Mental signs cannot then resemble general entities, for there are none such. In any case it is difficult to see how a process of mind can be like a thing. The phrase, *similitudo rei*, cannot mean any concession to Realism to which Ockham is unequivocally opposed.

V

We can now attempt to assess the Nominalism of William of Ockham; and in order to do so we must glance at some of the philosophical premises on which it rests. The conception of knowledge, of which a rough summary has been given, presumes an outlook on the world which breaks with the main tradition of scholastic thought. Its ancestry lies rather with Stoicism than

---

[1] Expos. Aur. Lib. Perierm. Abbagnano, p. 94 n.
[2] Sum. tot. log. i. 14; Tornay, p. 125.
[3] Sent. i, dist. 30, qu. 1; Abbagnano, p. 98 n.

with Plato and Aristotle. Since there are no common natures in things, existence is composed of individual items in various relations. Everything that is is an individual thing. In Ockham's language *ens* and *unum*, being and one, are identical. To be one is to be a substance; and to be a substance is to exist.

'It must be maintained undoubtedly that anything imaginable whatsoever, which subsists by itself, is without any addition to it a singular thing and one in number, so that no imaginable thing is singular through having something added to it, but this (i.e. being singular) is an attribute belonging immediately to everything, because everything is *per se* identical with or diverse from others.'[1]

We have seen that for St. Thomas essence is what the object really is. It is its universal nature expressed in its definition. An essence or quiddity can be understood without anything being known of its existence. Existence is a function of matter, by which the essences of composite things are multiplied in numerous individuals. But for Ockham there are no universal essences which require to be expressed in matter in order to become individuals. This is what he means by saying that the singular thing is singular without any addition to it. The singular thing requires no metaphysical 'principle of individuation'. And with the rejection of these distinctions the distinction between essence and existence, which occupies so vital a place in the philosophy and theology of St. Thomas, is abandoned.[2] The refusal to accept formal properties as realities affects the view of matter in other respects. The theory of primary matter had descended from Greek speculation through St. Augustine. The theory had sought to provide for the continuity and connexion of things in their material aspect, and also to supply a passive medium or context for the generation of things by form. As the universal amorphous medium in which definite substances were shaped by forms, it had been conceived as pure potentiality. This notion of a pure potentiality, possessing no actuality nor form, had been severely criticized in the thirteenth century, particularly at Oxford; and Ockham carries forward the criticism. He allows certain common features in all matter, such as its plastic adaptability to many types of substantial forms. But these features have no existence apart from particular things. Primary matter is always *in actu*; or, to speak more accurately, it always has some actuality and embodiment. And these embodi-

---

[1] Expos. Aur. i, Moody, p. 79.
[2] Sum. tot. log. iii. 2, 27; Abbagnano, p. 158 n.

ments are all uniquely different. 'In all generated and existing things the various primary matters are each distinct and different, just as various white objects are different. My primary matter is different from your primary matter.'[1] The positivist and phenomenal tendency of this philosophy is here apparent. In one passage Ockham's thought becomes even more prophetic, for he identifies matter with quantitative dimension. 'It is impossible to have first matter without extension, for matter cannot exist without having parts distant from part. But this amounts to asserting that matter is extended, quantitative and has dimensions.'[2]

The sense of dissatisfaction with the accepted principles of explanation is apparent in a further passage in the *Summulae* where he writes, 'And if it is asked why matter is potentiality and form act, the answer is that such is the nature of the thing, and there is no other cause for it, but that matter is matter and form is form.' This, in truth, is no proper cause, he adds; but we do not know any others.[3]

Other discussions on causation strikingly press the new empirical approach to knowledge. Ockham insists on the empirical origin of our knowledge of causal connexion, dismissing the orthodox belief in formal principles that control the connexion. He maintains that the notion of one particular object is never the sufficient cause of the notion of another particular object.[4] Causal connexion cannot be demonstrated. We find fire and burning present together, but we cannot assume that the burning is due to the fire. It may be due to God, who could produce other effects if He so willed.[5]

Substance, too, becomes unknowable. When we see a fire we know that it is fire; yet in reality we do not know fire in itself but only the accidents of fire, such as its heat.[6] A substance is understood only by negative descriptions, such as 'an entity which subsists by itself', 'an entity underlying all accidents'.[7] The position reminds us of Locke's 'supposition one knows not what support of such qualities which are capable of producing simple ideas in us; which qualities are commonly called accidents'.[8] The ancient doctrines concerning the mind are also challenged.

[1] Summulae i. 18 and i. 14; Tornay, p. 35, nn. 16 and 17.
[2] Summulae i. 14; Tornay, p. 36.
[3] Summulae i. 23; Tornay, p. 38.
[4] Sent. Prol. qu. 9; Abbagnano, p. 167 n.
[5] Sent. ii, qu. 5; Tornay, p. 69.
[6] Sent. i, dist. 3, qu. 2; Abbagnano, p. 162 n.
[7] Ib., dist. 3, qu. 2; Tornay, p. 59.   [8] Essay, bk. ii, ch. 23.

'Our understanding of the intellectual soul as an immaterial and incorruptible form which is totally in the whole and totally in every part cannot be accepted as evident from either reason or experience. We cannot know whether such form is in us, or that it is the nature of such substance in us to be intellectual, or that the soul is the form of the body. I do not care how Aristotle felt about this, because everywhere he himself appears on this point to be uncertain. We hold the three foregoing propositions only by faith.'[1]

In fine, he moves away at every point from the historic metaphysical interpretations of experience. Since there are no universal principles in things, principles are generalizations from particulars. His preference for particular sensible realities over metaphysical entities governs his contributions to physics. His observations on movement provide examples of this method. The accepted way of interpreting movement was to understand it as the realization of a Form. Ockham asserts that the moving body is the motion. There is no being inherent in bodies which is movement; there are simply the moving bodies which we perceive.[2] The characteristic note is struck again in the discussions on the nature of time. 'Time is not a latent unknowable thing.'[3] It is the measure of bodies in motion, the ultimate reference being the fixed stars. Such hints encouraged a profound revolution in the set of ideas which had descended from classical Greek thought. They were taken up by the school of Parisian Nominalists who followed Ockham, men such as John Buridan, Nicholas of Oresme, and Marsilius of Inghen. These Nominalist philosophers made important advances in physical theory. William of Ockham's influence on the birth of science is undoubted.

VI

But it was in the fields of philosophy and of theology that his views produced their most disturbing effects. Throughout the whole period of medieval thought the relation between the provinces of reason and revealed Faith had constantly occupied the attention of philosophers. The problem is present at every point of their work. Some authorities at each period completely severed rational inquiry from the traditional content of Revelation, in the interest of the former. The dogmas of the Faith are sufficient, and the exercise of rational inquiry beyond what is

---

[1] Summulae i. 14; Abbagnano, p. 179 n.
[2] Sent. ii, qu. 26; Tornay, p. 39.   [3] Summulae iv. 3; Tornay, p. 43.

necessary in order to accept them is unnecessary and dangerous. St. Bernard and Peter Damian are, in different ways, instances of this unspeculative piety. But the typical attitude of the masters of medieval thought is *Fides quaerens intellectum*. This is the programme of Augustine, of Anselm, of Thomas Aquinas. It is the task of reason to clarify in logical terms, as far as possible, the deliverances of Revelation. It is impossible that Christian beliefs should be unreasonable; and the whole aim of the *Summa Contra Gentiles* is to show how nearly human inquiry can approach to the teaching of theology. But Thomas went farther than his predecessors in allowing to the science of temporal things a free scope independent of theology. His definition of the provinces of Faith and Reason was provoked by the influence of Averroës who had argued that reason is incompetent in theological matters. But now, in the face of the work of Thomas, the sceptical teaching of Averroës was forcibly revived. Ockham denies that any of the central beliefs of religion can be logically demonstrated. He finds the argument which St. Thomas had elaborated in *Summa Contra Gentiles* inconclusive. Thomas had argued, after Aristotle, that movement entails an external agent which initiates the movement. If we are to avoid an infinite regress we are obliged to postulate a First Mover. Ockham replies that it is reasonable to hold that some things move themselves without the intervention of another agent. He adduces as instances not only the mind and the angels, but also weight (*gravitas*).[1] Nor does he accept the point that an infinite regress in the series of movers is a logical impossibility. On the contrary, an infinite regress is a plain fact in certain cases. For example, if a continuous surface is struck at one end motion is produced in the adjacent part; that part moves the next, and so on to infinity.[1] Ockham is willing to admit that Thomas's conclusion that there is an unmoved mover is a more probable position than its opposite; but he refuses to allow that it is proved by his arguments.

Even the belief in one God is shown to be not susceptible of demonstration. And a similar attitude is taken concerning the doctrine of the infinity of God. In a word, conclusive philosophical knowledge of God cannot be attained. Our concepts of Him suffer the defect of all concepts; they cannot establish existence. In order to know God as an existent being we should have to apprehend Him in intuition; and this is impossible.

[1] Cent. Theolog. i; Tornay, p. 190.

Scholasticism was inspired by the belief in the rational unity of philosophy and theology. In the schools of Paris and Oxford it now began to be openly asserted that Christian dogmas could not be supported by reasonable proof; natural reason could show them at the best to be probable inferences. At the worst, when philosophic argument led to the opposite conclusion, the believer was invited to embrace by Faith what his reason rejected. Masters became ready, both in disputations in the schools and in their treatises on the *Sentences*, to defend theories contrary to theological doctrine. These opinions were often put forward under the guise of dialectical exercises. In his work *On the Power of Emperors and Popes* Ockham excuses his heretical utterances by remarking that Catholics can be seen denying points of faith by way of exercise without incurring reproach.[1] But this outlook was a precarious one that heralded deep fissures in medieval culture. Many religious minds turned away from the dialectical theology of the schools towards a practical and devotional rule founded on the simple teaching of the Gospels. Such was Gerard Groote's ideal expressed in the Brotherhood of the Common Life at Deventer. The more speculative returned to the allegorical riches of Neoplatonism. Even during the lifetime of Ockham three great mystical writers— Eckhart, Suso, and Ruysbroeck—had expressed this form of the reaction against theological metaphysics. The agnosticism of Ockham contributed towards the theological pessimism characteristic of the last period of the Middle Ages. And when Luther struck his blow against the edifice of Catholic belief he hailed Ockham as his master.

VII

But our concern here is with the more strictly philosophical outcome of Nominalism. The successors of Ockham developed his sceptical treatment of knowledge. It was argued that we can be sure only of sensations and of the existence of our minds. Now began the repudiation of Aristotle which attained such extravagant heights in the following century. One of Ockham's disciples, Nicholas of Autrecourt, observed that 'in all his natural philosophy and metaphysics Aristotle has hardly reached two evidently certain conclusions, perhaps not even a single one'. And another Nominalist, Peter d'Ailly, asserted that Aristotle's doctrine merits the name of opinion rather than of knowledge. It is true that the

[1] Op. cit. iii.

writings of Nicholas were condemned; but Peter d'Ailly became a cardinal. The teaching of Ockham was condemned four times at Paris between 1339 and 1347. Yet it became ascendant everywhere in Europe. The obscure positive movement in this general repudiation of the standard authorities was the search for a new criterion of evidence. But Ockham's conception of thought had severed the general and formal elements from immediate apprehension. The principle that the universals which constitute the content of thought are terms which stand for cross-sections of individual things introduced a division in the schools which marked out two directions for the subsequent philosophy of knowledge. On the one hand, the formal treatment of terms in propositions produced an elaborate technique of symbolic logic. On the other, the narrowness of the field within which Ockham had confined certain knowledge of reality developed into a subjective empiricism. But later philosophers were confronted not only with the task of surmounting the abstractions of Nominalism. They were led by the general advance in scientific method to broaden the Scholastic conception of Realism. The universal in thought was perceived to include not only class notions, but to embrace other forms of essential connexions. Yet in the course of modern inquiry into the principles of knowledge Nominalism as well as Realism has been revived in terms which recall the great conflicts of the Middle Ages.

In particular, English philosophy has been dominated by Nominalist theories. Hobbes, Locke, Berkeley, Hume, Hamilton, and Mill express views on the nature of general ideas which are parallel to those of Ockham. Mill, for instance, maintains that 'we think by means of concrete phenomena, such as are presented in experience or represented in imagination, and by means of names, which being in a peculiar manner associated with certain elements of the concrete images arrest our attention on those elements'.[1] In contemporary discussion there is wide concentration on the relation of thought to language, and the work of these schools has brought about a revival of Nominalism. On the other hand, Realism has been a central note in other modern systems of thought. The debt of Descartes to Scholastic principles has been traced by Professor Gilson. And since the seventeenth century Realism has been asserted in many forms, notably by Hegel and his disciples in Germany, Italy, and England. And there are

[1] *Examination of Sir William Hamilton's Philosophy*, p. 330.

numbers of Realists among philosophers in our own day, some of whom (such as those belonging to the school of Husserl) acknowledge their obligation to their medieval predecessors. And in many discussions besides those concerned with the theory of knowledge the old issues are perpetually reappearing. Extreme Realism is maintained by numerous writers who investigate the nature of Goodness or of Beauty, who uphold the corporate character of the Church, or who press the claims of Nationality or Labour or the State. Nominalism is advocated by others in the name of individuality and democracy.[1]

The secular and scientific roots of modern speculation have transformed the problem. But it remains a vital issue. It seems reasonable to suppose that brownness or generosity or man refer to identities which are common to many different particular things. On the other hand, it appears equally clear that such characters are in each instance as particular as the particular things which they qualify. The brownness of curtains and tables and dresses is in each case distinct and separate; and even when it looks the same it is distinct in its various instances. If we pursue the question we are confronted on the one hand with the problem of the relation of a thing to its qualities, the problem of substance; on the other hand with the question of the status in reality of the abstract unities which thought and science apprehend. If Nominalist theories are to be accepted we must believe that the common principles sought for in particular things are fictions. But to abolish the objectivity of universals in *some* sense is to abolish, as St. Thomas would say, the possibility of exploring the nature of anything. He insisted that universals have their foundations in objects and so far are indisputably real. All thinking, he maintained, presupposes certain irreducible modes of unity, and these are not psychical patterns contributed by subjects but essential features of objects. But the exploration of the universal nature by means of general terms does not imply the self-subsistent entities, man-in-general or colour-as-such upon which the medieval and eighteenth-century

---

[1] Here is a surprising incursion of the debate into the field of law. 'It may seem a bold and reckless statement to assert that an adequate discussion of cases like *Berry* v. *Donovan, Adair* v. *United States*, or *Commonwealth* v. *Boston and Maine R.* involves the whole medieval controversy over the reality of universals. And yet, the confident assertion of "immutable principles of justice inhering in the very idea of free government" made by the writers of these decisions, and the equally confident assertion of their critics that there are no such principles, show how impossible it is to keep out of metaphysics.' Morris R. Cohen, *Harvard Law Review*, xxix, p. 628.

Nominalists poured their scorn. What is sought are systems which are intrinsic to the nature of things.

The issue cannot be further argued here. Our purpose in these brief accounts of medieval views on knowledge has been expository rather than critical. We have attempted no more than to indicate some of the questions relating to knowledge which occupied the schools, and to exhibit the way in which they were discussed by representative thinkers. In the philosophical passages of St. Augustine we have watched the rise of that enduring impulse in Christian reflection which is preoccupied with indestructible truth and the eternal reasons. We have followed the first great assault on the high Realism that had descended from Augustine to the Cathedral schools of the eleventh century. In the philosophy of St. Thomas we have witnessed, so far as a slight sketch allows, a comprehensive and subtle endeavour to combine the general and particular, the sensible and the intellectual, elements of experience into an harmonious scheme on Aristotelian lines. Finally, we have briefly surveyed the critical challenge to the assumptions of the main tradition of Christian metaphysics that appeared in the fourteenth century. The scepticism that was encouraged by the searching inquiries of Ockham and the Terminists into the bases of knowledge, contributed to the disruption of society in the fifteenth century. From that disruption there grew fresh principles of truth and new formulations of the ancient problems of the Realists and Nominalists. But even here the great schoolmen can stimulate and instruct us. And without acquaintance with their methods and opinions we lose sense of the continuity of European thought.

BIBLIOGRAPHY

General works on Medieval Philosophy:
E. Bréhier, *La Philosophie du Moyen Âge*. Paris, 1937.
E. Gilson, *La Philosophie au Moyen Âge*. Paris, 1922.
—— *L'Esprit de la philosophie mediévale*. 2 vols., Paris, 1932.
—— und C. Böhner, *Die Geschichte der christlichen Philosophie*. Paderborn, 1939.
R. McKeon, *Selections from Medieval Philosophers*. 2 vols., London, 1930.
F. Ueberweg, *Grundriss der Geschichte der Philosophie*, Vol. II, *Die patristische und scholastische Philosophie*, 11th edition, edited by B. Geyer. Berlin, 1928.
M. de Wulf, *Histoire de la philosophie mediévale*. Louvain, 1924.

St. Augustine:
C. Boyer, *Essais sur la doctrine de St. Augustin*. Paris, 1932.
E. Gilson, *Introduction à l'étude de Saint Augustin*. Paris, 1929.
H. I. Marrou, *Saint Augustin et la fin de la culture antique*. Paris, 1938.
H. Pope, *Saint Augustine of Hippo*. London, 1937.
E. Przywara, *An Augustine Synthesis*. London, 1936.
Various, *A monument to St. Augustine*. London, 1930.

Abaelard:
E. Gilson, *The Unity of Philosophical Experience*. London, 1938. (Chapter I.)
C. de Rémusat, *Abélard, sa vie, sa philosophie et sa théologie*. 2 vols., Paris, 1855.
T. G. Sikes, *Peter Abailard*. London, 1932.

St. Thomas Aquinas:
M. C. D'Arcy, *Thomas Aquinas*. London, 1934.
E. Gilson, *The Philosophy of St. Thomas Aquinas*, translated by E. Bullough. London, 1937.
G. Rabeau, *Species, Verbum*. Paris, 1938.
P. Rousselot, *L'intellectualisme de Saint Thomas*. 2nd ed., Paris, 1924.
A. D. Sertillanges, *Saint Thomas d'Aquin*. 2 vols., Paris, 1910.
—— *Foundations of Thomistic Philosophy*, translated by G. Anstruther. London, 1931.

William of Ockham:
N. Abbagnano, *Guglielmo di Ockham*. Lanciano, 1931.
E. Gilson, *The Unity of Philosophical Experience*. London, 1938. (Chapter III.)
E. A. Moody, *The Logic of William of Ockham*. London, 1935.
G. Prantl, *Geschichte der Logik im Abendlande*. Leipzig, 1867. (Vol. III, Chap. 19.)
S. C. Tornay, *Ockham, Studies and Selections*. La Salle, Illinois, 1938.

INDEX

PRINTED IN GREAT BRITAIN AT THE UNIVERSITY PRESS, OXFORD
BY VIVIAN RIDLER, PRINTER TO THE UNIVERSITY